Social Stratification and Mobility

Social Stratification and Mobility

K.L. Sharma

RAWAT PUBLICATIONS
Jaipur • New Delhi • Bangalore • Guwahati • Kolkata

ISBN 978-81-7033-262-6 (hardback)
ISBN 978-81-7033-263-3 (paperback)

Reprint, 2017

Published by
Prem Rawat for Rawat Publications
Satyam Apts., Sector 3, Jawahar Nagar, Jaipur - 302 004 (India)
Phone: 0141 265 1748 / 7006 Fax: 0141 265 1748
E-mail : info@rawatbooks.com
Website: rawatbooks.com

Delhi Office
4858/24, Ansari Road, Daryaganj, New Delhi 110 002
Phone: 011-23263290

Also at *Bangalore, Guwahati* and *Kolkata*

Typeset by Rawat Computers, Jaipur
Printed at Nice Printing Press, New Delhi

In loving memory of my nephew
late Surendra Sharma,
a genius, who excelled in every walk of life.

Preface

Social stratification being a societal phenomenon focuses on general issues relating to structuring of social inequalities in human societies. Variations in different societies relating to the structure and process of social stratification refer to specificities of its historical and contextual dimensions. In structuring of social stratification, a multiplicity of forces and factors operate including ideology, ascription, achievement, technology and economic development. How to understand the relative efficacy of all these factors has bothered the concerned scholars and intellectuals. Construction and application of concepts, frameworks and paradigms to influence social relations in a particular manner is a well known colonial device. A sociology of knowledge perspective uncovers deep layers of ideological moorings of the concepts such as caste, class, ethnicity and power.

The first three essays in this volume examine the main analytic standpoints with regard to theory, method and data in the study of social stratification in India. The main aim is to know the compelling facticity of social inequality as a persisting phenomenon. Late Surendra Sharma, whom this volume is dedicated, provides a comprehensive review of the studies on social stratification examining the questions of theory, method and data from the perspective of sociology of knowledge. He states that the main problem is still to find out a proper connection between theory, method and data.

What is 'caste model' of Indian society? A debate on this question is presented in chapter three. How caste refers to both structure and process? In what way is it a cultural system? How British rule and western social science have viewed India's caste system? A discussion on these and other related points finds space in chapters three and four. It is argued that caste and class inhere each other as aspects of India's social formation. More important is the realization of the nexus between caste and class and the continuity and change of the nexus. Dialectics, layers and levels of this nexus need to be studied more than mere as studies of caste and/or class. Caste has structural aspects and class is not without cultural constructs and practices. The way caste-class dichotomy is projected in the western literature is in fact found as a superimposition on Indian social formation.

Chapters five, six and eight are being published for the first time. No dialogue on social stratification would be complete without inclusion of a critical evaluation of Louis Dumont's *Homo Hierarchicus*. Salient features of this magnum opus are summarized in chapter five. The question why *Homo Hierarchicus* is dealt with briefly by way of some criticisms in this chapter. Chapters six, seven and eight emphasize on the substantive contexts of social stratification such as urban-industrial, rural-agrarian and tribal. Caste, class, power, and ethnicity are seen both as convergent and incongruent aspects of social stratification. Patterns of social mobility in these sectors in relation to different social groups, such as castes, classes and tribes have brought about definitional changes in the notions of caste, class, ethnicity, and power and their interrelationships.

Social mobility in caste structure in terms of 'levels' such as individual, family and group is discussed in terms of inputs from my study of six villages in Rajasthan. These are not just analytical distinctions, substantive differences are found in structural and cultural dimensions of social mobility. However, mobility does not imply only upward movements of individuals, families and groups. There is specific as well as generalized downward social mobility. Effective macro-structural forces and contradictions in micro-structural situations lead to structural as well as positional decline. Domain-specific decline as a result of 'status withdrawal' is illustrated as an example of structural changes such as the abolition of *jagirdari* and *zamindari* systems.

In the last two chapters, caste, class and social mobility among the scheduled castes has been analyzed. Role of constitutional safeguards and welfare measures and socio-cultural movements is discussed in relation to social mobility, consciousness and anti-upper caste-class attitude among the scheduled castes. How structural unevenness among the scheduled castes, within members of a scheduled caste, and between the scheduled castes and caste Hindus has affected social mobility is discussed in chapters eleven and twelve. Questions of 'class in caste' and 'caste in class' have surfaced in our reporting of several examples of exploitation, oppression, atrocities and rape inflicted upon the scheduled castes in different parts of India.

All the chapters except six, seven and nine included in this volume were published as articles at different points of time since 1969 onwards. Chapter two has been taken from late Surendra Sharma's book *Sociology in India: A Perspective from Sociology of Knowledge* (Rawat, 1985). An effort has been made to remove ambiguities which had remained, and to tighten the loose ends in the articles. However, some repetition could not be avoided as it became necessary for pursuing a particular line of argument. The selection of these essays for this volume has been guided by the sole objective of presenting a wholesome analysis of social stratification in India to the students, researchers and teachers. Care is taken in this endeavour to focus upon the basic conceptual, methodological and empirical issues relating to the study of social stratification. A balanced emphasis is placed on context-specific situations such as urban-industrial, rural-agrarian and tribal.

It will be highly gratifying for us if this endeavour contributes a little bit in carrying forward the unending debate on the issues relating to caste, class, ethnicity, power, and social mobility. The credit goes to Mrs. Prem Rawat and in particular to her husband Mr. Kailash Rawat who forced me to work on this project. I am grateful to them for publishing the volume with promptness.

K.L. Sharma

Contents

Contents

1

Towards a Framework of Relevance for the Sociology of Stratification in India

Questions have often been raised about the relevance of applying certain approaches and methods for studying social stratification. The foreignness of *theory* and *method* in the study of Indian society has been a point of discussion. Another question which has been under discussion is regarding the 'fit' between *theory, method* and *data*. Generally, the lack of fit between these three has been highlighted. Theories of social stratification, namely, Marxian, Weberian and Functional have ideological bearings, and have therefore corresponding influences on the understanding of social inequality. These questions are also important because social stratification is a very sensitive subject. Social stratification refers to unequal relations and their management. All the members of society including the researcher/analyst and his respondents are a part of this arrangement of unequal social relations. Those who have occupied lower position in this order of relations have often resented their underprivileged status, whereas those who have enjoyed a privileged status have been averse to concede any change in the existing system. Before we take up some specific theoretical issues, I would like to make a few points about some popularly held notions in regard to studies of social stratification.

I

No doubt the social scientists in India are well conversant, at least, with the apparent character of western theories and methods of study as they have amply used them in their analyses of Indian society. However, it is still an open question whether they have done so consciously, knowing well about their implications or have done so without a proper awareness of their deep-rooted implications—ideological, political and material. Even a cursory look at literature on social stratification shows that theories and concepts used by Marx, Weber, Durkheim, Sorokin, Pareto, Dahrendorf, Centres, Warner, Hollingshead, Mills, Dumont, etc., have been freely used by Indian scholars for studying social stratification and mobility without weighing their relevances. It has been more an exercise in sophistry and superfluousness than in genuine sociological research and understanding. If a question is posed about the relevance or otherwise of the Marxian and Weberian concepts and theories in the Indian context, I would prefer to maintain that both are partly relevant and partly irrelevant. However, about the dichotomous, trichotomous or the continua concepts, one would discover more of irrelevance than relevance. The concepts such as *vertical* and *horizontal mobility, reference group* and *sanskritization* are partly useful and partly futile.

The concepts of 'integration', 'conflict' and 'social mobility' have been at the centre of a large number of studies on caste, class and status-emulation in Indian society. Lack of 'indigenization' in these studies has been pointed out as a major drawback. The superiority of the western social sciences in the understanding of western societies is accepted by way of using it in the studies of Indian situation. I am not against accepting or borrowing explanatory models, concepts and methods from western social sciences, but one must ascertain their application in terms of time and space. Transnational and regional variations and historical-ideological moorings are basic to any scientific and objective study of social inequality.

A *sociology of knowledge* view of social reality is the foremost requirement for studying social stratification. Such a view is missing in most of the studies which emphasize either caste or class to the exclusion of each other. The protagonists of caste studies show a bias for its continuance and functionality (Hutton, 1963; Furnivall, 1939; Senart, 1930). The advocates of class studies have different ideological upbringings and look at everything from the point of class alone (Desai, 1948). A combination of concepts with analytic synthesis may ensure a deeper and realistic understanding of social stratification in India. These are concepts of culture, structure, history and dialectics (Sharma, 1982). Normative standards, social relations, specificity and levels of change in regard to social stratification can respectively be explained by these concepts. One can have a vision of social formation of Indian society or of a part of it by using the concepts of culture, structure, history and dialectics.

Marx gives us a call for the application of historical-dialectical materialism; Weber impresses upon us the value of using *verstehen*; Durkheim advocates the use of sociological positivism; Parsons advances the cause of structural-functionalism; and Popper declares that historicism is a poor method—a misconception, hence, the relevance for his brand of positivism (Sharma, 1983). We have been influenced by all of them at different points of time and in different contexts and sometimes in contradiction to each other in our attempts to understand Indian society. Therefore, the most important question continues to be: How to understand Indian social reality in an effective manner? Is there a congruence between theory, method and data in regard to the present studies on social stratification? This question could be posed even at the general level of the nature of sociology in India, but I do not intend to dwell upon this paper.

Whatever Louis Dumont (1970) might say about *caste as a method* of studying Indian society, he does support caste system and its allied sanctions. For him, caste is 'social', as religion is 'social' for Radcliffe-Brown and Durkheim. Dumont approvingly quotes from Hocart, Senart and Hutton, who have advocated for continuity of caste system by emphasizing the functions of caste system for individual members, for caste as a group, and for the entire Indian society or state (Hutton, 1963). Such an advocacy during the British days had led to the promotion of their colonial interests in India. However, this view of theirs stands contradicted when they make a sharp distinction between caste and class. Class is considered as a characteristic feature of the western society and the latter is characterized by its emphasis on democracy, individualism and openness. On the contrary, caste, as a core-feature of Indian society, is defined as an archaic institution lacking in democracy, individualism and freedom (Sharma, 1980). Such a dichotomous perspective on the part of the western scholars easily exposes them to the blemish of ideological particularism. They also have many camp-followers among the Indian scholars who have borrowed these deceptive and one-sided models deliberately and sometimes unwittingly. Dumont (1957, 1958, 1960, 1966) criticizes Saran's view as 'cultural solipsism', reactionary, obscurantistic and Hindu chauvinistic, but under the cover of 'external view', comparison and objectivity, Dumont brings in a mystic hallo around the caste system. Why Dumont accepts India's caste system as a datum for his understanding of all the rest? Why does he consider caste as a cultural form of social inequality? Is inequality based on racial criteria not of an extreme form? Continuance of monarchy in England or depriving women from contesting election for presidentship in USA are equally retrograde and archaic practices, but Dumont forgets them conveniently, not declaring them as 'extreme' type of institutions.

Thus, the question is not of preferring one approach against another. The question is also not of studying 'ideas' or 'relations' or both. The question is rather of studying social inequality and its ramifications—historically and contextually. The relevant questions to be posed in this connection are: (1) How far studies of social stratification have incorporated the historicity of Indian society? (2) What are the approaches, methods and techniques of research in regard to social stratification? (3) Where did they originate and how the experience behind their origination is different from the experience of Indian social reality? (4) What measures have been taken to ascertain a *priorism* of these tools of understanding? Does it not mean accepting them as academic cults? I shall refer to these questions while analyzing some selected though well-known studies of social stratification.

II

Let me make it explicit again that our aim is not to suggest that since functional approach to social stratification has been in vogue for long enough, therefore, dialectical approach should be accepted now. It is also not to make a plea for a synthesis of the two approaches so as to have a pluralistic or multidimensional approach for studying social stratification. I do not wish to assert that in the studies so far 'consequences' of social inequality have been emphasized more than its causes and processes, and therefore, the trinity of theory, structure and process should be studied now. More important than these endeavours would be the one which recognizes the historicity of Indian social stratification, and accordingly seeks to identify its present character. Why functional or dialectical approaches, either individually or in synthesis, are recommended for the understanding of social inequality in India since neither of these has emanated from the experience of social inequality in India? None of the theories and concepts of social stratification can be applied in any context without knowing their ideological moorings. Their presuppositions need to be analyzed in terms of new forms and expressions of social inequality in divergent- social situations. *Particularism* of theories and concepts under the garb of their *universality* should thus be uncovered.

The structural-functional theory of social stratification dominated in the 1950s. Congruence between caste, class and power was found in the village community. Division of labour among various castes in a given local situation was found desirable. Corporate character of caste groups was analyzed with regard to intracaste and intercaste relations. Structuralism and Marxism as explanations of and approaches to social stratification acquired prominence in the 1960s. Dumont is the spokesman of structuralism. Marxism has been advocated by A.R. Desai and Charles Bettelheim. However, in the 1970s, the historical perspective has been accepted by the Marxists as well as non-Marxists in their studies of social stratification. The non-Marxist adherents of structural-historical perspective have given more emphasis on indigenization of Marxist approach with an emphasis on understanding of Indian society in relation to its historicity (Singh, 1974, 1981).

Caste as the singular institution of social ranking was the characteristic argument during the fifties and sixties in the studies of Hutton, Ghurye, Hocart, Bougle, Myrdal, Leach, Srinivas, Marriott, Lewis, etc. All of them have treated caste as coterminous with the entire gamut of social relations and thought it to be an all-inclusive basis of social stratification (Beteille, 1969). Multidimensionality of social stratification is emphasized in the sixties and seventies in the studies conducted by Beteille (1966), Bhatt (1975) and Aggarwal (1971). Class and power along with caste are treated as economic and political dimensions of social inequality and hierarchy. Ramkrishna Mukherjee (1957), Gough (1960) and Mencher (1974), however, look at caste from a class point of view. Mencher feels that caste be studied from 'upside down' rather than through 'top down' view. In fact, caste is treated by all these scholars as a system of economic relations rather than merely as a system of ritual hierarchy. In my own study, I applied both structural and cultural perspectives to understand social stratification in six villages of Rajasthan (Sharma, 1974). Not only I could identify the structure of social inequality in divergent social settings, I could also analyze the ideological basis of social stratification, factors of change and social mobility, levels of caste and class consciousness, power structure and value orientations in my attempt to examine the relevance of 'caste' model to the study of Indian society.

Theory, method and data are generally in complementary alliance. Functional approach to the study of caste implied that it was a useful institution and it would not change, and also that it would adapt itself to meet the challenges and exigencies of a variety of situations. Caste was found as an adaptive and pragmatic system performing as an interest group for its members (Kothari, 1970). In such studies, however, several significant structural processes such as proletarianization of the ex-*zamindars* and bourgeoisiefication of the ex-tenants and *raiyats*, which have affected caste structure, have been ignored (Sharma, 1973). In fact, normative and cultural aspects of caste have received more attention through analysis of sanskritization and westernization (Srinivas, 1966). It also seems relevant here to recall that a couple of studies have comprehended contemporary changes in the caste system as a movement from its organic nature to its segmentary character, from its closedness to openness and from its emphasis on corporateness to individualism (Bailey, 1957; Miller, 1975). The central message of all these studies is that caste is continuing but bases of its continuity and forms of its functioning are quite different now from what they were four decades ago.

An overview of the studies on caste by the Indian sociologists suggests that we are competing with each other in imitating approaches, models and methods used by the British and American scholars. A study of the role of religion among the Coorgs (Srinivas, 1952) is clearly an extension of Radcliffe-Brown's functionalism. Religion is *sui generis* for Srinivas. Caste and religion are intertwined, hence religion becomes the basis of caste hierarchy. Beteille (1966a), in trying to go beyond caste through his 'caste-class-power' analysis, is explicitly guided and inspired by Weber's triology of 'class, status and party'. Whether study of caste alone is sufficient or class and power should also receive adequate attention is not a matter of concern here. No doubt application of Weber's trio is a step ahead of the application of the British functionalism to the study of caste system. Yet, the fact remains that in the understanding of Indian social stratification, structuralism, Marxism and positivism, along with their numerous variations, have been accepted more as fads than as relevant theoretical and methodological devices. History of social inequality has been the biggest casualty in regard to these approaches.

III

Beteille makes a distinction between caste, class and power on the pattern of 'class, status and party' as suggested by Max Weber (1970). The distinction between these three is justified by Beteille's observation of "the differentiation of institutional structures", and also because of the absence of "summation of statuses" (Beteille, 1966b; Bailey, 1963). Beteille also notes that there is a very little preoccupation with purity-pollution rituals in general. The problem is neither regarding application of Weber's approach to social stratification, nor is it in connection with incongruence between social, economic and political aspects of rural people. Instead, it is concerning *apriori* acceptance of Weber's theory and its inherent ideology. The theoretical core of Weber's formulation is constitutive of rationalism, subjectivity and objectification, whereas its substantive inspiration comes from his experience of Germany's political and economic situation. These points have not been kept in view while trying to understand the Indian situation through the application of Weber's frame of reference. Methodological appreciation of Weber's theory, namely, *verstehen* does not constitute a part of Beteille's research strategy. In fact, the research strategy adopted by Beteille is 'foreign' to Weber's theoretical apparatus. Hence, the contradiction between Beteille's approach and his method of study.

Anil Bhatt's study (1975) of caste, class and politics provides a clear theoretical exposition and a set of objectives. He has borrowed extensively from studies of 'comparative politics' and 'comparative functionalism', and in fact uses the phrase 'comparative social stratification'. His main focus is on the understanding of 'summation of statuses' between the contemporary social structure and politics. This he does by comparing the traditional Indian society with its contemporary setting. Quantitative analysis is his main source of objective understanding of social stratification. Generalization and quantification are closely linked. He has gone beyond 'village' in understanding social stratification, and also in avoiding ethnographic and anthropological-qualitative analysis. Through survey research, macro-national and regional-level analysis has been attempted. He writes: "I have tried to be very explicit in relating the evidences to the theory". However, one should also recognize that survey research is the most favourite technique of research for the American structural-functional positivists.

In most of the studies discussed above, a link between *theory* and *method* of study has remained unclear. Two reasons can be attributed to this vagueness: (i) the notion of scientism associated with a *method* of study; and (ii) convenient acceptance of a particular method of study (Sharma, 1983). Beteille accepted 'participant observation' as a method of study with a view to stay in the Brahmin locality in the village. He did not plan his field-work before hand, and as he says, he did not have "a battery of hypotheses and concepts" prior to the field-work. But why? Is it that he had not read Marx and Weber prior to his field-work? But this does not seem to have been the case as all through his work, he extensively borrows from both, and clearly opts for Weber's approach to social stratification.

In my study (1974) of social stratification in rural Rajasthan, I began with 'a battery of hypotheses' which I have listed in the study. I also had a very clear awareness that empirical substantiation for these hypotheses required an application of a variety of research techniques and devices. Comparison was made based on several variables. Data were gathered from both primary and secondary sources. Historical details about the villages were also collected. A variant of qualitative analysis was thought necessary before launching upon the field-work in the six villages from three districts.

Invariably certain specific notions about social reality have guided studies of social stratification. Needless to say that most of these notions are inept to understand social stratification in India. Some of them are: caste is a rural phenomenon; class is found in urban centres; individual is the unit of social ranking in cities; group is the unit of status-estimation in villages; ranking is flexible in urban areas and rigid in rural milieux; achievement is the hallmark of urban people; and ascription is the essence of life in the countryside. Such notions have not only led to biased formulation of hypotheses, even empirical observations have been distorted due to such simplistic uncritical statements.

D'Souza's study (1967) of caste and class in Chandigarh no doubt highlights significance of the continuum of the rigidity-fluidity dimensions and of the individual and his properties as the units of analysis, but all this exercise is implicitly patterned on the notion of positivism of the structural-functionalist variety. His emphasis is on constructing 'order' of classes based on education, occupation and income. Concrete interacting social groups, such as professionals, businessmen, mill-owners, industrial workers, etc., have not been studied in situations of concrete interaction. Caste groups and forms of corporateness have also been left out from his study of Chandigarh. D'Souza is perhaps influenced by Warner's SES approach more than anything else.

In pursuance of the command received from the British government, their agents in India propagated that caste was a useful institution for Hindus in particular and for Indians in general. Furnivall, Senart and Hutton listed a couple of functions of caste system in the books they wrote on caste. Recently, some more western scholars have also lent support to this verdict inferentially through the findings of their studies (Marriott,1965). They have stated that caste has a secular aspect. It has made people conscious and therefore it has had an integrating consequence. Kothari (1970) reports that one American scholar even talks of "the democratic incarnation of caste". According to some scholars, caste has even led to the modernization of India's polity. Kothari (1970b) accepts these statements and considers caste *apolitical.* In his study of politics, he uses the vocabulary of the American advocates of comparative functionalism.

Louis Dumont's *Homo-Hierarchicus* is the most well-known exposition of structuralist perspective on social stratification. The pivotal notions of Dumont's structuralism as noted by Yogendra Singh (1981) are ideology, dialectics, and transformation. The basic tenet of caste system is 'hierarchy'. Hierarchy encompasses all aspects of life including binary tensions and dialectics of the opposition between 'pure' and 'impure'. Dumont's view in terms of binary opposition is wanting both theoretically and substantively, since 'pure' in actual practice is often found fused in the 'impure' and vice-versa in many rituals (Gould, 1967). Besides this, Dumont's structuralist view lacks a conception of history and analysis of politico-economic dimensions of India's social reality. To think of structuralism independent of empirical reality is Dumont's main concern. However, structuralism of such a variety in regard to the study of caste and its allied aspects has resulted into propagation of caste ideology and caste-based inequalities. Dumont has never bothered to see the hiatus between the rules of the game and the actual game played and enacted in a given context.

IV

A couple of studies on caste and class have taken 'change' as the focal point of analysis. Stratification as a process is now a well conceived notion. Structural-historical perspective is being applied by those who lay emphasis on the study of differentiation, evolution and change in caste and class in India. Modes of production in agriculture and industry in relation to caste and class have been discussed both by economic historians and anthropologists (Frykenberg, 1969). The Marxists look at the origin or evolution of caste from the point of economic relations. Political activists like Dange (1949), Ranadive (1979) and Namboodiripad (1979) look at caste as a mechanism of exploitation in the hands of the upper castes. However, non-Marxists consider caste not as a superstructural entity, but mainly as a basic institution of division of labour and harmonic relations. Mode of production is the key to the Marxist theory of social stratification. But the mode of production and the differentiation of peasantry are old and familiar issues (Sharma, 1983). To find them in Indian society, one does not have to borrow from Marx and Mao. Doing so would mean ignoring analysis of the traditional structure and processes of change affecting that structure. One could find uneven structures of landlords, peasants and tenants before the advent of the British rule in India. Over a time, the said unevenness of the traditional social structure has been transformed into a new one. Land reforms, green revolution, adult franchise, etc., have contributed to this unevenness in many ways.

The essence of the Marxist method of study is that explanation emanates from the structure of social reality. Social reality is not static; hence, historical explanation. Marxist approach has also been called evolutionary, emancipatory and hermeneutic in nature. The problem does not lie in accepting its ethos, but in its transplantation in toto for studying Indian society. A.R. Desai's study (1982) is a well-known example of 'orthodox Marxism'. Other variants of Marxist analysis of caste, class and land relations are the studies by D.P. Mukerji(1958), Kathleen Gough (1980) and

Gail Omvedt (1982). Gough, for example, employs a mix of anthropological method, history and Marxism in her study of agrarian relations in South India. Mukerji combines tradition, history and Marxism as the three main components of his study of modern Indian society, economy and polity. He calls himself a Marxologist and not a Marxian. Class is viewed as a sociological concept and Marxism is treated as a study of the history of entire process of alienation. Thus, Mukerji is one who has moulded and modified Marxism in view of the nature of Indian society—its tradition and history.

The problem, therefore, is first to identify the genesis of theory and method and then to explore its relevance for the study of social stratification. This inquiry also calls for understanding of the conscious motives of the researchers in applying these theories and methods. 'Researcher' is a very significant variable in social research, particularly in a developing country like India. Marxian, Weberian, structural-functionalist and structuralist theoretic orientations and methods of study have generally analyzed here with a view to assess their relevance/irrelevance for a deeper understanding of social inequality in India.

In the studies of social stratification during the post-independence period, caste has been over-emphasized. Culturological or indological dimensions have been predominant in the studies of caste and social mobility. Colonialism brought about social mobility affecting the caste system; this fact has remained unanalyzed to a large extent. In the wake of colonialism, economic and political domains were affected due to changes in land tenure systems, emergence of professional classes, migration, education, law and bureaucratic organizations, but the notion of class which has been akin to Indian society remained in the background. Western notion of class was propagated as a secular and democratic concept of social relations. Class mobility was viewed as the opposite of mobility in the caste system. Simple facts such as class-like distinction within a caste, class considerations in hypergamy and coexistence of caste and class remained peripheral issues, whereas corporateness, pollution-purity and sanskritization were over-emphasized. So much so that caste mobility at the level of individual, family and *jati* (group) has not been adequately analysed as corporateness of caste has overshadowed all other dimensions. Once again, downward social mobility (proletarianization) has not received much needed attention due to overemphasis on upward social mobility. All these gaps could be filled up if theoretic orientations and methods of study could appropriately be suited for the study of Indian society. And this is possible only if theory and method could have their genesis in the ramifications of social inequality existent in Indian society. However, indiscreet indigenization or nativism is not a good substitute for borrowed theories, concepts and methods of study.

References

Aggarwal, P.C., *Caste, Religion and Power*, New Delhi: Shri Ram Centre for Industrial Relation, 1971.

Bailey, F.G., *Caste and the Economic Frontier*, Manchester: Manchester University Press, 1957.

Bailey, F.G., "Closed Social Stratification in India", *European Journal of Sociology*, 4(1), 1963.

Beteille, Andre, *Caste, Class and Power*, Bombay: Oxford University Press, 1966a.

———, "Closed and Open Social Stratification in India", *European Journal of Sociology*, 7, 1966b.

———, "Ideas and Interests: Some Conceptual Problems in the Study of Social Stratification in Rural India", *International Social Science Journal*, 21 (2), 1969.

Bhatt, Anil, *Caste, Class and Politics*, Delhi: Manohar Book Service, 1975.

Dange, S.A., *India from Primitive Communism to Slavery*, Bombay: People's Publishing House, 1949.

Das, Veena and J.P.S., Uberoi, "The Elementary Structure of Caste", *Contributions to Indian Sociology* (New Series), 5, 1971.

Desai, A.R., *Social Background of Indian Nationalism*, Bombay: Popular Prakashan, 1948.

D'Souza, Victor S., *Social Structure of a Planned City—Chandigarh*, New Delhi: Orient Longmans, 1967. See also his "Caste and Class: A Reinterpretation", *Journal of Asian and African Studies*, 2 (3,4), 1967a.

Dumont, L. and Pocock, D.F., "For a Sociology of India, *Contributions to Indian Sociology*, 1, 1957.

———, "A.M. Hocart on Caste, Religion and Power", *Contributions to Indian Sociology*, 2, 1958.

———, "For a Sociology of India: Rejoinder to Dr. Bailey", *Contributions to Indian Sociology*, 4, 1960.

Dumont, Louis, "A Fundamental Problem in Sociology of Caste", *Contributions to Indian Sociology*, 9, 1966.

Dumont, Louis., *Homo Hierarchicus: The Caste System and its Implications*, London: Weidenfeld and Nicolson, 1970.

Frykenberg, R.E. (ed.), *Land Control and Social Structure in Indian History*, Madison: University of Wisconsin Press, 1969.

Furnivall, J.S., *Netherlands, India: A Study in Plural Society*, Cambridge: Cambridge University Press, 1939.

Gough, Kathleen, "Caste in a Tanjore Village", in E.R. Leach (ed.), *Aspects of Caste in South India, Ceylon and North-West Pakistan*, Cambridge: Cambridge University press, 1960.

———, "Modes of Production in Southern India", *Economic and Political Weekly*, 11 (5,6,7), 1980.

Gould, Harold, "Priest and Counter-Priest: A Structural Analysis of Jajmani Relations in the Hindu Plains and the Nilgiri Hills", *Contributions to Indian Sociology* (New Series), 1, 1967.

Hutton, J.H., *Caste in India: Its Nature, Functions and Origin*, Bombay: Oxford University Press, 1963.

Kothari, Rajni, *Politics in India*, New Delhi: Orient Longmans, 1970a.

———, "Introduction: Caste in Indian Politics", in Rajni Kothari (ed.), *Caste in Indian Politics*, New Delhi: Orient Longmans, 1970b.

Marriott, Mckim, *Caste Ranking and Community Structure in Five Regions of India and Pakistan*, Poona: Deccan College, 1965.

Mencher, Joan P., "The Caste System Upside Down or the Not-So-Mysterious East", *Current Anthropology*, 15(4), 1974.

Miller, D.B., *From Hierarchy to Stratification: Changing Patterns of Social Inequality in a North Indian Village*, Delhi: Oxford University Press, 1975.

Mukherjee, Ramkrishna, *The Dynamics of Rural Society*, Berlin: Akademie Verlag, 1957.

Mukerji, D.P., *Diversities*, Delhi: People's Publishing House, 1958.

Namboodiripad, E.M.S., "Caste Conflicts Vs. Growing Unity of Popular Forces", *Economic and Political Weekly*, 14, (7,8), 1979.

Omvedt, Gail, *Land, Caste and Politics in India* (ed.), Delhi: Authors Guild Publications, 1982.

Ranadive, B.T., "Caste, Class and Property Relations", *Economic and Political Weekly*, 14(7,8), 1979.

Saran, A.K., "For a Sociology of India", *Eastern Anthropologist*, 15(1), 1962.

Senart, E., *Caste in India: The Facts and the System*, London: Metheun, 1930.

Sharma, K.L., "Downward Social Mobility: Some Observations", *Sociological Bulletin*, 22(1), 1973.

———, *The Changing Rural Stratification System: A Comparative Study of Six Villages in Rajasthan*, New Delhi: Orient Longman, 1974.

———, *Essays on Social Stratification*, Jaipur: Rawat Publications, 1980.

———, "Caste and Class in India: Some Conceptual Problems", *A Working Paper read at XVI All India Sociological Conference*, (Mimeo), 1982.

———, "Agrarian Stratification: Old Issues, New Explanations and New Issues, Old Explanations", *Economic and Political Weekly*, 18, (42,43), 1983.

Sharma, Surendra, *Sociology in India: A Perspective from Sociology of Knowledge*, New Delhi: M.Phil Dissertation, Jawaharlal Nehru University, 1983.

Singh, Yogendra, "Sociology of Social Stratification", in *A Survey of Research in Sociology and Social Anthropology*, Vol. I, ICSSR, Bombay: Popular Prakashan, 1974.

———, "Sociology of Social Stratification in India- II", Prepared for the *Second Survey of Research in Sociology and Social Anthropology*, ICSSR, New Delhi (Mimeo), 1981.

Srinivas, M.N., *Religion and Society among the Coorgs of South India*, Oxford: Oxford University Press, 1952.

———, *Social Change in Modern India*, Berkley: University of California Press, 1966.

Weber, Max, "Class, Status and Party", in H.H. Gerth and C. Wright Mills (ed.), *From Max Weber: Essays in Sociology*, London: Routledge and Kegan Paul, 1970.

2

Studies on Social Stratification: A Sociology of Knowledge Perspective

Surendra Sharma

Studies on social stratification in India reflect the same theory, method and data which we find in regard to the studies on other aspects of Indian society. Social stratification is a very sensitive field of study. The people, the researchers and the government agents (leaders and bureaucrats) are parts of the system of social stratification. The people are divided into different caste, class, occupational, professional and power groups or categories. The researchers are part of these divisions and study of social stratification by them may bring in subjectivity in understanding of positions of others *vis-a-vis* their own positions. The government has a policy about the nature of social groupings and categories of groups and relations between them. The criticisms of the government are that their policy and action have been at variance; that the rich are becoming richer and the poor are becoming poorer; and that the inequality is 'officially' institutionalized; and this speaks about the nature of the ruling classes and power elite. Thus, social stratification is a field of study which demands a critical analysis from the point of sociology of knowledge. Theory, method and data are the three main concerns in this paper.

A large number of studies on 'caste' have been brought out during the past half a century. A few studies have been published on 'class', particularly in the seventies. Some scholars have focused on the three 'orders', namely, social, economic and political in their studies on social stratification taking clues from Max Weber[1] and P.A. Sorokin.[2] Our objective is not to provide a chronology of the studies on caste, class and social stratification. Our main aim is to analyze these studies from the point of their theory, method and data.

Yogendra Singh has analyzed the studies on social stratification and social change[3] conducted in the 1950s and 1960s from the viewpoint of sociology of knowledge. In a recent study, Singh analyzes the studies on social stratification conducted in the 1970s.[4] It would, therefore, be desirable to give a brief resume of Singh's analysis of the studies on social stratification published in the fifties, sixties and seventies.

Main Questions in the Studies on Social Stratification

The issues in the sociology of social stratification relate to questions of theory, structure and process of social stratification.[5] "The theory of social stratification implies a set of concepts, propositions and assumptions that are verified and validated and constitute an explanatory system."[6] Singh observes that studies on social stratification rarely reach the formal level of theory. The two well-known orientations in the studies on social stratification are of 'functional' and 'conflict' theories. Singh refers to a couple of attempts made by sociologists towards a synthesis of the functional and the conflict theories. He observes: "Now the increasing tendency is to analyze social stratification from a pluralistic conceptual frame by treating both conflict and consensus as two dimensions of the same reality."[7] But Singh does not make this statement in regard to the studies on social stratification in India. Referring to Hans Zetterberg's distinction between the 'prepositional' and the 'dimensionalistic' theory in sociology[8], Singh mentions 'status, wealth, power' approach to the study of social stratification as this corresponds to the 'dimensionalistic' theory. The 'theory' of social stratification thus refers to 'why' of social stratification.

The 'structure' of social stratification could be seen in two ways: (i) the nominalist, and (ii) the realist.[9] The *nominalism* refers to role or status as the unit of social stratification. Davis and Moore and Parsons[10] (the well-known functionalists) consider 'positions' and 'roles' as the units of social stratification. Certain 'attributes' are the basis of classification of roles and positions. Social classes, elites, status groups or castes are taken as units in the *realist* frame of analysis.[11] The processes of social stratification are seen as "changes in the differentiation, evaluation, ranking and rewarding patterns."[12] Accretion, transformation and replacement are the consequences of the processual nature of social stratification. The questions which Singh has posed in regard to theory, structure and process of social stratification are as follows:

(1) What theoretical assumptions have guided studies in social stratification in India?
(2) How far have the functional or dialectical (conflict) theoretical postulates been used either for analysis or selection of problems in social stratification?
(3) Which are the major structural foci in social stratification studies, and has the focus been comprehensive enough to cover most strategic structural units or components of the system of stratification?
(4) Has the focus been biased for historical or other disciplinary reasons towards studies in a specific or particular direction?
(5) Have these studies been sociologically relevant?
(6) Do these studies focus upon the most strategic processes of social stratification?
(7) Have the studies highlighted in a representative manner the processes of social stratification, their causes, consequences and impact upon the overall social order and change in the Indian social system?[13]

Singh analyzes 'caste system and social stratification', 'scheduled castes and social stratification', 'class structures and social stratification', 'agrarian class stratification and change', and 'elites and social stratification' in India in the first trend report published in 1974.[14] The studies in the fifties and sixties have been grouped under these headings.

In *Sociology of Social Stratification in India-II*,[15] Singh provides a sharper analysis of sociology of knowledge perspective about social stratification. The headings are evidence of the concern for the sociology of knowledge perspective. The main points are: 'ideological debate', 'changing theoretical orientations', 'structuralist approach', 'structural-historical approach', 'Marxist analysis of social stratification', 'other social sciences and stratification', 'social stratification in non-Hindu communities', 'tribes and scheduled castes', and 'sociology and social change'. These points compared to the points in the earlier trend report are definitely indicative of change in the theoretic orientations and themes of study in social stratification. Singh clearly exposes the sociology of knowledge perspective for studying social stratification in India.

New theoretical and substantive issues in the studies on social stratification in the seventies have come up due to self-awareness of Indian sociologists. New social situation and evaluation of the national ideology of social stratification have led to the emergence of self-criticism and search for relevance among the Indian sociologists.[16] Singh identifies the following new trends in the studies of social stratification:

(1) increased debates on the ideological moorings of concepts and theories;
(2) efforts to re-schematize conceptual systems and their presuppositions in the light of shifting paradigms;
(3) the new substantive concerns in stratification studies; and finally
(4) fruitful convergence of multidisciplinary interests, both substantive and theoretical, in the studies of social stratification.[17]

The colonial background of the methodological and theoretical legacy of social sciences was attacked along with sociological positivism of the West. The quest for indeginization of paradigms and for relevance[18] became a focal point of attention among Indian social scientists. A broad framework of sociology of knowledge was rooted into experiential reality of Indian society and its historicity. The shadow of colonialism and positivism has been haunting Indian sociology for a long time. Why its harmful impact is realized in the seventies and not in the fifties and the sixties is a question to be examined carefully. Concepts and frameworks given by the British scholars during India's colonization and by the American social scientists in the fifties and sixties have led to perpetuation of colonization, academic and intellectual dependency and mystification of knowledge.[19] A serious 'rethinking' is required. It is not true that all the sociologists and social anthropologists were influenced by American sociological positivism or British functionalism. Iravati Karve's work on kinship[20], I.P. Desai's study of family[21], A.R. Desai's study of nationalism[22] and some other studies remained unaffected by western theoretical and methodological thinking. However, departments of sociology at the universities in Delhi, Jaipur and Chandigarh have had the imprints of such influences.[23]

The crux of the ideological debate is that the concepts, frameworks and paradigms which have dominated the academics are being challenged, refuted and revised or replaced. Mencher suggests that caste be studied from 'upside down' rather than 'top down' perspective.[24] Use of historical material is emphasized by Saberwal.[25] Sharma pleads for structural-historical perspective accepting Indian society as a 'social formation',[26] The bias of the upper caste and class sociologists in their studies has been highlighted.[27] An alternative perspective is offered in the form of a shift of emphasis. Caste model of Indian society[28] is being questioned. The question of evolution of caste and class in India is again looked at afresh by Myrdal[29], Klass[30], and Sinha.[31] Arguments of Srinivas and Dumont for 'sociology for India' are considered not only irrelevant but also harmful.[32] They are blamed for putting wrong priorities and emphasis in sociological studies.

Theoretical Orientations

Yogendra Singh classifies the theoretic concerns in the stratification studies of the seventies as: (i) structural-functional, (ii) structuralist, (iii) structural-historical, and (iv) historical-materialist or Marxist.[33] During the fifties, there was dominance of the structural-functional theory of stratification. Towards the end of the fifties, structuralism and Marxism emerged in the studies of social stratification. In the seventies, the historical perspective was adopted by both Marxists and non-Marxists.[34] Before we take up the studies on social stratification for our analysis, it may be noted that the evolution of approaches to stratification cannot, in fact, be characterized only by structural-functionalism in 1950s, structuralism and Marxism in 1960s, and structural-historical (both Marxists and non-Marxists) in 1970s. Structural-historical perspective was adopted by A.R. Desai[35], a noted Marxist in 1940s; structuralist view could be seen in the 1950s in the writings of Bougle[36],Dumont[37] and Hocart.[38] The 1950s and the 1960s were dominated by structural-functionalism (both American and British) and structuralism[39] (both British and French). Structural-historical perspective has ideological overtones of both borrowed and modified Marxism and indeginization in the form of a reaction to Marxist perspective and rejection of western positivism and culturology.[40] Even today, there are people engaged in studies from the viewpoint of western positivism, culturologism and orthodox Marxism.[41]

K.L. Sharma divides the studies on stratification into two categories: (i) the studies on caste stratification; and (ii) the multidimensional studies.[42] The studies in the first category are by Kroeber, Weber, Hutton, Ghurye, Hocart, Myrdal, Dumont, Leach, Srinivas, Dube, Bailey, Lewis, Mayer, Mathur, Majumdar, Marriott, etc.[43] These sociologists and social anthropologists have focused on caste as the sole institution of social ranking. What is known as 'caste model of Indian society' is their theoretical perspective. Caste is treated as an extreme form of class or as a closed community. Some others have given premium to socio-religious and ritualistic considerations. The ideas related to pollution-purity and religion are treated as the basis of caste ranking. 'Elaboration' of caste ranking has also been compared in various zones of India. None of these studies refer to the phenomena of class and power. They, in fact, consider caste as synonym with social structure. These studies were carried out in 1950s and in the first half of the sixties.

The multidimensional studies on social stratification do not consider caste as an all-inclusive basis of social stratification. Economic position, style of life, education, occupation and personality attributes are evaluated for assessing a person's rank in his community or caste. Beteille refers to the emergence of 'differentiated institutional structures of various kinds' and 'case free' areas.[44] Later on he explains the necessity for studying 'ideas and interests'.[45] One finds a shift in Beteille's emphasis from 'caste-oriented' studies to 'class-oriented' studies of stratification. Bhatt's study of caste, class and politics[46] and Aggrawal's study of caste, religion and power[47] also emphasize the multidimensionality of social stratification. However, studies by Gough[48] and Ramakrishna Mukherjee[49] are different in their theoretic orientation compared to the studies by Beteille, Bhatt and Aggrawal. Gough and Mukherjee look at caste from a class point of view with Marxist disposition. But, it is clear that even in the sixties 'caste alone' view was questioned. Sharma's study of six villages in Rajasthan[50] in the sixties highlighted the role of ascription, units of ranking, dimensions of stratification, ideological bases of stratification, factors of change in stratification and its emerging patterns. Both 'structural' and 'cultural' perspectives were used to facilitate analysis of caste, class, caste and class consciousness, occupational and social mobility, power structure and value- orientation. Land tenure systems, land reforms, *panchayati raj*, educational achievements, occupational opportunities and networks were studied in particular in view of the multidimensionality of social stratification and limitations of the 'caste model'.

The studies of social stratification in the fifties and the sixties were guided by structural-functionalism and structuralism barring a few studies which had variants of structural-historical perspective. Yogendra Singh observes that the basic premises of structural-functional studies have implied a *systemic teleology* based on the Brahminic or 'hierarchical' model of caste society, harmony or consensus as the system state from which change, differentiation or fission was studied emphasised on a micro-structural or communitarian scale of reality.[51] The caste system would not change. It would absorb all tensions and changes generated by polity and economy. 'Summation of roles' was its basic feature, hence consensual ideology. Historicity was a casualty in these studies of caste system.[52] However, the structural-functional studies in

1970s have shown two tendencies: (i) deeper substantive and theoretical concerns in respect of processes of change, and (ii) increased diagnostic orientation.[53]

The notions of social mobility advanced by Srinivas[54] have been examined afresh. Downward mobility, proletarianization and bourgeoisiefication as processes of structural change[55] have been reported. Relations between caste and class, caste and religion, caste and tribe, etc., have also been questioned. Dumont and Srinivas have ideologized (in their differing characteristic styles) resilience of the caste system and its principle of hierarchy.[56] Bailey[57], Kolenda[58] and Miller[59] refer to changes in the caste system from its 'organic' nature to its 'segmentary' character, but hold the view that caste continues to be the focal point of hierarchial relations in Indian society.

Let us take up a few studies from the viewpoint of their theoretical positions. Srinivas' emphasis on the role of religion in the Coorg society is clearly an extension of Radcliffe-Brown's functionalism. Srinivas observes that everything could be seen in terms of pure and impure. The entire life is organized around religion. Thus, it is the social organization of religion that encompasses everything else. Srinivas does not look at village polity, economy, consequences of religion on people's existence as the points necessary for investigation.

Weberian Approach

Srinivas' perspective has inspired several scholars for undertaking their doctoral researches on similar lines. However, some students of Srinivas have differed from him. Beteille's study of social stratification in a village in Tamil Nadu may be cited here.[60] Beteille poses the question: "What is the central theme of the study here presented?" He answers this question by saying: "Broadly speaking, our concern is with the phenomena of caste, class and power with their changing relations."[61] Beteille refers to 'caste-free' areas. He writes: "The social system has acquired a much more complex and dynamic character, now there is a tendency for cleavages to cut across one another." "The hierarchies of caste, class, and power in the village overlap to some extent, but also cut across."[62] Beteille justifies his use of the concept of 'class' as he finds "the differentiation of institutional structures". Weber's notion of class is found useful to understand emergence of market economy. Beteille's perspective is also evident when he states that "...there is a very little preoccupation with purity, pollution, and rituals in general."[63] This is a qualitatively different position compared with that of Srinivas. Beteille not only treats caste, class and power as abstract categories on the pattern of 'class, status and party' as given by Weber, he also finds diversity at empirical level between economic, social and political distinctions among the people.

The problem with Beteille's formulation is not that distinctions are not there, but *a priori* acceptance of Weber's theory and its implicit ideology creates problems in proper understanding of social reality in a village of Tamil Nadu. Methodological individualism, *Verstehen* or interpretative understanding and rationalism (or psychologism) are fundamental bases of Weber's trio (class, status and party). These are neither stated nor exemplified by adopting certain research strategies. Surreptitious adoption of Weber's schema is evident in Beteille's study. Diversity between Indian village and German society (which was basis of Weber's formulation) is overlooked. Application of Weber's approach for studying social stratification by Beteille implies a contradiction between theory and method.[64]

There are two more studies, one by P.C. Aggarwal[65] and other by Anil Bhatt[66], which may be treated along with Beteille's study discussed above. Aggarwal also does not formulate his theoretical proposition like Beteille; however, we can perceive it from some of the statements and data reported in Aggarwal's book. Let me also mention that Aggarwal's book is more of a village monograph rather than a study of social stratification based on caste, religion and power. He has studied the Meos of Mewat with a holistic perspective. Meos are a Muslim community. Structural-functional orientation is implicit as Aggarwal gives a detailed account of the region, people, village, caste system, economic life, family and kinship, religion, life cycle rites and political organization. Some historical glimpses have also been provided. Participant observation and unstructured interviews were used for gathering data. Scaling technique was also used in analyzing data. Integration of Meos with the wider society and with the Hindus was also investigated.

Though Aggarwal uses ethnography as a methodological device, his emphasis is on the understanding of social structure of the Meos in Chavandi Kalan, a village in Alwar district of Rajasthan. Aggarwal concludes that ritual status is insignificant in social ranking. Unequal distribution of power and economic resources is the crucial basis. However, Aggarwal's study lacks an understanding of 'class relations' among the Meos. Thus, only inferentially, we consider Aggarwal's study as structural-functional, but in form as the title suggests, it is more of a Weberian study.

A clear exposition of theoretical formulation is found in Bhatt's study of caste, class and politics. He states that the objectives of his study are: (i) to compare and correlate ascriptive, socio-economic and political dimensions of social stratification; (ii) to study the interaction between traditional social structures and modern democratic politics; and (iii) to examine the extent to which the traditional model of social stratification in India obtains today.[67] The model of social stratification in traditional India is that of 'summation of statuses'. All aspects become subservient to the basis of this model. The implications of this model are that caste encompassed all other aspects; there was no differentiation within the caste groups; it was a homogeneous but complex social organization; and there were non-antagonistic strata. Thus, the traditional India had closed, highly hierarchical, combinative, non-competitive social stratification.[68] Bhatt writes: "For my purpose, the first view serves as a benchmark in contrast to the democratically ordered society envisioned by the constitution of Independent India."[69] Like 'comparative politics', Bhatt uses the phrase 'comparative social stratification'[70]. The writings which are cited by Bhatt are of Robert Dahl, L. Rudolph and S. Rudolph, Bernard Barber, McKim Marriott, Neil Smelser and S.M. Lipset, M. Tumin, A.C. Mayer, F. Barth, Andre Beteille, F.G. Bailey, Rajni Kothari and S. Verba and N. Pie, etc.[71] in support of his structural-functional perspective.

Bhatt puts the question: "Can India realize this new order in such a deep-rooted and pervasive traditional social structure?" In view of this question, Bhatt explores relationship between society and politics. "Social system is conceptualized as a larger system and political system as its subsystem."[72] Bhatt's conceptual framework conceives of society as a separate and larger system instead of an aggregate of interacting subsystems. Such a framework considers social structures as independent variables and political factors as dependent variables.[73] Bhatt's study is an 'ideal' illustration of structural-functionalist positivism. Analysis of the pattern and degree of relationship between caste, class and politics, the degree of status congruence, the extent of socio-economic and political inequalities, the degree of internal differentiation, the impact of caste status on socio-economic and political positions and conversely the impact of democratic political structures on processes of the caste system reveals the notion of 'whole' and 'parts' relationships. We shall refer to methodological and substantive aspects of this study later on it this chapter.

Structural-Functional-Positivistic Approach

Victor S. D'Souza applies the structural-functionalist-positivistic approach to the study of social stratification. His study of Chandigarh[74] and analysis of caste and class[75] emphasize the significance of the continuum of the rigidity-fluidity dimensions and the individual and his properties as the units of analysis rather than castes as endogamous groups. Class and individual as the bases of social stratification in place of caste and group are considered significant in the present context. In his study of Chandigarh, D'Souza considers educational, occupational and income hierarchies as predominant features of urban social stratification. These are significantly related with each other. A scale of prestige is constructed based on these variables. Following L. Warner and Richard Centres, D'Souza classifies classes as upper, middle, working class and lower class based on the prestige of individual members.[76] The data are based on survey method and attitudinal responses. This approach is generally known as 'attributional' approach.

A crude application of structural-functionalism is found in Rajni Kothari's book *Politics in India*.[77] Kothari and Bhatt provide a similar perspective, however, their data-base and research strategies are not the same. Kothari analyzes politics at macro-level based on secondary sources, published researches and other materials. Bhatt's study is rooted into typical American sociological positivism, hence a comparative study based on sampling and questionnaire from four states of India. Structural-functionalism in Kothari's study is evident from the following statements taken from the first chapter of his book:

(1) India is a relatively open political system, hence no congruent development. Discrepancy between ideal and real creates inequalities including the political ones.

(2) The social system in India provides a key to political stability. Any change in power relations should be seen in this perspective as well.

(3) The traditional political culture seeks to incorporate into its womb the best elements of the culture of the modern world, without destroying the age-old traditions and diversities.

(4) Thus, Indian society operates still largely as apolitical society.

(5) Politics in India is preeminently the politics of *integration*, e.g., structural continuity exists in the sphere of power.[t78]

Kothari refers to the processes of 'nation-building'. He writes: "What is being stressed is the increasing political orientation of social interests, in which the political process provides the inclusive setting within which these interests are found to interact."[79] However, this perspective of Kothari has been belied even before this was published. The elections of 1967 witnessed defeat of the Congress in more than half of the states. Of late, the emergence of regional forces and culture of politics in Tamil Nadu, Andhra Pradesh and Punjab[80] have also falsified the basic tenets of Kothari's thesis. What was not accepted said by Selig Harrison about the emergence of regional forces[81] perhaps could be accepted after the recent Akali movement and the emergence of Telugu Desham in Andhra Pradesh.

Kothari uses the vocabulary of American 'functionalists' in

particular without any sort of inhibition or objection in both *Politics in India* and in his 'Introduction' to *Caste in Indian Politics*.[82] I cite a few statements to show the conservatism of functionalist approach *vis-a-vis* of Kothari. "Politics is a competitive enterprise, its purpose is the acquisition of power for the realization of certain goals, and its process is one of identifying and manipulating existing and emerging allegiances in order to mobilize and consolidate positions."[83] Politics is mass based. Politics must strive to organize through such a structure (caste structure).[84] *Politicization of caste* is necessary for modernizing India. Politics is an instrument for a group to consolidate its position.[85] Kothari accepts an American author's view—*the democratic incarnation of caste*.[86] Caste has the *secular aspect*,[87] it has the integration aspect, and the *aspect of consciousness*.[88] These aspects led to the *modernization* of India's polity.[89] Let us quote again: "Finally the politicization of caste makes for outward looking, upward moving orientations and as this results in the phenomenon of multiple memberships and overlapping identities, the result is highly secular for the polity as well as the society at large."[90] This not only speaks of theoretical, methodological and epistemological apriorism and determinism, but also reveals an utter lack of understanding or realization of historicity of Indian society and polity. Kothari does not debate the relevance or irrelevance of the functionalist perspective before accepting it for studying Indian society. He does not compare it with alternative perspectives and frameworks. The quite acceptance of a theoretical perspective smacks of an academic conspiracy and ideological propaganda. We leave the debate at this point.

Let us now make a brief mention of two books, namely, F.G. Bailey's *Caste and the Economic Frontier*[91] and T.S. Epstein's *Economic Development and Social Change in South India*.[92] Both of the studies focus on social change in village. Since the structural aspect of change is duly taken into account, it would be relevant to make a reference about them. Bailey looks at the caste system in a village in Orissa under a new economy. The new frontiers are economic, political and administrative. Transfer of land from the ex-landowners is a significant fact which makes land a market commodity, and other occupations which were tied with landlordism also become part of a market situation. Bailey gives details about new economy, land transactions, services and trade. He writes: "The mercantile economy has impinged on the system of agriculture, because those who profited as merchants, traders and earners of salaries invested their money in land."[93] Bailey puts three questions: (1) Why did they do so? (2) What made it possible for them to buy land? (3) What has been the effect of the redistribution of land on the social structure of the village? These questions support the position which Bailey took about Dumont and Pocock's position regarding Indian sociology. Bailey looks at 'culture' from the perspective of 'structure'.

Epstein's study also emphasizes on social change, but from a comparative perspective. Epstein follows by and large Bailey's line of research. The main argument of Epstein's study is that a structural innovation (irrigation) consolidates village economy, but it restricts social change, namely, migration, contacts, education and politicization, etc. Conversely, a lack of such an innovation results into widespread social change without corresponding economic development. Epstein's study of two villages in Karnataka from this structural perspective provides us details about crops, houses, landholdings, livestock, family incomes and expenditures, market networks, etc. This study also like that of Bailey focuses on changes in the traditional social structure and hierarchy in the village community.

Structuralist Approach

Levi-Strauss' structuralist principle of complimentary dualism or logical principle of opposition as a fundamental feature of human mind[94] is applied by Louis Dumont in his study of hierarchy and marriage alliance.[95] Pure and impure, consanguinity and affinity are examples of this logical dualism. These also refer to the notion of hierarchy. Graded statuses are entrenched into all spheres including kinship. Dumont sees intercaste, intracaste and intrafamilial ranking as projections of the same intellectual and ideological principle. Dumont emphasized necessity of looking for *cultural meaning* of affinity and consanguinity. The structuralist stance of Dumont is clearly seen in his assertion that it is hierarchy which is pervasive principle of Hindu society and the caste system is only one expression of it. There is hierarchy of principles and values of occupations, food and clothes, and also of 'bride givers' and 'bride takers'.

It is this thinking of Dumont which he had about Indian society in 1950s that found its fuller expression and exposition in his subsequent writings in *Contributions to Indian Sociology* and in *Homo Hierarchicus*.[96] Yogendra Singh observes that the pivotal notions of structuralism are: *ideology, dialectics, transformational relationship and comparison* in regard to social stratification as particularly found in Dumont's *Homo Hierarchicus*. The basic tenet of caste system is 'hierarchy'. The opposition between pure and impure defines its binary tension, its dialectics. Dumont observes that "hierarchy also inheres the relationship of 'encompassing' and being 'encompassed'."[97]

Dumont's theoretical perspective is clear in the statement: "I think that this view of the duality as one of form and content is mistaken, and that hierarchy, especially in its exemplary Indian form, teaches us a better way of looking at it."[98] Dumont makes three points about this:

(1) A hierarchical relation is a relation between larger and smaller, or more precisely, between *that which encompasses and that which is encompassed*. "The duality that plagues us is not one of form and content but that of the *encompassing and the encompassed*." The duality is real in so far as *we come to know* the two kinds of aspects in a different way: (i) basic values related to kinship, caste, status, etc., and (ii) political or economic aspects as observed in actual situations.

(2) Opposition is found between the orientation to the whole (*holism*) and the orientation to the element (*individualism*). Caste represents the holistic orientation and equality refers to the individualistic orientation. The 'whole' is something religious (or philosophical), while 'economy' is a matter of the individual. The division of labour in the Indian village is not an economic fact; it is a holistic (religious) fact.

(3) The third point refers to ritual status and power. The king as sovereign is the high priest and the ruler in one person. It is a fact. But in *principle*, the priest and the king are absolutely distinguished—the priest is highest in status even if he is dependent materially. Thus, priesthood encompasses rulership; and at the same time these 'twin forces' together encompass all the rest.[99]

Dumont's conception of social change or the principle of transformational relationship is moulded by his frame of reference. He observes that there has been change *in* the society and not *of* the society. Dumont postulates that *comparison* is possible within a cultural type, it is also possible within such types. He does not emphasize on the uniqueness of a society. Comparison is possible between logically opposite types, hence comparison of India with West and *vice-versa*.

Dumont's structuralist view on India's social stratification in terms of pure and impure or binary opposition (encompassing and encompassed) is found lacking theoretically as well as substantively. The 'pure' is found in the 'impure', and *vice-versa*. Gould's concept of 'contrapriest'[100] explains the fusion of purity or priesthood in the 'impure' or 'untouchable'. In a symposium on Dumont's *Homo Hierarchicus*, it is suggested by Veena Das[101] and Veena Das and J.P.S Uberoi[102] that the pure and impure are fused in many rituals. It is suggested that the dichotomy of 'sacred' and 'non-sacred' and the notion of 'reciprocity' would be more appropriate for analyzing caste system in India.

Dumont's structuralist perspective lacks a conception of history.[103] His view also suffers from the neglect of the politico-economic dimensions of Indian reality.[104] However, Dumont makes a clear distinction between the substantivist and the structuralist modes of thinking. He draws a distinction between dialectics and hierarchy, contradiction and complementarity. Pure and impure are not of a dialectical nature; they are complementary opposites.[105] Singh observes that Dumont's view has created a high self-consciousness among Indian sociologists about the study of caste and class in India.[106]

Recent Alternative Perspectives

There are a few studies in which differentiation, evolution and change in caste and class over a period of time have been focused. We could say that the emphasis in these studies could be seen as on caste, caste and class, class alone, again caste, and now caste and class as parts of social formation. Besides sociologists and social anthropologists, historians and economists have taken up studies from structural-historical perspective particularly of the agrarian and industrial stratification, and mode of production in agriculture *vis-a-vis* rural class structure. Mortan Klass[107] and S. Sinha[108] have analyzed once again the origin and evolution of caste system in India. The continuity of caste system has been possible mainly due to support of economic factors and internalization of the hierarchical norms among people. The question of origin of caste has also been raised by the Marxists, namely, S.A. Dange, B.T. Ranadive and E.M.S. Namboodiripad.[109] They all look at caste as an institution based on exploitation of the lower castes by the upper castes. Mencher sees caste as a form of class.[110] The non-Marxist scholars do not treat caste as a superstructural entity, whereas the Marxist scholars treat it as a superstructural phenomenon. The latter are certainly not correct, but the former also should not ignore the role of economic factors in the evolution and resilience of caste system.

Studies of social and agrarian movements have been undertaken with structural-historical perspective by M.S.A. Rao[111], Rajendra Singh[112], P.N. Mukherji[113], K.L. Sharma[114], and of caste and class relationship by Satish Saberwal[115], S. Sivakumar and Chitra Siva Kumar.[116] All of them have emphasized the element of *time* and the influences which economic, political and ideological forces had upon caste and class. These studies are 'historical', but they are different from those of historians as they have studied neither the remote past nor the immediate present in *detail* based on primary sources. Most of these studies are of contemporary period and cover a vast canvas. They refer more to 'levels' and 'breakthroughs' for getting insights into the emergence of the present structures. Thus, the historically oriented studies give emphasis to the understanding of the present by conducting field studies. Singh also shows his preference for structural-historical approach[117], but he has not conducted an empirical study based on this approach.

Yogendra Singh outlines the main features of Marxist analysis of social stratification as follows: "The treatment of stratification in Marxist theory has distinctive features: it is systematic; it is dialectical; it treats structures (stratification) as historical product; it locates historical forces in the mode of production, reflection of the specific nature of man which under certain historical conditions creates contradictions of classes; it is essentially evolutionary and developmental, since mode of production and the relationship that it generates are endowed with dialectical quality of self-transformation."[118] Mode of production is the key of the Marxist theory of social stratification.

Systematic studies based on this approach began with A.R. Desai's study of 'nationalism' in 1940s, but more of such studies have been taken up recently as a reaction to the studies based on structural-functional and structuralist approaches. Singh refers to the studies by J. Pathy[119], P.K. Bose[120], Hira Singh[121], D.N. Dhanagare[122], D. Gupta[123] and Kathleen Gough.[124] The mode of production debate[125] highlights the issues related to the nature of agrarian class structure and differentiation of peasantry. These studies refer to the forces and factors of class polarization, exploitation, bourgeoisiefication of the peasantry and pauperization of the rural working class. Thus, the basic concern is the study of origin, structure and change in caste and class in India.[126] Caste and kinship are analyzed from a class point of view.[127] Caste is not treated as culture-specific system, but a reflection of class relationships.

Now we may refer to a few illustrative studies from the point of their conceptual framework. While analyzing the social and economic structure of rural India, Bettelheim writes: "Throughout its existence, the colonial system grafted new legal ties and property rights into the existing framework of production."[128] The laws created privileged social classes and also enforced the *status quo*. Bettelheim analyzes rural class structure in the post-independence period in view of Zamindari, Mahalwari, Ryotwari and Jagirdari systems of land tenure. Borrowing from D. Thorner[129], Bettelheim analyzes *mazdoors, kisans* and *maliks*. The change is seen towards *capitalism*. In the same way, Bettelheim analyzes India's industrial structure, the bourgeoisie and capital, the proletariat and the petty bourgeoisie, and the nature of Indian State. A similar analysis is found in a collection of essays by A.R. Desai.[130]

In a recent study of a village in Tamil Nadu, John Harris discusses the issue of capitalism and peasant farming.[131] He uses the Marxist approach with a difference. Harris writes: "I argue that the expanded reproduction of capital in agricultural production is subordinated to that of merchant and finance capital, in a form of economy like those described by Marx as 'intermediate' forms of capitalism. The process of 'differentiation of the peasantry is thus 'blocked' both because of the character of the economy and by the ideological structures of caste and kinship which reinforce the existing relations of production and the power structure."[132] Thus, Harris examines the question of relationship between caste and mode of production. Control of land by members of a caste is considered as a decisive determinant of 'dominance'. Harris finds that class of rich peasant-merchant-moneylenders came to dominate both agriculture and trade, and this is shown up in the dominance of the members of the same caste in both agriculture and trade.[133]

Some of the essays in a recently edited book *Land, Caste and Politics in India* by Gail Omvedt[134] clearly show that caste is not merely a cultural category. Atrocities on Harijans, movements of Dalits, unity moves among the Kulaks, and that the dominant castes are less of castes and more of classes—have amply shown class genesis of the social relations among people. Omvedt writes: "Class should be basically defined in terms of the *social* Marxist concept of the social *relations of production*."[135] Omvedt feels that "caste is not only form but also concrete material context."[136] The Indian feudal social formation was actually based on a *caste, feudal mode of production*. Castes and classes are found in a mix, and both have 'feudal' and 'capitalist' forms and affect each other, hence a social formation perspective.[137] Omvedt agrees with Gough's classification of the pre-British South Indian society into five major classes: (1) the state class; (2) the state servants, (3) commodity producers and merchants, (4) peasants, herders, fishermen and attached village servants, and (5) agricultural and menial slaves.[138] The last could be called *dalit* labourers. The first four classes are seen as equivalent of four *varnas*, and the fifth with the untouchables.

In a recent article, K.L. Sharma writes: "The understanding of caste and class demands an approach which has: (1) dialectics, (2) history, (3) culture, and (4) structure as its essential features."[139] Dialectics does not mean binary tension, it refers to change through time as a result of contradictions. History gives an account of levels and events in the structure of society. Culture refers to the norms which define the patterns of relations. Structure is seen as a product of dialectical, historical and cultural forces. Therefore, caste-class polarity is a misplaced one. The idea of change from caste to class is a wrong perception. Caste as an ideology is a dangerous move and perhaps so is the case with 'class alone' perspective as the basis of study of Indian society. However, no serious studies have been carried out by sociologists and other social scientists considering Indian society as a social formation *vis-a-vis* social stratification.

Methodological Orientations

Indian sociologists and social anthropologists have not been quite sensitive to research methodology and field of study. Broadly speaking, they have been swept (barring a few exceptions) by currents of theory and method in the western countries. Even if it was not the case at an early phase of Indian sociology, a large number of sociologists followed the methods of study adopted by a few leading sociologists of that period. Thus, one could say that indological survey, participant observation and historical methods (or techniques) have dominated sociological researches in India. A clear link between a method of study and a given theoretical perspective has generally remained vague in a large number of researches. Thus, the theoretical perspectives adopted by Indian sociologists have not remained rooted in Indian social reality. The methods of study have remained unrelated to these perspectives.

The methods have been adopted mainly due to two reasons: (i) the notion of scienticism has compelled a researcher to accept a particular method; and (ii) convenience of accepting a method of study. We hardly find any study on social stratification which explains the correspondence between its theoretical perspective, method of study and data.

Beteille's study of caste, class and power in Sripuram village of Tanjore district in Tamil Nadu is based on intensive field-work (participant observation). Beteille writes: "I did my field-work in Sripuram while living with people as one among them. I was permitted to live in the *agraharam* in a Brahmin house—a privilege, as I was often told, never before extended to an outsider and a non-Brahmin. I dined with the Brahmins and had access to most of their houses. I was perhaps the only non-Brahmin ever to have sat and eaten with the Brahmins in Sripuram on ceremonial occasions. I was identified with the Brahmins by my dress, my appearance, and the fact that I lived in one of their houses."[140]

Beteille admits that his identification with the Brahmins was not an unmixed blessing. The non-Brahmins and Adi-Dravidas took Beteille like as one of the Brahmins of the village. Consequently, he could not elicit properly the required information about the non-Brahmins and the Adi-Dravidas. The reason for staying in *agraharam* as given by Beteille is: "Had I lived with the non-Brahmins the Brahmins would not have moved freely with me. Had I lived with the Adi-Dravidas, the *agraharam* would have been unaccessible. I chose to live with the Brahmins for practical reason and also because this gave me an opportunity to gain some insight into the literate cultural tradition of the region."[141]

Beteille admits certain limitations of his study. "Had I lived with the Adi-Dravidas this study would perhaps have had a different focus."[142] The other point is that "the study is qualitative in its character and emphasis."[143] The village has not been understood "in quantitative and statistical terms." Beteille says that he has understood the village's social life "from within, in terms of the values and meanings attributed to it by the people themselves."[144] It is mentioned by Beteille that his status as a resident of *agraharam* was curiously ambiguous one of 'outsider' as well as 'insider'. As

Beteille claims it gave him the advantage of both insider and outsider. He writes: "My field-work was not done in a very planned or organized manner. I did not enter the field armed with a battery of hypotheses."[145] Beteille feels that formulation of hypotheses "would have done more harm than good."[146] Beteille writes in an article that "in adjusting oneself (Beteille himself) to a stratified community one learns much about the nature of stratification itself."[147] The points raised in the article—"The Tribulations of Field Work" by Beteille[148] are the same which he makes in his study of caste class and power. Some observations given by P.N. Mukherji on participant observation in the form of criticism of Beteille's[149] view may be mentioned below.

Mukherji formulates three questions: (1) By what criteria does the researcher select his community or small group for study? (2) Does the researcher enter the field first and then let the investigation take 'shape' or does he approach the field with a clearly formulated plan of investigation? (3) What indeed is the method of participant observation, and how are we to assess its utility in the Indian context?[150] Our interest is in the first two questions more than the third one. Simply an interest to understand a community's social life cannot be the basis for an extensive study. Also some knowledge about the people cannot be the basis of an insightful investigation. The point is that some research objectives are always thought of beforehand. However, our concern is still more for the second question and we tend to agree with Mukherji's observation on that question. We, like Mukherji, do not agree with Beteille's statement that he went to Sripuram without a definite preference for any particular aspect of its social life; that he did not have an interest in the problem of social inequality. Beteille's assertion that he got interested in the study of social inequality after seeing the marks of stratification in virtually every sphere of life.[151] The danger in acceptance of Beteille's position is that it is not the cognitive understanding of society and explanations about society that determine our interests of research, but it is the observation of field that determines the object of study.

A number of questions could be raised about Beteille's method of study. Why did he not plan his field-work? Was his village a unique one? Did he not have any idea of a village in India? Did he not read Max Weber or Karl Marx before conducting the present study? Did he relate his data with the formulations of Weber in particular and of Marx and others in general after field-work? Beteille perhaps knows about these questions relating to his study. There is no connection whatsoever between the 'battery of hypotheses' and 'concepts' which he has formulated (may be after he completed his field-work) and the method of study. Beteille's study lacks required *historical* perspective. The formulations of Weber and Marx would demand a historical understanding of caste, class and power. Beteille has also ignored (perhaps unwittingly) the ideological implications of Max Weber's conceptual framework. The ghost of Marx was the basis of Weber's distinction between class, status and party. Where was such a ghost before Beteille? However, it is true that analysis of rituals and religion finds a negligent place in Beteille's study of Sripuram, but it is not clear whether it was consciously planned to chase the ghost of Louis Dumont's binary opposition of pure and impure or Srinivas' emphasis on the study of religion in Rampura. Certainly, Srinivas' impact on Beteille is seen in the advocacy of participant observation, but Beteille is unable to relate it with Weber's theory of social stratification and its implicit ideological moorings.

K.L. Sharma's study of the changing rural stratification system has been guided by 'a battery of hypotheses'.[152] He expresses his concern for scarcity of multidimensional studies of social stratification. His study raises questions about 'caste' as an overreaching stratification, vertical or pyramidal arrangements of caste groups and caste (or group) as the unit of social ranking. Sharma questions the thesis of 'corporateness' about social ranking and social mobility. He uses both structural and cultural criteria in understanding of social stratification.

Emphasis on comparison based on variables such as economic conditions, geographical factors and cultural distinctiveness along with land tenure systems is the hallmark of Sharma's-study of social stratification in six villages of Rajasthan. The study is based on census and enumeration method, sampling, interview, case study, secondary data, and historical records. Participant observation alone is not the standpoint of Sharma's study. Since the study was based on a well-thought of plan, these techniques were found useful for gathering a variety of information.[153] The study provides a 'mix' of qualitative and quantitative analysis of social stratification.

Anil Bhatt's complaint is that ethnographers and social anthropologists have made 'qualitative' studies of single villages or single or multiple castes and communities. They do not provide quantification, but have a tendency to generalize or typify their limited observations and studies. Generalization and quantification are closely related. A large part of Bhatt's study is based on quantitative data gathered through survey research and deals with macro-national and regional levels of social stratification. He talks of 'degrees' and 'amounts' instead of 'generally', 'approximately' and 'mostly', etc. in his analysis of data. Bhatt deals with individuals as members of a caste, caste as a group in relation to other castes and the caste system as a dimension of social stratification in relation to socio-economic and political dimensions. He has collected large-scale data in more substantive and relevant contexts.[154] Bhatt writes: "I have tried to be very explicit in relating the evidences to the theory." Perhaps Bhatt has done more justice to Weber's conceptualization than Beteille in regard to substantiation, unit of study and range of analysis.

There are a few village studies based on information collected by questionnaire.[155] Computerization of data has also been reported in village studies. Techniques of scale analysis have been applied. In several studies, interview schedule has been used for data collection. However, most of the studies on social stratification concerning rural India are based on participant observation, interview and case study method. Studies of social stratification relating to urban India are based on survey method and questionnaire.

Let us now discuss briefly the Marxian method of study. The essence of this method is that the explanation comes from the conditions and structure of social reality. Marxian approach is a historical explanation. It takes into account the course of events over a period of time in a given society in regard to class relations among the people. It is an evolutionary approach. Some have called it emancipatory and hermeneutic in nature. For studying social stratification in the British period, A.R. Desai has analyzed economy, agriculture, handicraft industries, means of transport, modern education, political and administrative set-up, class structure, role of press, social and reform movements etc. The perspective is dialectical-historical.[156] Bettelheim's study of caste and class structure in post-independence period uses the same approach. But, between the two, Desai does more justice with Marxist approach and method of study.

The variants of the Marxist theory and method of study are found in the studies of D.P. Mukerji[157], Kathleen Gough[158], Gail Omvedt[159] and Ramakrishna Mukherjee[160]. As we know that Mukerji has analyzed Indian tradition from the Marxist approach, but he collected a different sort of research material compared with that of Desai and Bettelheim. He was more interested in understanding of the cognitive and meaning structures which formed Indian tradition than the concrete classes itself. Gough and Omvedt consider caste as an important aspect of Indian society, and the study of caste along with class structure and mode of production is characterized by this method. Gough has done this in her recent studies of South India,[161] and Omvedt has done this in her recent studies of *dalits* in Maharashtra.[162] Mukherjee has combined historical and census data with the data relating to the present class and caste structure in his study of rural society in Bengal. Several other sociologists with Marxist and non-Marxist dispositions have used historical method in their analysis of caste and class and agrarian movements.[163] Among the non-Marxists (or even anti-Marxists), Dumont is one who combines the method of indology, abstracted empiricism and pseudo history in his well-known study—*Homo Hierarchicus*.[164]

The method of study largely determines the nature of data in a given study. As we know, a large number of studies on caste have used ethnographic accounts prepared by the British officers. Some others have used scriptural texts as source of their analyses. Historical accounts and studies are found as data in some studies. However, in the post-independence period, generation of data by sociologists and anthropologists in both rural and urban areas has been a pronounced practice. This has been done through field studies based on techniques such as survey, interview, observation and case study.

The main problem is still to find out a proper connection between theory, method and data. Field studies with the use of research techniques such as survey, interview and observation and some statistical devices became so fashionable that researchers remained 'unarmed' or 'unaware' about the intrinsic connection between theory, method and data. In other words, the false notion of making a study scientific simply by adopting these techniques of research has created innumerable problems. Secondly, the notion of 'science' in social sciences has been distorted by implementing it in a vulgarized and unrealistic way. However, such a problem is seen more in the case of 'commercialization' of social research. It is this sociology of knowledge perspective, which is lacking, that is, sensitization about nature of theory and its implications for method and data.

Notes

1. Max Weber, "Class, status, party" in H.H. Gerth and C. Wright Mills (eds.), *From Max Weber: Essays in Sociology*, London: Routledge & Kegan Paul Ltd., 1970, pp. 180-185.
2. P.A. Sorokin, *Social and Cultural Mobility*, London: The Free Press, 1964.
3. Yogendra Singh, "Sociology of social stratification", in *A Survey of Research in Sociology and Social Anthropology*, Vol. I (ICSSR), Bombay: Popular Prakashan, 1974, pp. 311-383.
4. Yogendra Singh, "Sociology of social stratification in India-II," prepared for the *Second Survey of Research in Sociology and Social Anthropology* (ICSSR), New Delhi, 1981 (mimeographed). Now it is published.
5. Yogendra Singh, op.cit., 1974, p. 311.
6. Ibid., p. 311.
7. Ibid., p. 312.
8. Cf. Y. Singh, Ibid., p. 313.
9. Ibid., p. 313. See also Raymond Aron's two definitions of class in Andre Beteille (ed.), *Social Inequality*, Penguin Books, 1969, pp.

67-68. The two definitions of class are: (i) the American, in which the emphasis is on *nominalist* character, prestige and status determined by class, and (ii) the French, in which the *realist* tendency is there—class represents total reality, collective consciousness and class is different from stratum.

10. See, for example, Kingsley Davis and Wilbert E. Moore's "Some principles of social stratification," *American Sociological Review*, Vol. 10, No. 2, 1945, pp. 242-49; and Talcott Parsons, "An analytical approach to the theory of social stratification", and "A revised analytical approach to the theory of social stratification", in Talcott Parsons, *Essays in Sociological Theory*, Glencoe: The Free Press, 1964. However, for the debate on the functional approach to social stratification, see Celia S. Heller (ed.), *Structured Social Inequality*, New York: The Macmillan Co., 1969.
11. Social classes are treated as concrete interacting groups in a given social situation. They are not treated as categories. The French sociologists and the Marxist social scientists have taken up this view.
12. Y. Singh, op.cit., 1974, p. 314.
13. Ibid., p. 314.
14. Ibid., pp. 311-82.
15. Y.Singh, op.cit., 1981.
16. Ibid., p. 1.
17. Ibid., p. 2.
18. See, R.S. Khare, "'Inside' approaches of 'outside': Some implications of a sociological debate", in Giri Raj Gupta (ed.), *Main Currents in Indian Sociology*, Vol. I, Delhi:Vikas Publishing House, 1976, pp. 20-58; S.C. Dube, "Social sciences for the 1980s: From rhetoric to reality," *International Social Science Journal*, Vol. XXXIV, No. 3, 1982, pp. 495-502; and Y. Singh, "The role of social sciences in India: a sociology of knowledge," *Sociological Bulletin*, Vol. 22, No. 1, 1973, pp. 14-28.
19. See, Yogendra Singh, "Role of social sciences in India: A sociology of knowledge", in S.C. Dube (ed.), *Social Science and Social Relations:Role of the Social Sciences in Contemporary India*, Simla:Indian Institute of Advanced Study, 1976; and K.L. Sharma, *Essays on Social Stratification*, Jaipur:Rawat Publications, 1980, pp. 1-25.
20. Iravati Karve, *Kinship Organisation in India*, Bombay, Asia Publishing House, 1958.
21. I.P. Desai, *Some Aspects of Family in Mahuwa*, Bombay:Asia Publishing House, 1964.

22. A.R. Desai, *Social Background of Indian Nationalism*, Bombay:Popular Book Depot, 1948.
23. The department of sociology at the University of Delhi came into existence in 1959 with Professor M.N. Srinivas as its head. Professor Srinivas initiated studies in the areas of village community, family life, caste and kinship from the point of the British functionalism. However, the department of sociology at the University of Rajasthan, which was established in 1961, had influence of American social science positivism as it was evident in its courses and researches. More or less similar orientation has been there in the case of the sociology department at Chandigarh.
24. John P. Mencher, "The caste system upside down, or the not-so-mysterious east," *Current Anthropology*, Vol. 15, No. 4, 1974, pp. 469-93.
25. Satish Saberwal, "Sociologists and inequality in India: The historical context," *Economic and Political Weekly*, Vol. XIV, Nos. 7 and 8, 1979, pp. 243-54.
26. K.L. Sharma, *Essays on Social Stratification*, op.cit., 1980, and "Caste and class in India:some conceptual problems," a working paper read at XVI All India Sociological Conference, 1982 (mimeographed).
27. C. Parvathamma, "The remembered village: Brahminical odyssey," *Contributions to Indian Sociology*, New Series, Vol. 12, No. 1, 1978, pp. 91-96.
28. Andre Beteille, "Ideas and interests: Some conceptual problems in the study of social stratification in India," *International Social Science Journal*, Vol. 21, No. 7, 1969, p. 17.
29. Gunnar Myrdal, *Asian Drama:An Inquiry into the Poverty of Nations*, Vol. I, Penguin Books, 1968.
30. Mortan Klass, *Caste:The Emergence of the System in South Asia*, Philadelphia:The Institute for the Study of Human Issues, 1980.
31. S. Sinha, *Caste in India:Myth, Reality, Challenge*, New Delhi: B&R Publishing Company, 1982.
32. See, for example, E.R. Leach, "Introduction: What should we mean by caste?", in E.R. Leach (ed.), *Aspects of Caste in South India, Ceylone and North-West Pakistan*, Cambridge:Cambridge University Press, 1960, pp. 1-10. M.N. Srinivas replies Leach's criticism of his concept of 'dominant caste' in "Future of Indian caste," *Economic and Political Weekly*, Vol. XIV, Nos. 7 & 8, 1979, pp. 237-42, after a lapse of 19 years. See also C. Parvathamma and R.K. Jain's

criticism of M.N. Srinivas in *Contributions to Indian Sociology*, op.cit., 1978; F.G. Bailey and A.K. Saran's criticisms of Louis Dumont's position on how to study Indian society are given in Surendra Sharma, Sociology in India, Jaipur, Rawat Publications, Chapter IV.

33. Y. Singh., op.cit., 1981, p. 10.
34. Ibid., pp. 9-10.
35. A.R. Desai, op.cit., 1948.
36. Celestin Bougle, *Essays on the Caste System*, Cambridge: Cambridge University Press, 1971.
37. Louis Dumont, *Homo Hierarchicus*, London: Paladin, Granda Publishing Ltd., 1970.
38. A.M. Hocart, *Caste*, London: Mathew & Co., 1950.
39. Structural-functional orientation is predominantly found in village studies in 1950s and 1960s. All the aspects of village life have been studied in terms of their interrelationships and village as a 'totality'. However, the British social anthropologists and sociologists have more in-depth studies than their American counterparts. Louis Dumont has been a pioneer of the structuralist perspective in regard to the study of caste system in India.
40. D.Thorner in particular has suggested the use of native concepts and categories for the study of agrarian stratification. D.P. Mukerji also refers to indeginization of Marxist approach for studying Indian society. Recently, studies of agrarian structure and social movements in particular have shown interest in historico-sociological analysis.
41. Studies on Hindu religion, urban settings and class character of Indian state are illustrative of the concurrent interests in positivism, culturology and orthodox Marxism.
42. K.L. Sharma, *The Changing Rural Stratification System*, New Delhi: Orient Longman Ltd., 1974, p. 15.
43. These studies have highlighted *caste* as the most predominant institutional factor in Indian society. Some of them have analyzed caste rank as the basis of social status, others have found it as an obstacle in economic development, as an interest group and as a basis of social solidarity and security.
44. Andre Beteille, *Caste, Class and Power*, Bombay:Oxford University Press, 1966, p. 4. See also Beteille, "Closed and open social stratification in India," *European Journal of Sociology*, Vol. 7, 1966, pp. 224-46.
45. Andre Beteille, "Ideas and interests: Some conceptual problems in the study of social stratification in India," op.cit., 1969.

46. Anil Bhatt, *Caste, Class and Politics*, Delhi: Manohar Book Service, 1975.
47. P.C. Aggarwal, *Caste, Religion and Power*, New Delhi: Shri Ram Centre for Industrial Relations, 1971.
48. K.E. Gough, "Caste in a Tanjore village", in E.R. Leach (ed.), op.cit., 1960, pp. 11-60.
49. Ramakrishna Mukherjee, *The Dynamics of Rural Society*, Berlin:Akademie Verlag, 1957.
50. K.L. Sharma, op.cit., 1974, p. 24.
51. Y. Singh, op.cit., 1981, p. 10.
52. Ibid., p. 10.
53. Ibid., p. 11.
54. See M.N. Srinivas' concepts of sanskritization and westernization in his *Social Change in Modern India*, California:University of California Press, 1966.
55. See K.L. Sharma, *Essays on Social Stratification*, op.cit., 1980.
56. See Louis Dumont, op.cit., 1970; and M.N. Srinivas, *Cast in Modern India and other Essays*, Bombay: Asia Publishing House, 1970.
57. F.G. Bailey, "Closed social stratification in India," *European Journal of Sociology*, Vol. IV, No. 1, 1963.
58. Pauline Kolenda, *Caste in Contemporary India, Beyond Organic Solidarity*, California: Benjamin Cummings Publishing Company, 1978.
59. D.B. Miller, *From Hierarchy to Stratification*, Delhi:Oxford University Press, 1975.
60. Andre Beteille, *Caste, Class and Power*, op.cit., 1966.
61. Ibid., p. 3.
62. Ibid., pp. 4-5.
63. Ibid., p. 12.
64. K.L. Sharma, op.cit, 1980, p.x.
65. P.C. Aggarwal, op.cit., 1971.
66. Anil Bhatt, op.cit., 1975.
67. Ibid., p. 1.
68. Ibid., pp. 1-4.
69. Ibid., p. 5.
70. Ibid., p.5
71. Characteristics of structural-functional studies have been mentioned earlier in this essay.
72. Anil Bhatt, op.cit., 1975, p. 9.
73. Ibid., p. 9.

74. Victor S. D'Souza, *Social Structure of a Planned City, Chandigarh*, New Delhi:Orient Longmans Ltd., 1968.
75. Victor S. D'Souza, "Caste and class: A reinterpretation," *Journal of Asian and African Studies*, Vol. 2, Nos. 3-4, 1967.
76. Ibid., p. 48.
77. Rajni Kothari, *Politics in India*, New Delhi:Orient Longman, 1970.
78. Ibid., pp. 1-20.
79. Ibid., p.10
80. The emergence of the DMK and the ADMK in Tamil Nadu, the Telugu Desham in Andhra Pradesh, the Akali movement in Punjab and several 'sons-of-soil' movements in other parts of India have falsified the basic assumptions of Kothari's hypothesis about 'integration' politics in India.
81. Selig S. Harrison, *India:The Most Dangerous Decades*, Princeton:Princeton University Press, 1960.
82. Rajni Kothari, "Introduction: Caste in Indian politics," in Rajni Kothari (ed.), *Caste in Indian Politics*, New Delhi:Orient Longman Ltd., 1970.
83. Ibid., p. 4.
84. Ibid., p.4.
85. Ibid., p.5.
86. Ibid., p. 6.
87. Ibid., p. 8.
88. Ibid., p. 10.
89. Ibid., p.11.
90. Ibid., p. 20.
91. F.G. Bailey, op.cit., 1957.
92. T.S. Epstein, *Economic Development and Social Change in South India*, Manchester:Manchester University Press, 1962.
93. F.G. Bailey, op.cit., 1957, p. 239.
94. C. Levi-Strauss, *The Elementary Structures of Kinship*, Oxford:Alden Press, 1969 (English edition).
95. L.Dumont, *Hierarchy and Marriage Alliance in South Indian Kinship*, Occasional Paper No. 12, London:Royal Anthropological Institute, 1957.
96. Dumont's view on how to study Indian society is discussed in detail in Surendra Sharma, op.cit., chapters 2 and 3.
97. *See* Y. Singh, op.cit., 1981.
98. L. Dumont, "Caste: A phenomenon of social structure or an aspect of Indian culture?", in Anthony de Reuck and Julie Knight (eds.),

Caste and Race: Comparative Approaches, London: J&A Churchil Ltd., 1967, p. 33.

99. Ibid., pp. 33-35.
100. Harold A. Gould, "Priest and contrapriest: A structural analysis of Jajmani relationships in the Hindu plains and the Nilgiri Hills," *Contributions to Indian Sociology* (NS), No. 1, 1967.
101. Veena Das, *Cognition and Reality*, Delhi:Oxford University Press, 1977.
102. Veena Das and J.P.S. Uberoi, "The elementary structure of caste," *Contributions to Indian Sociology* (NS), No. 5, 1971.
103. E.R. Leach, "'Espirit' in Homo Hierarchicus," *Contributions to Indian Sociology* (NS), No. 5, 1971, p. 16.
104. T.N. Madan, "On understanding caste," *Economic and Political Weekly*, Vol. VI, No. 34, 1971. See also T.N. Madan et.al., "On the nature of caste in India: A review symposium on Louis Dumont's Homo Hierarchicus," *Contributions to Indian Sociology* (NS), No. 5, 1971, pp. 1-81.
105. Y. Singh, op.cit., 1981, p. 17.
106. Ibid., p. 18.
107. Mortan Klass, op.cit., 1980.
108. S. Sinha, op.cit., 1982.
109. See S.A. Dange, *India from Primitive Communism to Slavery*, Bombay:People's Publishing House, 1949;E.M.S. Namboodiripad, "Caste conflicts vs. growing unity of popular democratic forces," *Economic and Political Weekly*, Vol. XIV, Nos. 7 & 8, 1979, pp. 329-336; and B.T. Ranadive, "Caste, class and property relations," *Economic and Political Weekly*, Vol. XIV, Nos. 7 & 8, 1979, pp. 337-348.
110. Joan P. Mencher, op.cit., 1974.
111. M.S.A. Rao, *Social Movements and Social Transformation*, Delhi:Macmillan Co., 1979.
112. Rajendra Singh, "Politicisation, protest and peasant movement in UP: A case study in the politics of land control in District Basti", in M.S.A. Rao (ed.), *Social Movements in India*, Delhi: Manohar Book Service, 1977.
113. P.N. Mukherji, "Social movement and social change: Towards a conceptual clarification and theoretical framework," *Sociological Bulletin*, Vol. 26, No. 1, 1977.
114. K.L. Sharma, op.cit., 1982.
115. S. Saberwal, op.cit., 1979.

116. S. Sivakumar and Chitra Sivakumar, "Class and Jati at Asthapuram and Kanthapuram: Some comments towards a structure of interests," *Economic and Political Weekly*, Vol. XIV, Nos. 7 and 8, 1979, pp. 263-286.
117. Y. Singh, op.cit., 1981, p. 24.
118. Ibid., p. 27.
119. Jaganath Pathy, "Social stratification in an Orissa village," *Economic and Political Weekly*, Vol. X, June 7, 1975, pp. 893-901.
120. P.K. Bose, "Agrarian structure, peasant society and social change: A study of selected regions in West Bengal," Ph.D. thesis, JNU, New Delhi, 1979.
121. Hira Singh, "Decline of feudalism: Marwar from 1870s to 1940s," Ph.D. thesis, University of Delhi, 1981.
122. D.N. Dhanagare, "Social origins of the peasant insurrection in Telengana," *Contributions to Indian Sociology* (NS), No. 8, 1974.
123. Dipankar Gupta, *The Shiva Sena Movement*, 1966-1974: *A Sociological Analysis*, Ph. D. thesis, JNU, New Delhi, 1977.
124. K.E. Gough, "Indian peasant uprisings," *Economic and Political Weekly*, Vol. IX, Nos. 32-34 (SN), pp. 1391-1412.
125. See a summary of the debate on the mode of production in Indian agriculture by Alice Thorner, "Semi-Feudalism or capitalism: Contemporary debate on classes and modes of production in India," *Economic and Political Weekly*, Vol. XVIII, Nos. 49, 50 & 51, 1982.
126. K.E. gough, "Colonial economics in South-East India," *Economic and Political Weekly*, Vol. VIII, No. 13, 1977, pp. 551-554. See also E.K. Gough, "Modes of production in southern India," *Economic and Political Weekly*, Vol. XV, Nos. 5,6 & 7, 1980, pp. 337-364.
127. See Joan P. Mencher, op.cit., 1974, K.E. gough, op.cit., 1977 and 1980, and A.R. Desai, op.cit., 1948 and *State and Society in India:Essays in Dissent*, Bombay:Popular Prakashan, 1975.
128. Charles Bettelheim, *India Independent*, London: Mac-Gibbon & Kee Ltd., 1968, p. 128.
129. Alice Thorner and Daniel Thorner, *Land and Labour in India*, Bombay: Asia Publishing House, 1974.
130. A.R. Desai, op.cit., 1975.
131. John Harris, *Capitalism and Peasant Farming*, Delhi:Oxford University Press, 1982.
132. Ibid., p.9.
133. Ibid., p. 49.

134. Gail Omvedt (ed.), *Land, Caste and Politics in India*, Delhi: Authors Guild Publications, 1982.
135. Gail Omvedt, "Caste, class and land in India: An introductory essay", in Gail Omvedt (ed.), op.cit., 1982, p. 13.
136. Ibid., p. 14.
137. Ibid.
138. K.E. Gough, cf. Gail Omvedt, op.cit., 1982, p. 42.
139. K.L. Sharma, op.cit., 1982, p. 36.
140. Andre Beteille, *Caste, Class and Power*, op.cit., 1966, p. 9.
141. Ibid., p. 10.
142. Ibid.
143. Ibid.
144. Ibid.
145. Ibid., pp. 10-11.
146. Ibid., p.11.
147. Andre Beteille, "The tribulations of field work," *Economic and Political Weekly*, Vol. VII, Nos. 31, 32 and 33 (SN), 1972, p. 1510.
148. Ibid.
149. Partha N. Mukherji, "Some observations on participant observation," *Economic and Political Weekly*, Vol. VIII, No. 1, 1973, pp. 27-30.
150. Ibid., p. 27.
151. Andre Beteille, op.cit., 1972, p. 1510.
152. K.L. Sharma, op. cit., 1974, p. 24.
153. Ibid., pp. 22-27.
154. Anil Bhatt, op.cit., 1975, pp. 17-19.
155. P.C. Aggarwal, op.cit., (1971), p. 14.
156. A.R. Desai, op.cit., 1948.
157. D.P. Mukerji, *Diversities*, Delhi: People's Publishing House, 1958.
158. K.E. Gough, op.cit., 1980.
159. Gail Omvedt, op.cit., 1982.
160 Ramakrishna Mukherjee, op.cit., 1957.
161. K.E. Gough, op.cit., 1977 and 1980.
162. Gail Omvedt, *Cultural Revolt in a Colonial Society: The non-Brahmin Movement in Western India*, 1870-1930, Pune:Scientific Socialist Education Trust, 1976.
163. See, for example, R. Singh, op.cit., 1977; K.L. Sharma, "Jharkhand movement in Bihar," *Economic and Political Weekly*, Vol. XI, No. 2, 1976; and Satish Saberwal, op.cit., 1979.
164. Louis Dumont, op.cit., 1970.

3

Caste and Class in India: Some Conceptual Problems

There are a number of points which have so far remained unclarified in regard to the nature of caste and class in India. Some misconceptions are: Caste and class are polar opposites; caste is being replaced by class; caste is a rural phenomenon whereas class is found in urban-industrial settings; caste is an ascriptive system while class is based on the achievement principle; caste is a closed system and does not permit mobility for its members whereas class is an open system and allows mobility for its members; India has/had a caste system, hence a 'caste model' for studying Indian society and the West has/had classes, hence a 'class model' for studying western societies. However, these notions are rooted in the historicity of Indian society and its culture including British and post-independence academic colonialism.

The other points refer to the debate regarding approaches to the study of caste and class in India. The various approaches can be classified as: (i) interactional versus attributional; (ii) structural versus cultural; and (iii) Marxist versus functional. These approaches have been borrowed from the West, and are clearly reflected in the studies of social stratification in India. Rural versus urban stratification, corporate vs. individual mobility, caste versus class relations, and ritual versus secular hierarchy are found as main issues in most of the studies on social stratification. The studies range from the study of caste or class alone to caste and class, caste and power, class and power, and caste, class and religion. I wish to analyze these issues in view of the available studies on caste and class from the point of theory, method and data. Both caste and class have been analysed in terms of theory, structure and process. Earlier Singh (1974) made this observation about social stratification in India. There is no epistemological apriorism in this sort of exercise. The studies can be seen from the point of their requirements as well as from the point of caste and class relations in India.

I

A certain conception of 'model' of traditional Indian society has emerged. This model has/had implications for studying Indian society. The main features of this caste model are: (i) it is based primarily on the ideas held or expressed by certain sections of society and not on the observed or recorded behaviour of people; (ii) it attaches a kind of primary and universal significance to caste as this has been conceived in the classical texts; (iii) the entire system is viewed as being governed by certain more or less explicitly formulated principles or 'rules of the game'; and (iv) the different castes which are the basic units in the system are conceived as fulfilling complementary functions and their mutual relations as being 'non-antagonistic' (Beteille, 1969).

No doubt, the 'caste model' brings into focus some of the significant features of the traditional Indian society, but it fails on two counts: (i) when it is made too general it can be applied to almost every society and therefore does not tell us very much about the specific properties of any society; and (ii) when it is made too specific it fails to take into account certain crucial features of economic and political life (Ibid.). Beteille observes that the model has been more systematically elaborated by Dumont as it is concerned essentially with ideas and values. It has failed, however, in providing a proper place to material interests in social life. Beteille argues a case for the study of material interests along with the study of ideas and values in terms of the dialectical relations between the two. But Beteille does not offer a 'class analysis' of Indian society as an alternative to the caste model. In fact, Beteille suggests a sort of modification of the caste model by putting an emphasis on the study of economic and political conflict with a certain degree of autonomy for the economic and political activities of intercaste relations. However, he points out that it would be wrong to consider India as a 'caste society', and the United States as a 'class society', and Europe as an 'estate society'.

Beteille denies the validity of a sociology of values and ideas. He emphasizes the role of material interests in the studies of traditional society and culture in India. Beteille takes a clue from Leach (1960), Bailey (1963), and Dumont (1970), who have offered a 'caste model' of Indian society. The essence of the views of Leach, Bailey and Dumont is that caste is a non-competitive system, the castes are 'non-antagonistic' strata. Leach (1960) writes: "Wherever caste groups are seen to be acting as corporations in competition against like—groups of different castes, then they are acting in defiance of caste principles." Competition refers to class and co-operation refers to caste. This is really a very erroneous view about both class and caste, and more so about the understanding of caste in India. Western scholars (including Leach) look at the caste system from the viewpoint of class in western societies. Leach refers to castes as groups which co-operate and do not compete. Leach finds competition within the 'dominant caste' and not between the dominant caste and other castes. The latter would refer to a class situation, and the former to a class-like situation without affecting the caste system. The idea of non-antagonistic strata has come from Ossowski (1963) who refers to the Polish situation in terms of status gradations and not as classes based on antagonism.

Thus, the western notions of class as well as non-antagonism have been used for analyzing the structure of Indian society. The historicity of Indian society is the real casualty, and reductionism has been the hallmark of 'caste model'. Everything is reduced to the all-pervasive principle of caste hierarchy. However, factually, this was not the situation in ancient, medieval and British India. Migration, mobility and defiance have been reported in historical researches (Thapar, 1974; Panikkar, 1955; Stein, 1968; Habib, 1974; and Desai, 1948). These researches have been ignored by anthropologists and sociologists perhaps due to British colonialism and an overwhelming impact of American and British social science research.

British ethnographers have defined caste in terms of its assumed or real functionality to Indian society and culture. The salient features given by them (including some Indian sociologists) are that a caste has a common name, common descent, and the same hereditary calling and communitarian living (Risley, 1969). Ketkar (1909) mentions hereditary membership and endogamy as the most striking features of the caste system in India. Senart (1930) writes: "A caste system is one whereby a society is divided up into a number of self-contained and completely segregated units (castes), the mutual relations between which are ritually determined in a graded scale." The uniqueness of the system is prominently emphasized in the above definitions of the caste system. Furnivall (1939), Hutton (1946) and Sherring (1974) observe that the caste system is 'functional' for Indian society. Furnivall applauds the 'pluralism' of the caste system. Hutton speaks of its functions for the individual, community and society as a whole. Sherring refers to cleanliness and order and a bond of union among Hindus promoted by the caste system. Ghurye (1950) refers to six features of the caste system and upholds endogamy as its essence.

Other students of Indian society have also provided a view which either refers to the uniqueness of the caste system or they have viewed it from the viewpoint of their own society. Marx (1945) related the (Asiatic) mode of production to the stability of the caste system in India. Maine (1890) referred to caste as an example of a non-contractual 'status-society'. Senart (1930), Hocart (1950), and Dumont (1970) have emphasized ritual criteria and pollution-purity as the bases of Hindu society. Weber (1947) considered caste as a system of 'status groups' based on the other-worldly doctrines of Hinduism.

Sinha (1974), in a report on caste, notes the following trends:

(i) Speculative theories about the origin of the caste system have practically been given up.

(ii) The bulk of the work on caste is done by the method of social anthropology on the basis of a study of multicaste villages.

(iii) Considerable interest is shown in these studies on an understanding of the adaptability of the caste system to view situations and forces of changes.

(iv) Study of interethnic status ranking is done through an analysis of data collected through a rigorous methodology.

(v) Literature on social mobility in the caste system has grown in abundance and improved in quality.

(vi) The concept of hierarchy based on the binary polarity of purity-pollution has received much attention.

(vii) There is a felt need for interregional comparison.

(viii) The comparability of caste beyond Indian society has been examined.

(ix) The emergent non-caste phenomena are left unanalyzed because of the obsession with caste.

(x) The number of scholars interested in the study of caste has grown considerably.

Sinha does not reflect upon caste and class polarity, the 'caste, class and power' approach to stratification, and caste as a cultural or structural phenomenon (Sharma, 1977). Sinha also ignores the analysis of the entrenchment of caste into politics, education, industry and ethnicity. A sociology of knowledge perspective would demand an understanding of theory, structure and process of the caste system and this is lacking in Sinha's trend report. Sinha considers caste basically as a cultural phenomenon. "The cultural system of caste thus naturally promotes an infinite variety of stable crafts and ritual styles" (Sinha, 1967). Sinha further observes: "The social and cultural systems of caste thus segment the total society into many Jati groups committed to particular britis and styles of life, arranged in a social hierarchy defined in terms of the cultural value of the purity and impurity of these occupations and styles of life" (Ibid.). Sinha's plea for combining structural and cultural perspectives on caste stratification will not stand the test of validity in view of his clear preference for considering caste as a cultural phenomenon.

Thus, the studies on caste aimed at the legitimacy and justification of the caste system itself. Caste was pronounced as an all-inclusive and encompassing functional system. The 'pluralism' of caste was glorified with the intent of establishing British rule on a sounder footing. This was an exercise in befooling the Indian people and the leaders of various castes and even intellectuals. At the same time, the scholars of the West glorified the class system with a view to establishing the superiority of western society and culture (Sharma, 1980). "Class was considered as an open system, the individual was given freedom of movement under the system, and achievement was the essence of the system. In contrast, the caste system was considered as a closed system, the individual could not move up in the hierarchy, and it was a system based on ascription. Caste and class were polar opposites, caste was considered a feature of an archaic society like India, and class was considered a characteristic feature of the industrially advanced achievement-based western society" (Ibid.). This clearly shows that the western scholars (mainly American and British) tried to establish their hegemony by academic propaganda.

MacIver and Page (1967) do not define class strictly in the economic sense. They refer to 'status' as the basis of what they call 'social class'. Marshall (1934), Parsons (1954), Davis and Moore (1945), Bottomore (1964: 148) and Centres (1961: 27) define class either in terms of 'status' or in psychological terms (attitudes and consciousness). The quintessence of the definitions of caste *vis-a-vis* class is that caste is found in India and class is a feature of the western world. The important point is that caste is used as a double-edged weapon, namely, keeping it intact by declaring it as a 'functional' system, and by pronouncing its inferiority or subordination to the class system of the West. Two consequences followed from this academic propaganda:

(i) the indoctrination of social scientists in terms of theorization, methodology and field studies; and
(ii) legitimation of British hegemony and the superiority of their understanding of Indian society. Consequently, social science research in India in the fifties and the sixties was clearly directed by the western social scientists and was patterned in terms of their perspectives.

Literature on caste was produced in abundance in the fifties and sixties. The emphasis was on the overwhelming role of caste in

Indian society, caste ranking and mobility in the caste system. Some writings also dealt with class in India. A brief resume is given here. The higher castes revolted against any attempt to challenge their status and power, and the lower castes were content with their lower status, believing that it was due to their *karma* (Prasad, 1957). Srinivas's collection of essays on caste (1962) and his earlier essay on caste (1959), Mathur's book on the role of caste and ritual (1964), Marriott's study of caste and kinship in Central India (1960), and Kothari's edited work on the role of caste in politics (1970) are some of the important studies on the theme.

Dube (1955) writes that the main criteria for the ranking of castes are ritual and not economic. Srinivas's work on religion and society among the Coorgs of South India (1952) is also an attempt towards caste ranking based on the criterion of pollution and purity. Marriott's essay (1959) is on the criteria of caste ranking whether they are 'interactional' or 'attributional' or both. Later on Marriott (1965) has used the concept of 'elaboration' for examining the rigidity and flexibility of the caste system in five regions of India. Mahar (1959) and Hazlthurst (1968) have referred to multiple criteria for caste ranking. Dube (1968) and Gardner (1968) refer to 'levels' of caste dominance and highlight the role of the individual in caste mobility and refute the utility of the concepts of 'dominant caste' and 'sanskritization' as advocated by Srinivas. There are other studies in which 'structural mobility' has been noted. Sharma (1969, 1970, 1974, 1980) discusses stresses in caste stratification, modernization and rural stratification, and bourgeoisiefication, proletarianization, downward social mobility and levels of social mobility in village India. He also discusses the crystallization of class relations in the countryside.

A number of studies on caste mobility have been reported by Majumdar (1958), Silverberg (1968), Lynch (1968) and Singer (1968). Silverberg, Singer and Cohn have brought out several studies on caste and mobility in their edited volumes with particular emphasis on the relevance of concepts of reference group and relative deprivation, etc. Saberwal (1976) discusses mobility among the Rampurias of a Punjab town who belonged to the lower stratum but took up trade and commerce as their main occupation. Berreman (1979) has published his essays on caste written over a period of two decades. The emphasis in Berreman's essays is that caste-based inequalities in India are not different from race-based inequalities in the United States of America.

Gough has highlighted the class basis of the caste system in India. She refers to conflicts and litigations between different castes in a Tanjore village (1960) based on economic inequalities. The mix of caste and class in East Bengal (now Bangladesh) is referred to by Ramakrishna Mukherjee (1957). Bose (1967) refers to the class genesis of the caste structure in Bengal. Changes from caste to class are noted by Misra (1960), Beteille (1969), Miller (1975), and Kolenda (1978). But none of them deny the resurgence of caste in the new situation. A class analysis of Indian society in general and the caste system and village community in particular is found in Desai's edited work on rural sociology (1978) and in his book on Indian nationalism (1948), and in Bettelheim (1968), Harris (1982), and in an edited work by Omvedt (1982).

II

Caste is a unique system; it pervades the whole of Hindu society in India; and it is an encompassing system. These are the views upheld by Bougle, Srinivas and Dumont in particular and several others in general. Bougle (1971) writes: "To sum up on these points: hereditary specialization, hierarchical organization, reciprocal repulsion: as far as any social form can realize itself in its purity, the caste system is realized in India. At the very least it penetrates Hindu society to a level unknown elsewhere. It plays some part in other civilizations but in India it has invaded the whole. It is in this sense that we may speak of the caste system as a phenomenon peculiar to India." Srinivas (1952) following Bougle, notes the pre-eminence of religious values in the caste system. The religious values among the Hindus centre in the ideas of pollution and purity. Bougle follows Hocart in regard to the role of rituals in the caste hierarchy. However, Hocart (1958) finds that religion encompasses power, hence the priesthood is not 'absolute' in nature. Relations between Brahmin and Kshatriya are defined in terms of a certain reciprocity, namely, the Brahmin represents the 'religious' authority and the Kshatriya enjoys 'political' power.

Srinivas notes various types of purity and impurity among the Coorgs of South India. Ritual impurity, normal ritual status and ritual purity form a hierarchy based on the notion of pollution and purity. Normal ritual status is the one which a person normally enjoys; it is a mild form of impurity. However, Dumont and Pocock (1959) discard the expression of 'normal ritual status'. Hierarchy based on pollution-purity does not include 'mildly impure', it includes only 'pure' and 'impure'. Ephemeral purity or impurity after purification do not guide intercaste relations. Ritual purification or impurification is a generalized phenomenon among all Hindus.

However, Srinivas feels that the concept is absolutely fundamental to the caste system. Sanskritization is the only way to remove impurity or to minimize it. While commenting on a book by Srinivas (1976), Parvathamma (1978: 91) writes: "In all the writings of Srinivas, the Brahmin-non-Brahmin values are juxtaposed." Hierarchy based on pollution-purity remains intrinsic to Srinivas's thinking in regard to all aspects of human life, even if it is actually not so pronounced. That sanskritization can also cause tensions and contradictions manifestly or latently is overlooked by Srinivas. His main emphasis remains on dominance and solidarity. It is not only Srinivas who has heavily endorsed 'Brahminical' sociology, several others including Dumont (1970), Marriott (1955) and Singer (1968) have emphasized disproportionately the phenomenon of caste in Indian society. Pollution-purity, religion and rituals are the central foci of their studies. Today, social structure is not considered beyond the parameters of the notions of pollution-purity, hierarchy and dominance.

Compared to Leach, Dumont and Srinivas, a different view is provided by Bailey (1963). Bailey refers to three types of definitions of caste. These are: (1) the 'rigidity' type; (2) the 'cultural' type, and (3) the 'structural' type. The first type of definition is found inapplicable as it refers to status immobility, hence 'analytic'. The second type is found 'useful' as it refers to religious ideas, namely, opposition based on purity and pollution and hierarchy. The pollution-purity opposition implies (i) hereditary specialization, (ii) hierarchy, and (iii) opposition of parts. Caste as a system based on beliefs and ideas becomes a closed unique system of social stratification. The third type of definition refers to exclusiveness, exhaustiveness and ranking as the 'structural' criteria of the caste system. The 'cultural' criteria limit comparison and the structural ones facilitate cross-cultural comparison.

Thus, according to Bailey, caste is a unique system so far as its cultural criteria are concerned, and it shares certain features with other systems of social stratification so far as structural criteria are concerned. Bailey disapproves Dumont's view about caste as he considers it in terms of 'finality' and 'completeness'. Bailey considers Dumont's definition of caste 'analytic' rather than 'synthetic'. The latter refers to the existence of the caste system at the micro-level. The analytic statement tends to become axiomatic. However, Bailey also accepts the analytic statement of Dumont as the starting point of his analysis. Bailey does not refer to 'class analysis' or inherence of class in caste. Like Leach and Dumont, Bailey's view also refers to 'organicism'; competition and equality are not found in the caste system. Bailey's attempt at formulating a 'compromised definition' of the caste system is not different from the understanding of the caste system provided by Dumont, Leach and Srinivas.

Thus, ultimately, Bailey also tends to formulate an 'analytic' statement about the caste system, and in effect, not so different from that of Dumont and Srinivas. Bailey fails to recognize the historicity of the caste system which brings to light innumerable adaptations and contradictions faced by it. For Bailey, the caste system is an inviolate system, hence closed and organic in nature. Inviolate systems are found in simple societies, or in relatively insulated enclaves of complex societies. Caste is also seen by Bailey as an organizing principle of competition, and not the one by which politico-economic groups are recruited. Castes are not corporate or organic political groups, hence caste is a closed segmentary stratification. 'Segmentation' refers to change from organicism. However, such a conception of change does not explain the change of the caste system. Segmentation does not lead ultimately to equality or castelessness. Bailey's notion of change in caste is thus based on a sort of false consciousness about change (Sharma, 1980). Increasing segmentation does not mean emergence of class-based relations, and the latter do not mean equality or egalitarianism. Singh (1968: 170) observes that Bailey's analysis is based on a static and abstract model of caste, and on the same type of 'analytic' statements as those of Dumont. Beteille's notion of the emergence of 'differentiated structures' (1966) also does not provide a class-view of social stratification or/of the village community.

III

Marriott (1959) was the first to make a reference to the 'interactional' and 'attributional' approaches to the study of the caste system. Later on it was exemplified in great detail by Singh (1974) in a trend report on social stratification. Marriott is the one who has promoted 'culturology' by studying Indian tradition and the interaction between what he calls 'Great Tradition' and 'Little Tradition'. Marriott's study (1955) substantiates the interactional approach to the study of Indian society in terms of the relations between 'Sanskritic' and 'oral' traditions. The study of relations between higher and lower castes in basic to the 'interactional' approach. However, this approach has also been vigorously applied by Marxist scholars to the study of class relations in village India.

Emphasis in the 'attributional' approach is on 'order' rather than 'relation'. The configuration of elements constituting a system of hierarchy is the essence of the attributional approach. The attributes are, for example, income, occupation, education, positions of power, etc. These attributes have sufficient measurability, and they facilitate construction of categories such as upper, middle and lower. Thus, an attempt is made to work out the indicators of status, and the variations are measured on different types of scales and indices. The 'composite status' of individuals is worked out. 'Corporateness' of status is ruled out as the individual's attributes are the basis of constructing the 'order'.

That caste is not an exclusively cultural system is the view held by D'Souza (1967). Caste and class are different forms of social stratification. Groups (caste groups or *jatis*) are ranked in the caste system, whereas positions are ranked in social stratification (particularly with reference to class stratification). The ranking of endogamous groups and not endogamy as the rule of marriage, is the hallmark of the caste system. D'Souza's contention is that changes in the caste system have brought about changes in the properties of individual members. A 'hereditary group' might continue in the caste system as a 'class'. This fact explains the similarity between caste and class. In fact, D'Souza emphasizes the significance of the continuum of the rigidity-fluidity dimensions in regard to both caste and class. Thus, the individual and his properties are the real units of analysis rather than the endogamous groups.

D'Souza decisively concludes that class is replacing caste, and the individual is replacing the group. A certain place for the individual as a unit of status, and a certain level of social mobility at that level are the basic assumptions of D'Souza's formulation. Even if the role of the individual and the fact of social mobility are admitted, class would not take the place of caste inspite of the fact that caste has undergone significant changes. It would be untenable to infer that change is taking place from caste to class, from hierarchy to stratification, from closed to open system, and from an organic to a segmentary system of social stratification (Sharma, 1977; 1980). Singh (1968) rightly points out that a 'prismatic model' of change is suitable where traditional segments of caste and kinship undergo adaptive transformation without completely being 'diffracted' into classes or corporate groups. Thus, class segments operate within the frame of caste categories with a new sense of identity, and they also violate caste norms, hence contradictions. Caste has been a dynamic system full of adaptations, accretions, contradictions and transformations, hence resilience and change.

Having realized that caste alone is not the totality of social stratification and that caste is not being replaced by class as the two are not necessarily antithetical to each other, Beteille (1965), following Weber's trio of 'class, status and party', analyzes patterns of social stratification in a Tanjore village in terms of 'caste, class and power'. Beteille is not quite clear about the phenomenon of class. He says that "classes are categories rather than groups," but he contradicts this statement when he writes that "by class we mean a category of persons occupying a specific position in the system of production" (1965). The first statement has the overtones of the Weberian notion of class and the second has those of Marx's conception of class. However, Beteille by no means intends to provide a Marxian analysis of social stratification, nor he does justice to Weber's ideas of rationalism and *verstehen*. Beteille's study, therefore, also falls short of the 'attributional' or 'interactional' criteria of social ranking.

In fact, it is Anil Bhatt (1975) who has done more justice to the attributional approach in studying social stratification. Bhatt's trio comprises 'caste, class and politics.' He observes that social stratification in India has deviated considerably from the traditional caste model. Caste does not encompass economic position and political power. A caste is internally differentiated in terms of class and power of its members. Thus, Bhatt finds status incongruence, relative openness, mobility, and competition as the salient features of the emergent system of social stratification. Bhatt has relied on secondary data and attitudinal responses. It is more of a 'formalistic' approach and does not go into actual details regarding the functioning of institutions related to caste, class and power. Aggrawal (1971) and recently Chauhan (1980) have also followed the viewpoint adopted by Beteille. There is no doubt that Beteille has presented a new approach to the study of social stratification in India, but without realizing the incongruity between the his approach and the method of his study (Sharma, 1980).

Whether caste is a cultural aspect of the Indian tradition or a structural form was discussed in a symposium (Reuck and Knight, 1967) in which Myrdal, Leach, Dumont, Berreman, Sinha, Cohn, Mayer and Tambiah participated along with some others. I have already referred to the view that caste is considered a cultural aspect of the Indian tradition. Dumont, Leach, Srinivas and Marriott consider castes as corporate groups, found exclusively in Indian society, particularly among Hindus. Beteille and Bailey partly agree with this view; however, D'Souza and Bhatt clearly advocate the application of an attributional approach (class approach in a non-

Marxian sense). Caste as a cultural phenomenon is seen as a system of values and ideas. Srinivas's (1966) notions of sanskritization and westernization are examples of 'intrasystemic' or 'positional changes.'

Caste as a structural phenomenon is considered as a part of the general theory of social stratification. Barth (1960) writes: "If the concept of caste is to be useful in sociological analysis, its definition must be based on structural criteria, and not on particular features of the Hindu philosophical scheme." Barth considers caste in general as a system of social stratification. The principle of status summation seems to be the structural feature of caste stratification. In other words, caste should label not a particular social system but a general social subsystem. Opposition, segmentation and hierarchy are universal criteria of social stratification, and are expressed in different cultural idioms including caste. Berreman (1967) also refers to three universal elements of all castes, namely, stratification, culturalism and interaction. Harper (1968) and Nadel (1957) have expressed the view that caste stratification is one of the various forms of social stratification.

As we have stated earlier that D'Souza (1967) draws a polar distinction between caste and class, but he does not consider caste as an exclusively cultural system. D'Souza's main concern is that changes in the caste system are ultimately brought about by changes in the properties of the individual members. The emphasis in D'Souza's view is on the significance of the continuum of the rigidity-fluidity dimensions to the understanding of both caste and class. Leach (1960) also refers to emergence of 'caste grades' as class-like changes in the caste system.

Studies on caste mobility refer to the structural dimension of caste stratification. Thapar (1974), Panikkar (1955) and Stein (1968) refer to caste mobility in spatial and status contexts rather than in the context of rituals. Bailey (1957) and Epstein (1962) also consider economic factors responsible for changing intercaste relations. Kothari (1970) mentions caste as a variable in politics in independent India. Singh (1974) analyzes caste in terms of cultural and structural factors and considers it as a 'structural-particularistic' type of social stratification. The essence of the structural approach is that caste should be seen in terms of a system of 'relations' between different castes, and structural factors bring about changes in the vertical and horizontal gradations in the caste system. Mencher (1974) analyzes caste from a Marxist (also structural) point of view. She considers the exploitation of the low castes and the prevention of the formation of classes as the two main features of the caste system. Thus, caste is, in fact, a system of class relations, and at the same time, its functioning idiom does not allow it to operate as a class system.

IV

Class in India is generally seen as a consequence of change in the caste system and not as a concomitant and co-existent system inseparable from caste. Several questions can be raised about the studies of caste hierarchy and social mobility. For example, why did Srinivas and his associates often study caste structure, positional changes, village community, and family life and kinship; and why did they leave out the studies of class relations, vertical mobility, urban community, industry and formal organizations from their sociological purview? Culturology is given primacy over the structural perspective in the understanding of the caste system in most studies carried out by Srinivas and his followers. Structural changes are visualized only latently and that too due to sanskritization and westernization. Emphasis on the study of social mobility in terms of upward movement in the caste hierarchy further legitimizes the culturological approach to the study of society and culture in India. The concepts of dominant caste and sanskritization remain central to this view. Corporate mobility and the study of the social and cultural aspects receive greater attention instead of mobility at the level of family and individual and economic and political aspects. Resentment, opposition and conflict in the study of intergroup relations remain inactive notions.

Dube (1976) and Singh (1979) both realize that the concepts of caste and class have been basically 'western', and therefore, ignore the historicity of Indian society in their formulations. Indigenization of social science paradigms would ensure a proper input of historical substance in the concepts and theories related to Indian society. Both Marxist and non-Marxist scholars (Thorner, 1974; Saran, 1962) have pleaded for the use of native concepts and categories, respectively. D.P. Mukerji (1958) has argued vehemently for making the Indian tradition as the sole basis of analyzing social change. Desai (1948) has strongly opposed to the application of the non-Marxist approaches. Srinivas has been blamed for an inappropriate application of British structural-functionalism by Mencher (1974) and Saberwal (1979).

Caste has been taken as synonym with the social formation of Indian society and therefore class is treated as an alternate system to caste. However, the fact is that neither does caste refer to the totality of social formations nor is class the polar opposite of caste. Studies such as caste and class (D'Souza, 1967); caste, class and power (Beteille, 1965); caste, religion and power (Aggrawal, 1971); and caste, class and politics (Bhatt, 1975) do not provide a corrective to the 'caste alone' approach. These studies are rooted in the falsity of the western dichotomy of tradition and modernity and the trio of 'class, status and party' (Weber, 1947). They do not incorporate the experience of Indian society into the concepts of caste, class and power, hence inadequate in rescuing us from these alien concepts and theories.

Class in India has existed along with caste and power. Caste incorporates class and class incorporates caste in the Indian context. Neither the 'caste alone' view nor the 'class alone' perspective can help in a proper and fuller understanding of Indian society. It has been noted that there was never a perfect congruence between caste, class and power. Mobility and migration were quite normal activities in ancient and medieval India. However, Bailey, Beteille and Bhatt give the impression that a congruence prevailed between caste, class and power in the pre-independent India, and land reforms and politicization have brought about incongruities and caste-free areas.

Historians of the Marxist disposition have realized that there is an intertwining of caste and class in India, but they prefer to look at caste from a class point of view. Kosambi (1956) makes a class analysis of the Aryans after the Rig Veda. Thapar (1974), Habib

(1974:), and Desai (1948) have also done a class analysis of Indian society. According to Desai, caste inheres in an underdeveloped but potentially explosive class character. In another study, Desai (1975) has analyzed the Indian State from a class (Marxist) point of view. But class does not necessarily mean openness, mobility and a combination of certain attributes as generally perceived by western social scientists and their followers in India. Castes have been functioning as classes for all practical considerations. Class relations are as old as caste relations or even older than caste relations. Lamb (1975) reports the prevalence of class relations as early as 600 B.C. in India. Material and cultural traditions existed with a sort of congruity, and class transformation had been a vital fact in the form of new kingdoms, settled agriculture, trade, cities and banking and guild organizations.

The non-Marxist scholars in general have relied on analytical abstractions in the form of statistical-mathematical indicators or analytical topologies (Singh, 1981). D'Souza (1975) treats class as a conceptually abstracted category. Class does not exist as a community like caste. Class is defined operationally in terms of certain indices. D'Souza applies the attributional approach to class purely in terms of constructing an 'order' comprising upper, middle and lower class categories. The following points have been made about classes in India:

(1) Classes are not found as a system of stratification in the same way as castes are rooted in the Indian society.
(2) Class is not a universalistic phenomenon of social stratification.
(3) There are no objective criteria of class identification.
(4) It is not clear whether class is a category or a concrete unit of interaction with other units.

One could affirm that these points have been put forth in order to prevent a class analysis of Indian society. Caste has created numerous problems of a class nature related to economic domination and subjugation, privileges and deprivations, 'conspicuous waste' and bare survival. However, these problems have not been taken up as central concerns of social research. Pollution-purity and the encompassing power of caste have been taken up as a positive dimension of the caste system. The usual pretension is that class antagonism, class consciousness and class unity are not found as Karl Marx had seen, hence no class analysis. However, this is not true. Caste is a system of harmonic relations from a particular perspective only, it is also a system of opposition and antagonism from another perspective, and the latter has not been taken up seriously.

The mode of production and class contradictions are essential features of the Marxian approach to social stratification. Gough (1980) considers the mode of production as a social formation in which she finds interconnections of caste, kinship, family, marriage and even rituals with the forces of production and production relations. Gough's study of Thanjavur explains the emergence of a new bourgeoisie, the polarization of the peasantry, and the pauperization of the working class due to historical transformations in the mode of production. The totality of contradictions in social stratification can be seen through the contradictions in the mode of production. Marxist ideologists like Namboodiripad (1979) and Ranadive (1979) consider class relationships as a domain assumption in the treatment of caste and kinship in India. Even *varna* and the *jajmani* system can be explained in terms of class relations as they are embedded in the mode of production (Meillassoux, 1973). Others who have used the mode of production as the framework for analysis of class relations in village India are: Djurfeldt and Lindberg (1975), Heera Singh (1979), Thorner (1969), Saith and Tanakha (1972), and Bhardwaj and Das (1975).

The main classes today in India are: (i) agrarian, (ii) industrial, (iii) business and mercantile, and (iv) professional. Contradictions can be found between various classes in terms of continuance of the old classes and the emergence of new ones at the same time. Industrial, business and professional classes characterize urban India, and landowners, tenants, sharecroppers and agricultural labourers are found in the countryside. These classifications have ideological overtones. The classification comprising landowners, moneylenders and labourers does not refer necessarily to class antagonism. But the other classification comprising the bourgeoisie, capitalist-type landowners, rich peasants, landless peasantry and agricultural labourers necessarily refers to class interaction, dependence-independence and conflict as the basic elements of class structure.

V

Approaches to the concepts of caste and class bear ideological contents. The methodology and data used in the studies of caste and class provided legitimacy to these approaches. Caste was treated not as a 'social formation', but as an encompassing institution which encompassed all other aspects of Hindu society. However, caste, in fact, was more than a 'ritualistic' mechanism, and it could face a variety of forces and constraints due to its all-inclusive character. If it were simply a ritualistic arrangement, it would have crumbled down long ago due to its very cumbersome nature. The social formation of Indian society comprises class, ethnicity, power, religion and economy along with caste. All these aspects of the social formation are incorporated into each other. They provide an understanding of the historicity of Indian society including that of caste and class. Indigenization of the concepts of caste and class must come from the realization of such a formation and the totality of its historicity.

The approaches such as the functional, dialectical, psychological and structuralist are inadequate for explaining the historicity of the Indian situation as they are rooted in the experience of the situations that are unfamiliar with India's historicity. Issues relating to caste and class were raised and debated elsewhere and subsequently passed on to Indian scholars through the mechanism of the academic hegemony of western scholars. Whether caste is a cultural phenomenon or a structural aspect, whether it should be studied by participant observation or by using survey method, whether it should be treated as the sole representative institution or class, power and religion should also be studied, whether 'caste alone' should be studied—have been raised by western scholars and later on taken up by their Indian counterparts with the tacit understanding of promoting certain ideas upheld by them. We must examine carefully why structural-functionalism has become so popular, why participant observation is regarded as a sacrosanct technique of research, why Redfield's notions of 'little community' and 'peasant society' or Marriott's notions of Little and Great Traditions and parochialization and universalization have gained currency. One view is that the Brahminocentric sociology produced by Srinivas is due to such indoctrination by these academic forces.

In an earlier study, Singh (1974) provides a paradigm of social stratification in the light of cultural versus structural and particular versus universal characteristics. The types that emerge from these criteria are: (i) cultural-universalistic; (ii) cultural-particularistic; (iii) structural-universalistic; and (iv) structural-particularistic. This paradigm is based on Parson's analysis of social structure. Singh's analysis shows relevance of the structural-particularistic type for analyzing social stratification in India. However, Singh does not provide reasons for the suitability of such a classification. Nomology is the obvious reason for Singh's scientism. However, in a recent study, Singh (1981) provides another classification of the studies on social stratification carried out in the 1970s. The main theoretic concerns are: (i) structural-functional; (ii) structuralist; (iii) structural-historical; and (iv) historical-materialist or Marxist. I have already referred to some of the studies which have been analyzed under the rubric of these approaches. Caste is the central concern of all the researchers including the Marxists.

Caste is an all-inclusive institution and it subsumes class relations. Any departure from caste is treated as incongruence between caste, status, wealth and power, hence the emergence of class relations. Such a view is known as the structural-functional. Change within the caste (sanskritization), resilience and consensus are the hallmarks of structural-functionalism. Dumont is the most well known proponent of structuralism. The pivotal notions of this approach are reflected in Dumont's *Homo Hierarchicus* (1970). Singh (1981) points out ideology, dialectics, transformational relationship and comparison as the salient features of Dumont's study of caste. For Dumont, hierarchy is ideology, and hierarchy implies ranking based on the notion of purity-impurity. The opposition between pure and impure refers to binary tension or dialectics. Pure and impure imply exclusion as well as inclusion in regard to caste hierarchy. Hierarchy also refers to the relationship of the 'encompassing' and the 'encompassed'. The 'pure' encompasses the 'less pure' and so on. This applies to all the sections and aspects of society. Thus, change is in the society and not of the society.

Dumont's view falls short of all those points which have been indicated in regard to structural-functionalism. In addition to these points, Singh (1981) comments that Dumont's structuralism suffers both theoretically and substantively. Gould's notion of 'contra priest' (1967) also negates the dichotomy or binary opposition between the pure and impure. The lower caste men also function as priests, hence they become pure. But they remain impure being lower in the caste hierarchy. The implication of Dumont's treatment of caste is that caste and class are in binary opposition. Singh's (1981) comments on structuralism are as follows: "The structuralist's treatment of dialectics is dissociated from history. History, indeed, links essence to existence, form to content, superstructure to infrastructure and theory to practice. Devoid of such a sense of historical conjecture structuralism amounts to a set of conceptual schema, devoid of a basis in evolutionary changes in society. Its transformational relationships being a historical abound in tautologies."

In a study, Klass (1980) has raised the question of origin of caste. Klass projects a paradigm of the possible development of the caste system. The main idea is that clans exchange women, whereas the caste system exchanges goods without exchanging women. The explanation given by Klass is that India has developed ecosystems in which people have different modes of life, and the various human groups (corporate groups) would have a minimum of intercourse and not exchange women with outside groups. Thus, corporate groups form marriage circles. Klass relates caste with physical force and economic power. However, the corporateness of caste groups is equated with their egalitarian character, and this might be historically and substantively incorrect.

The understanding of caste and class demands an approach which has such as: (i) dialects, (ii) history, (iii) culture, and (iv) structure. Dialectics refers to the effective notions which bring about contradictions and highlight relations between unequal segments and men and women. Thus, it does not simply mean binary fission in the cognitive structure of Indian society as perceived by structuralists in terms of pure and impure. History provides a substantial account of the conditions of human existence. It is not a conjectural construction based on mythology, scriptures and ideations. Culture defines the rules of the game, the nature of relations between the haves and the have-nots. Thus culture does not include only cultural practices, rituals, *rites de passage*, etc. Structure is a product of dialectical contradictions, historical forces, and a certain 'formation'. Once it has emerged, it becomes a sort of force in determining the course of history, the nature of contradictions and the evaluational standards. Thus, structure refers to relations between social segments at a point of time as a historical product and as an existent reality.

Dialectics, history, culture and structure refer to a combination of theory, structure and process about the social formation (both caste and class) of Indian society. Together they explain the historicity of Indian society from the point of its genesis. The debates today are: whether changes in caste and class are 'transformational' or they are 'replacements', whether caste is 'closed' and class is 'open'; whether caste is 'organic' and whether class is 'segmentary'; and whether caste is replaced by class. These are questions which have come up quite often as the idea of 'social formation' has not gained currency in our understanding of caste and class. The obsession of considering caste and class as polar opposites has prevented us from thinking of caste and class as dimensions of the historicity of India's social formation.

Several scholars have denied the 'congruence' version about caste, class and power in the ancient India. They have conclusively established that social mobility existed in ancient and medieval India. The *jajmani* system was never completely 'organic' in practice. The idea of the contrapriest exposes the hollowness of the concepts of hierarchy and pollution-purity. In the place of sanskritization, westernization and dominant caste etc., it is necessary to study downward mobility and proletarianization, upward mobility and embourgeoisiement, urban incomes for the rural people and the migration of the rural rich to towns, and rural non-agricultural income and mobility etc.

Caste has inhered in class and class has inhered in caste for centuries in the Indian context, and Indian society continues to have this inseparable mix even today. Role of caste and class in elections is an evidence of this mix. However, caste operates as a 'marriage circle' in a different way from the way it functions in other arenas. Hypergamy explains the role of status and wealth within caste. Class-like distinctions within caste and caste-like styles within a class are part of the people's life situations. 'Class' has been an in-built mechanism within caste, and therefore, caste cannot be seen simply as a 'ritualistic' system, and class cannot be seen as an open system as it has often been influenced by the institution of caste. In order to go deep into such a phenomenon the structural-historical perspective becomes inescapable.

References

Aggarwal, P.C., 1971, *Caste, Religion and Power*, New Delhi, Shri Ram Centre for Industrial Relations.

Bailey, F.G., 1957, *Caste and the Economic Frontier*, Manchester, Manchester University Press.

———, 1963, "Closed Social Stratification in India," *European Journal of Sociology*, Vol. 4, No. 1.

Barth, Fredrick, 1960, "The System of Social Stratification in Swat, North Pakistan," in E.R. Leach (ed.), *Aspects of Caste in South India, Ceylon and North-West Pakistan*, Cambridge, Cambridge University Press.

Berreman, Gerald D., 1967, "Stratification, Pluralism and Interaction: A Comparative Analysis of Caste", in Anthony de Reuck, and Julie Knight (eds.), *Caste and Race: Comparative Approaches*, London, J & A Churchill Ltd.

———, 1979, *Caste and Other Inequalities*, Meerut, Folklore Institute.

Beteille, Andre, 1966, *Caste, Class and Power*, Bombay, Oxford University Press.

———, 1966, "Closed and open social stratification in India", *European Journal of Sociology*, Vol. 7.

———, 1969, "Ideas and Interests: Some Conceptual Problems in the Study of Social Stratification in India", *International Social Science Journal*, Vol. 21, No. 7.

———, 1969, *Castes: Old and New*, Bombay, Asia Publishing House.
Bettelheim, Charles, 1968, *India Independent*, London, Mc-Gibbon and Kee Ltd.
Bhardwaj, Krishna and Das, P.K., 1975, "Tenurial Conditions and Mode of Exploitation: Study of Some Villages in Orissa", *Economic and Political Weekly*, Vol. 10, No. 5-7.
Bhatt, Anil, 1975, *Caste, Class and Politics*, Delhi, Manohar Book Service.
Bose, N.K., 1967, *Culture and Society in India*, Bombay, Asia Publishing House.
Bottomore, T., 1964, *Sociology*, London, Allen and Unwin.
Bougle, Celestin, 1971, *Essays on the Caste System*, Cambridge, Cambridge University Press.
Centers, Richard, 1961, *The Psychology of Social Classes: A Study of Class Consciousness*, New York, Russel and Russel.
Chauhan, S.K., 1980, *Social Stratification in Assam*, New Delhi, Classical Publishing Company.
Davis, Kingsley and Wilbert E. Moore, 1945, "Some Principles of Stratification", *American Sociological Review*, Vol. 10, No. 2.
Desai, A.R., 1948, *Social Background of Indian Nationalism*, Bombay, Popular Book Depot.
———, 1975, *State and Society in India: Essays in Dissent*, Bombay, Popular Prakashan.
———, 1978, *Rural Sociology in India*, Bombay, Popular Prakashan.
D'Souza, V.S., 1967, "Caste and Class: A Reinterpretation", *Journal of Asian And African Studies*, Vol. 2, Nos. 3-4.
———, 1975, "Social Inequalities and Development in India", *Economic and Political Weekly*, Vol 10, No. 19.
Dube, S.C., 1955, "Ranking of Castes in Telengana Villages", in D.N. Majumdar (ed.), *Rural Profiles*, Lucknow, The Ethnographic and Folk Culture Society.
———, 1968, "Caste Dominance and Factionalism", *Contributions to Indian Sociology*, New Series, No. 2.
———, 1976, *Social Science and Social Realities: Role of the Social Science in Contemporary India*, Simla, Indian Institute of Advanced Study.
Dumont, Louis, 1970, *Homo Hierarchicus*, London, Paladin Granada Publishing Ltd.
Dumont, Louis and D. F. Pocock, 1959, 'Pure and Impure", *Contributions to Indian Sociology*, Vol. 3.

Epstein, T.S., 1962, *Economic Development and Social Change in South India*, Manchester, The Manchester University Press.

Furnivall, J.C., 1909, *The Netherlands, India: A Study of Plural Economy*, Cambridge, Cambridge University Press.

Ghurye, G.S., 1950, *Caste and Class in India*, Bombay, Popular Book Depot.

Goran, Djeelrfeldt and J. Lindberg, 1975, *Behind Poverty: The Social Formation of a Tamil Village*, London, Curzon Press.

Gough, E. Kathleen, 1960, "Caste in a Tanjore Village", in E.R. Leach (ed.), op.cit., 1960.

———, 1980, "Modes of production in Southern India", *Economic and Political Weekly*, Vol. 15, Nos. 5, 6 and 7, Annual Number.

Gould, A. Harold, 1967, "Priest and Contrapriests: A Structural Analysis of Jajmani Relationships in the Hindu Plains Nilgiri Hills", *Contributions to Indian Sociology*, New Series, No. 1.

Habib, Irfan, 1974, "Social Distribution of Landed Property in the Pre-British India: A Historical Survey", in R.S. Sharma (ed.), *Indian Society: Historical Probings*, New Delhi, Peoples Publishing House.

Harper, E.B., 1968, "Social Consequences of an 'Unsuccessful' Low Caste Movement", in James Silverberg (ed.), *Social Mobility in the Caste System in India*, The Hague, Mouton Publishers.

Harriss, John, 1982, *Capitalism and Peasant Farming*, Bombay, Oxford University Press.

Hazlthurst, L.W., 1968, "Multiple Status Hierarchies in Northern India", *Contributions to Indian Sociology*, New Series, No. 2.

Heibert, Paul G., 1969, "Caste and personal Rank in an Indian Village", *American Anthropologist*, Vol. 71, No. 3.

Hocart, A.M., 1950, *Caste*, London, Mathew & Co.

Hutton, J.H., 1946, *Caste in India*, Oxford, Oxford University Press.

Ketkar, S.V., 1909, *The History of Caste in India*, Ithaca, New York, Cornell University Press.

Klass, Mortan, 1980, *Caste: The Emergence of the System in South Asia*, Philadelphia, Institute for the Study of Human Issues.

Kolenda, Pauline, 1978, *Caste in Contemporary India: Beyond Organic Solidarity*, California, Benjamin Cummings Publishing Company.

Kosambi, D.D., 1958, *An Introduction to the Study of Indian History*, Bombay, Popular Book Depot.

Kothari, Rajni, 1970, *Politics in India*, New Delhi, Orient Longman Ltd.

———, 1970 (ed.), *Caste in Indian Politics*, New Delhi, Orient Longman Ltd.

Lamb, Helen, 1975, "The Indian Merchant", in Milton Singer, *Tradition India: Structure and Change*, Jaipur, Rawat Publications.

Leach, Edmund R., 1960, "Introduction: What Should We Mean By Caste", in E.R. Leach (ed.), op.cit.

Lynch, Owen M., 1968, "The Politics of Untouchability: A Case from Agra, India" in Milton Singer and B.S. Cohn (eds.), *Structure and Change in Indian Society*, Chicago, Aldine Publishing Company.

Maine, Sir Henry, *Village Communities in the East and the West*, London.

MacIver, Robert M., and Page, C.H., 1967, *Society*, London, Macmillan Co.

Majumdar, D.N., 1958, *Caste and Communication in an Indian Village*, Delhi, Asia Publishing House.

Marriott, McKim, 1955, "Little Community in an Indigenous Civilization", in McKim Marriott (ed.), *Village India, Studies in the Little Community*, Chicago, Chicago University Press.

———, 1959, "International and Attributional Theories of Caste Ranking", *Man in India*, Vol. 34, No. 2.

———, 1965, *Caste Ranking and Community Structure in Five Regions of India and Pakistan*, Poona, Deccan College.

———, 1968, "Caste Ranking and Food Transactions: A Matrix Analysis", in Milton Singer and B.S. Cohn (eds.), op.cit.

———, 1968, "Multiple Reference in Indian Caste System", in James Silverberg (ed.), op.cit.

Marshal, T.H., 1963, *Sociology at the Crossroads and Other Essays*, London, Heinemann Educational Books Ltd.

Marx, Karl, 1945, *Articles on India*, Bombay, People's Publishing House.

Mathur, K.S., 1964, *Caste and Ritual in a Malwa Village*, Bombay, Asia Publishing House.

Mayer, Adrian C., 1960, *Caste and Kinship in Central India*, Berkeley, University of California Press.

Meillassoux, C., 1973, "Are There Castes in India", *Economy and Society*.

Mencher, Joan P., 1974, "The Caste System, Upside Down the Not-so-Mysterious East", *Current Anthropology*, Vol. 15, No. 4.

Miller, D.B., 1975, *From Hierarchy to Stratification: Changing Patterns of Social Inequality in a North Indian Village*, Delhi, Oxford University Press.

Misra, B.B., 1964, *The Indian Middle Classes*, London, Oxford University Press.

Nadel, S.F., 1953, *Foundations of Social Anthropology*, London, Cohen and West.

Namboodiripad, E.M.S., 1979, "Caste Conflicts Vs. Growing Unity of Popular Democratic Forces", *Economic and Political Weekly*, Vol. 14, Nos. 7 & 8, Annual Number.

Omvedt, Gail, 1982, (ed.), *Land, Caste and Politics in Indian States*, Delhi, University of Delhi.

Ossowski, Stanislaw, 1963, *Class Structure in the Social Consciousness*, London, Routledge and Kegan Paul.

Panikkar, K.M., 1955, *Hindu Society at the Crossroads*, Bombay, Asia Publishing House.

Parsons, Talcott, 1954, "A Revised Analytical Approach to the Theory of Social Stratification", in T. Parsons, *Essays in Sociological Theory*, Glencoe, The Free Press.

Parvathamma, C., 1978, "The Remembered Village: A Brahminical Odyssey", *Contributions to Indian Sociology*, New Series, Vol. 12, No. 1.

Ranadive, B.T., 1979, "Caste, Class and Property Relations", *Economic and Political Weekly*, Vol. 14, Nos, 7 & 8, Annual Number.

Risley, H.H., 1969, *The Peoples of India* (2nd edn.), Delhi, Orient Books.

Reuck, De Anthony and Julie Knight, 1967, (ed.), *Caste and Race: Comparative Approaches*, London, J & A Churchill Ltd.

Saberwal, Satish, 1976, *Mobile Men*, New Delhi, Vikas Publishing House Ltd.

———, 1979, "Inequality in Colonial India", *Contributions to Indian Sociology*, Vol. 13, No. 2.

———, 1979, "Sociologists and Inequality in India: the Historical Context", *Economic and Political Weekly*, Vol. 14, Nos. 7 & 8.

Saith, Aswani and Ajay Tanakha, 1972, "Agrarian Tensions and the Differentiation of the Peasantry: A Study of West UP Village", *Economic and Political Weekly*, Vol. 7, No. 14.

Senart, Emile, 1980, *Caste in India: The Facts and the System*, London, Metheun & Co.

Sharma, K.L., 1969, "Stresses in Caste Stratification", *Economic and Political Weekly*, Vol. 4, No. 3.

———, 1970, "Modernization and Rural Stratification: An Application at the Micro-Level", *Economic and Political Weekly*, Vol. 5, No. 37.

———, 1974, *The Changing Rural Stratification System*, New Delhi, Orient Longman Ltd.

———, 1977, "New Introduction", *Review of Caste*, by J. Murdoch, Jaipur, Rawat Publications.

———, 1980, *Essays on Social Stratification*, Jaipur, Rawat Publications.

Sherring, M.A., 1974, *Hindu Castes and Tribes*, Delhi, Cosmo Publications.

Silverberg, James, 1959, "Caste Ascribed Status Vs. Caste irrelevant Roles", *Man in India*, Vol. 39.

———, 1968, *Social Mobility in the Caste System in India*, The Hague, Moulton Publishers.

Singer, Milton and Bernard Cohn, 1968, *Structure and Change in Indian Society*, Chicago, Aldine Publishing Company.

Singh, Hira, 1979, "Kin, Caste and Kisan Movement in Marwar: Some Questions to the Conventional Sociology of Kin and Caste", *Journal of Peasant Societies*, Vol. 7, No. 2.

Singh, Yogendra, 1968, "Caste and Class: Some Aspects of Continuity and Change", *Sociological Bulletin*, Vol. 17, No. 2.

———, 1974, "Sociology of Social Stratification", in *A Survey of Research in Sociology and Social Anthropology*, Vol. I (ICSSR), Bombay, Popular Prakashan.

———, 1979, "Ideology, Theory and Method in Indian Sociology", in Stein Rokkan (ed.), *A Quarter Century of International Social Science*, New Delhi, Concept Publishing House.

———, 1981, "Sociology of Social Stratification in Indian-II", *Second Survey of Research in Sociology and Social Anthropology*, ICSSR, New Delhi.

Sinha, Surajit, 1967, "Caste in India: Its Essential Pattern of a Socio-Cultural Integration", in Anthony De Reuck and Julie Knight (eds.), op.cit.

———, 1974, "Caste in India", in *A Survey of Research in Sociology and Social Anthropology*, Vol. I (ICSSR) Bombay, Popular Prakashan.

Srinivas, M.N., 1952, *Religion and Society Among the Coorgs of South India*, Oxford, Clarendon Press.

———, 1959, "The Dominant Caste in Rampura", *American Anthropologist*, Vol. 61, No. 1.

———, 1962, *Caste in Modern India and Other Essays*, Bombay, Asia Publishing House.

———, 1966, *Social Change in Modern India*, Berkeley, California University Press.

———, 1976, *The Remembered Village*, New Delhi, Oxford University Press.

———, 1979, "The Future of Indian Caste", *Economic and Political Weekly*, Vol. 14, No. 7 & 8.

Srinivas, M.N., Damle, Y.B. and Beteille, Andre, 1959, "Caste, A Trend Report and Bibliography", Current Sociology, Vol. 8, No. 3.

Stein, Burton, 1968, "Social Mobility and Medieval South Indian Sects", in James Silverberg (ed.), op.cit.

Thapar, Romila, 1974, "Social Mobility in Ancient Indian Society", in R.S. Sharma (ed.), op.cit.

Thorner, Daniel, 1969, "Capitalist Farming in India", *Economic and Political Weekly*, Vol. 4, No. 52.

———, 1974, *Land and Labour in India*, Bombay, Asia Publishing House.

Weber, Max, 1948, *From Max Weber: Essays in Sociology*, London, Routledge and Kegan Paul.

———, 1964, *The Theory of Social and Economic Organisation*, London, The Free Press.

4

Caste and Class in India: Nexus, Continuity and Change

Both caste and class have been debated from narrow ideological standpoints. One extreme view, for example, is that Indian society can be best studied from a 'caste model' or 'caste perspective'. Caste is viewed as an overarching ideological system which pervades over all aspects of social life of Hindus in particular and of other communities in general. One of the implications of such a view is that caste is basically an infrastructural basis of Indian society; and occupation, division of labour, rules of marriage, interpersonal relations etc. are superstructural in nature as they emanate from the ideology of caste. A very pertinent question is: Whether caste is a normative system, or a system of actual social-structural relations? Perhaps the answer would be both yes and no. In certain arenas caste adheres to its normative sanctions whereas in some others caste groups and their members have taken up activities which have no traditional sanctions of the caste system. The crux of the matter is: what do we mean by caste system? It is a very complex and complicated system. One finds that members of a caste compete with each other; and they are also found co-operating with each other. Class-based distinctions within the caste are found in a pronounced form. Members of a caste in a given village can sometimes be representative of India's class structure. While observing all the pertinent rules of marriage members of a caste may still give premium to class-status in matrimonial alliances.

Caste refers to inequality in theory as well as in practice. Dumont[1] considers inequality based on the caste system as a special type of inequality. 'Ideas and values' are considered by Dumont as basic for knowing actual and observable behaviour of the people. For Dumont, therefore, the idea of the pure and the impure is basic to the understanding of caste. This idea is the basis of hierarchy in Hindu society. Dumont's main concern is with the traditional social organization of India from the viewpoint of values and ideas. He constructs an ideal type of the caste system based on ethnographic and indological research materials. Madan[2] upholds Dumont's view that hierarchy is a 'universal necessity'. Society in India has remained static; change in society has taken place, but the change of society is absent.

The basis of understanding of caste system as an empirical reality is to locate caste groups as *jatis* in a specific rural/urban context. Caste is seen as a status group in these contexts. It is a source of placement in the social set-up. But at a macro-level, caste is also a means of identity. At this level it is not a functioning reality of informal, day-to-day relations. Caste does not become a basis of marriage between a Tamil Brahmin and a Kanyakubja Brahmin of Uttar Pradesh. But still a Tamil Brahmin and a Brahmin from Uttar Pradesh can always have a sense of belonging to the same stock and even may co-operate for common good of the two in situations of crises and challenges. Is caste an interest group? Can common interests bring together men of different castes from various regions and states more smoothly than those of the same caste? Caste is certainly a resource, but its resourceability varies from caste to caste depending upon the status of a given caste in a given area. Caste identity/membership has become a liability for the members of upper and middle castes in recent years because a certain percentage of jobs, seats in parliament and state legislatures and admissions in institutions of higher learning have been reserved for the 'weaker sections' of Indian society.

The view that caste and class are polar opposites is not correct. Both have been inseparable parts of India's social formation, hence the study of their nexus, continuity and change. The view that recent processes of change have given way to a change from caste to class in Indian society is also not quite tenable and convincing. Caste is a very complex system as it is not simply a system of power relations and economic activities for namesake. If it gets weakened in one aspect, it also gets strengthened in an other with certain alterations, additions and accretions. Therefore, what we need is to study the dynamics of this complexity of the system. One obvious inference is that there is caste-basis of class and class-basis of caste, hence both are cause as well as consequence of one another. There is a class basis of rituals, pollution-purity and other apparently non-material aspects of social life. We may give an example of some associations. Jat Sabha is not a simple caste association; in effect it is a peasant's organization. Kisan Sabha is not a simple peasant's organization; it is very much an association of castes engaged in agriculture, particularly of Jats in northern India and their counterparts in other states. The same logic applies to the Vaishya Sabha, Kshatriya Mahasabha, Bhooswami Sangh etc.

It is a myth that caste is mainly a rural phenomenon, and class is found generally in towns and cities. We may cite here an example of caste-elections in Jaipur. The annual elections of Khandelwal Vaishya Mahasabha were being held at the time of one of my visits. To my utter surprise in the heart of the city, opposite to the Central Reserve Police Lines on the Station Road, hundreds of cars, jeeps, auto-rickshaws and two-wheelers were parked and an equally large number of vehicles were plying around, all engaged in the elections. At least 50 to 60 stalls were installed for electioneering on both sides of the road. Traffic was diverted and the police pickets were also posted to watch/control the situation. It was not only a show of casteism, but also of factionalism within the caste. Why all this show? What elected people would get out of this by spending thousands of rupees on these elections? One should seriously take up these questions to understand caste-class nexus in urban India. We know that there is no uniform pattern of caste structure in actual terms throughout India. The same can be said about class structure. Both caste and class bear ideological contents as conceptual elements. Both have substantive elements as existential and mundane schemes of relations. There are thousands of castes in India with different names and nomenclatures, but there are only about five or six classes throughout the country. The number of castes or classes is not so important in determining basic relations—social or economic or both. More important is that these apparently distinct bases of social division in Indian society are not realistically very different from each other. There are numerous middle classes which are not directly related to production processes, they are an offshoot of the modern Indian state apparatus.

In India, class-struggle is also in effect caste-struggle and *vice-versa*. Separation of the two seems to be superfluous and mechanistic. An anomological plea that the two are different as they refer to 'social' and 'economic' realities cannot be accepted because it has been proved with ample substantive support and evidence that caste and class are found not as separate entities. For example, caste mobility movements are also class mobility movements, both manifestly and latently.

We suggest that the frame of reference and the methodological device for studying India's social formation should comprise dialectical reasoning, structural processes, historicity, and ideological (cultural) and political consciousness. The goal is not really to study the totality of social formation in the literal sense of the term, but to discern both the dominant as well as the not-so-dominant elements of a given situation. The dominant causality would certainly mean ascertaining whether the causation is mainly social or economic or political etc. or it is a certain combination of these or/some other factors and forces.

II

Undoubtedly, due to multidimensionality and complexity of the caste system, one encounters numerous difficulties in giving a precise definition of caste. Structural aspect of caste is explained by accepting it as a general principle of stratification.[3] Caste as a cultural system is understood in terms of prominence of ideas of pollution-purity and notions of hierarchy, segregation and corporateness.[4] Caste is also viewed as a 'closed system' of stratification[5], whereas Beteille[6] considers caste system as both 'closed' and 'open'. He finds that caste is becoming increasingly 'segmentary' because of the emergence of differentiated structures in India. These analytic variations hinder a common definition of caste. However, these variations also explain the fact that caste is like all other systems of stratification in some ways while it is quite unique in some other respects. Caste is not really a very flexible system, yet a caste permits mobility in certain areas to its members. A given caste is guided by norms of the caste system, hence intercaste dependence; but a given caste has also its autonomy in regard to observance of its practices, rituals and protection of its rights in relation to other castes. In fact, caste has adapted itself as it has confronted innumerable varied situations, forces and constraints. Caste has evolved simultaneously in several directions and adjusted with ideologically antagonistic systems. It has not allowed the emergence of an alternative system of stratification and social relations though it has undergone significant changes from time to time.[7] There is no point, therefore, in enumerating features and functions of the caste system with their descriptions as done by Risley, Ketkar, Senart, Hutton, Furnivall, Sherring, Ghurye, etc.[8] Caste has been eulogized as a positive and functional system in the writings of the British ethnographers and some Indian scholars. Srinivas[9] notes that even today agricultural production requires co-operation of several castes. The use of the caste idiom is quite widespread. Even Marx[10] related the Asiatic mode of production to the stability of the caste system in India. Similarly, Maine[11] considered caste as an illustration of a non-contractual 'status-society'. Dumont and Bougle[12] thought of caste as an ideological system of a unique nature. Such a view was earlier held by Hocart[13]. Weber[14] too considered caste as a system of status stratification. None of these views and explanations offers a properly diagnosed understanding of the adaptive capacity and dynamic nature of the caste system. They explain caste basically as a cultural system implying that significant structural changes have not occurred in the Indian society due to its stable character and cultural dictum.

It has been inferred that a 'caste model' of Indian society has emerged as a result of implicit and explicit ideas and values. Beteille[15] blames Dumont in particular for encouraging a 'caste view' of Indian society. 'Caste model' as viewed by Beteille does not provide an analysis of material interests along with the study of ideas and values. There is a dialectical relationship between the two, and Dumont and Pocock's[16] notion of 'binary opposition' is far from the notion of 'dialectics' as given by Marx. Beteille also suggests that economic and political conflicts occur with a certain degree of autonomy of their own, hence they could be studied independent of caste and religious beliefs and ideas. Caste model would not permit such a path of understanding. The view that castes co-operate with each other is also a misconceived one. Non-antagonism and hierarchy both are nomological constructions. In reality defiance and conflict among castes are not uncommon. Leach's understanding that co-operation refers to caste and competition refers to class is naive and unconvincing. Not only families of dominant castes compete with each other to extend patronage to the lower castes for maintaining their dominance, but the lower caste families too compete to seek favours from the families of the dominant castes. Such a competition is really not a new phenomenon. Even feuds were quite common among the Kshatriyas and Brahmins for seeking power over a territory in ancient and medieval India. Leach's view that caste was simply 'caste' and a 'class-like situation' emerged only when the patrons started competing with each other ignores the fact that intercaste conflicts and revolts by the lower castes against the upper castes have been a historical fact.

There are two serious but erroneous consequences of upholding caste as a unique, closed and corporate system of social ranking: (i) caste and class are polar opposites; and (ii) 'caste view' could explain everything in India. Srinivas' concept of dominant caste[17] and his collection of essays on caste,[18] Mathur's[10] book on caste and ritual, Marriott's[20] studies on caste, and Kothari's[21] works on role of caste in India's politics are some of the notable examples of the 'caste view' model. Emphasis in these studies has been singularly on the hegemony or over-determination of caste by cultural/normative criteria rather than economic and political. However, in late sixties and seventies, 'multiple criteria',[22] 'levels of caste dominance'[23] and 'levels of mobility in caste system, structural processes of change and downward mobility'[24] were discussed with a conscious intent to counter the falsity of the culturological concepts like dominant caste, pollution-purity, sanskritization, westernization, etc. Some of these studies also repudiate the over-emphasized significance of the concepts of 'reference group' and 'relative deprivation' in analyzing social mobility in the caste system in India.

Those who draw a sharp line between caste and class observe that the two are different forms of social stratification. The units ranked in the class system are individuals, and those ranked in the caste are groups. D'Souza[25] draws a simple and mechanical distinction between caste and class obviously guided by the American notion of class. In other words, class for D'Souza is a result of what he calls objective rating of positions based on certain attributes. Here D'Souza refers to the rigidity-fluidity dimension of social stratification implying class as a case of fluidity and caste as referring to rigidity. Description of caste through the concepts of status rigidity and immutability, organic solidarity and functional interdependence, *homo Hierarchicus* and pollution-purity; and description of class by the ideology of individualism, competition and equality, are grossly erroneous. Caste as a system of social stratification represents a semblance of rigidity and fluidity, co-operation and competition, holism and individualism, organic and segmentary divisions, interdependence and autonomy and inequality and equality, etc., The genesis of these polar characteristics lies in the notion of superiority of the non-caste western society. These are 'analytic' explanations of caste, hence 'historic' and experiential contents are lacking in these writings. No static and abstract model of caste or class would help in the understanding of Indian society.

Not only caste has been thought as antithetical to class, but the notions of both caste and class have been guided by the experience of alien situations. Weber's notion of 'status group' has been equated with 'caste group', and his notions of 'class,' 'class situation' and 'market situation' have been found relevant for studying class in India. The other observation is that caste is 'real' phenomenon, whereas class is a category, an attributional construction. We may state that if caste is a 'real' phenomenon, class is also equally 'real' and empiric, if not more. Both caste and class are real and empiric in the same situations and human transactions. Both are interactional and hierarchical, and one incorporates the other. Another fallacy is to bestow 'class' only the Marxian meaning for studying the Indian society. What about 'unity' and 'harmony' among the patrons and clients, landlords and tenants, the upper caste 'haves' and the lower caste 'have nots', etc. These also refer to contradictions and consequent conflicts between the powerful and the lesser ones. Power is not a zero sum reality in Indian society as the Marxists would perhaps think of it. Thus, to reduce the totality of social relations to two simple layers, namely, the top and the bottom would be too crude a way of understanding the multilayered and intricate social formation of Indian society.

Since caste incorporates class and class incorporates caste, neither 'caste view' nor 'class view' alone would explain the totality of India's social reality. Researches by Stein, Panikkar and others have shown that a perfect congruence between caste, class and power never existed in the pre-British India.[26] Mobility and migration were quite normal activities particularly resulting from warfare for acquiring powers and revolts against the atrocities committed by the rulers and upper caste priests. In recent years, land reforms, adult franchise and certain constitutional provisions have brought about incongruities in summation of statuses. Since 'caste view' has been given unwarranted and undue emphasis, it is quite appropriate to make a note of 'class view' of Indian society. Kosambi[27] analyzes the Aryans in the post-Rig Veda period from the point of their economic formation. Thapar, Habib and Desai have analyzed class character of Indian society in ancient, medieval and modern India, respectively.[28] Lamb[29] reports prevalence of class relations as early as 600 BC in India. Material and cultural traditions existed in a congruent form, and class transformation had been a vital fact in the form of new kingdoms, settled agriculture, trade, cities and banking and guild organizations. Desai's approach is, however, more of a doctrine rather than an empirically relevant frame of reference. Caste inheres an underdeveloped but potentially explosive class character. Desai also analyzes character of the Indian State from the Marxist point of view and calls it 'capitalistic' in its essence and reality.

Both caste and class are real dimensions of India's social formation, hence inseparable from each other. Class is not simply a conceptually abstracted category. It is not a construct based on certain attributes or indices, operationally arrived at. Classes of landowners, landless labourers, traders and moneylenders are not abstractions, but they are existential structural components of India's class structure. Interactional ties (both conflict and co-operation) between them refer to their life-situations. Caste and class nexus is highlighted by Gough[30] in her analysis of mode of production as a social formation in which she finds interconnections of caste, kinship, family and marriage with forces of production and production relations. The Marxist ideologues[31] Namboodiripad and Ranadive consider class relations as domain assumption in the treatment of caste and kinship in India. Even *varna* and *jajmani* systems have been explained in terms of class relations and mode of production.[32] A 'class view'[33] of social structure and social relations is found in the analyses of several others including Djurfeldt Goran and J. Lindberg, Singh, Thorner, Saith and Tanakha and Bhardwaj and Das.

Caste and class represent to a large extent the same structural reality. Singh rightly comments on caste and class nexus: "The situation corresponds to a 'prismatic' model of change where traditional sentiments of caste and kinship undergo adaptive transformation without completely being 'diffracted' into classes or corporate groups. Classes operate within the framework of castes."[34] Caste conflicts are also class conflicts as the gap between the upper and the lower castes is also the same that one finds between the high and the low classes. Castes also function as classes as they are geared for performing their class interests. Therefore, common class consciousness among the members of a caste is mainly due to their common economic deprivations. Caste associations, particularly in urban context, perform economic and political functions for the benefit of their respective members. Thus, castes are more of interactional groups rather than attributional constructs. Mencher[35] finds caste as a very effective system of economic exploitation of the lower castes. Precisely due to this, the upper castes (in the garb of exploiting classes) have not allowed emergence of class consciousness among the lower classes as they feared a threat to their entrenched status in India's social structure.

III

Marxist notions of class and class-conflict have become hallmarks of the studies of India's agricultural and urban-industrial structures. Marx himself stated about caste and traditional ethos of village communities in his two articles on India in 1853 in the *New York Daily Tribune* (1951). Initially, Marx thought of Asiatic mode of production by which he meant absence of private property in land and static nature of economy due to a certain tie-up between caste, agriculture and village handicrafts. However, Kurian[36] observes that the analysis of Asiatic mode does not deny the role of class contradictions and class structures. India's precapitalist economic formation was neither classless nor static. Social relations and exploitation were based on both caste and class side by side. Now it is viewed that different forms of communal societies, forms of slavery and bondage, and feudal relations have existed in different combinations in the same areas at the same time.

Two questions are relevant for a discussion on class: (1) How to analyze the class structure in Indian society; and (2) what is class-caste nexus and its ramifications and interrelations in each region? The purpose of discussing these questions is not to accept or reject the Marxian approach for studying Indian society, but to understand the concept and reality of class in Indian context, and how it has been different from or similar to the concept and reality of caste. Rudra[37] while analyzing the class composition of the Indian agricultural population observes that there are only two classes in Indian agriculture, one of which is termed 'the class of big landlords', the other 'the class of agricultural labourers'. These two classes are in antagonistic contradiction with each other, and this contradiction constitutes the principal contradiction in Indian rural society. Similar to Rudra's view is the view held by Desai[38]. Rudra and those who adhere to his view do not accept the view that class differentiation in terms of agricultural labourers, poor peasants, middle peasants, rich peasants, landlords, etc. exists today and even existed in medieval India.[39] Rudra's view is that Indian agriculture has capitalist relations and capitalist development, hence two classes—'haves' and 'have nots'. State in India has assumed property norms of capitalist society as the axis of developmental strategy. One of the implications of this formulation is that the frame of reference which applies to the rest of the world also applies jolly well to the Indian society. The other inference is that the dominant causality in Indian society is 'economic' in nature in all situations and contexts.

Kosambi[40] accepts modes of production as the basis of understanding of class relations, but does not accept the hypothesis of 'economic determinism' and universal application of Marxism as a monolithic frame of reference and a method of study. Concepts specifically relevant for studying Indian society could be evolved from its historicity and experience. Mukerji and Thorner, for example, have used indigenous concepts drawing from agrarian relations and Indian's cultural heritage.[41] Even Patnaik[42] who uses notions of mode of production and differentiation of peasantry rejects a mechanical acceptance of Marx's model of study. She observes that several modes of production coexist in India, and there has been a limited and distorted development of capitalism. Lin[43] makes a reference regarding interpenetration and integration of precapitalist and capitalist relations.

Dandekar[44] examines nature of class and class-conflict in Indian society. Five major classes in India, according to Dandekar, are: (1) pre-capitalist (cultivators, agricultural labourers and household industry); (2) independent workers in capitalist society; (3) employers; (4) white-collar employees; and (5) blue-collar workers. The main classes today in India can also be referred to as: (1) agrarian, (2) industrial, (3) professional, and (4) business and mercantile. The emergence of these classes in modern India cannot simply be explained by the Marxist approach. Dandekar states that large-scale industry and monopoly capitalism have not been seen fully in terms of their implications in India. Marx did not see that capitalism would change due to trade unions and collective bargaining power of workers. Class antagonism is the kernel of Marxism, but class harmony is also a fact of life, and multiplicity of classes in-between the haves and the have nots, cannot escape our attention. There is a 'middle class' inevitably in all societies, and it has a class higher and a class lower to it—this has not received Marx's serious attention. Proletarian is propertyless, but he has also a chance for embourgeoisiement, and this is not stated by Marx. In India strikes by wage-earners is a very common feature, and they include those earning from Rs. 200 to Rs. 2,000 per month, hence wage-earners (proletariat) are a heterogeneous category. About fifth-sixths of the total workforce are left out by the Marxian yardstick. Indian State, being a welfare state, is the largest employer today. Is the Indian State a capitalist, exploitative and oppressive agency just like an industrialist or an employer of wage-earners? About 10 million workers are engaged in small-scale industries and family-owned concerns, and these workers generally do not witness class antagonism and strikes. The organized labour in India is one-ninth of the total workforce. Can we accept the Marxian approach in toto in view of these vital facts mentioned by Dandekar? Besides these points, overlapping of class, caste and occupation, and elite conflict, pressure groups and factions, influence of middle classes, and prevalence of mixed classes like 'gentleman farmers' are some other important points to be taken into account for a serious analysis of India's class structure.

IV

Gough[45] has analyzed conflicts and litigations based on economic inequalities between different castes in a Tanjore village. The 'mix' of caste and class in East Bengal[46], class genesis of caste structure in Bengal[47], and changes from caste to class by Misra, Beteille, Miller, and Kolenda have been reported[48], but none of them have studied resurgence of caste in the new situations with its multiple facets. Some scholars[49] have undertaken a class analysis of India's social formation considering caste, religion, family and politics as subservient to class relations. However, Harris and Omvedt[50] have analyzed class relations as a dominant causality within which they explain caste and other cultural aspects in Indian society. They have objected to the culturological determinism as advocated by Srinivas[51], Dumont[52] and several others of their persuasion. Parvathamma, while commenting on Srinivas' *Remembered Village*, writes: "In all the writings of Srinivas, the Brahmin-non-Brahmin values are juxtaposed."[53] Hierarchy based on pollution-purity remains intrinsic to Srinivas' thinking in regard to all aspects of human life even if it is actually not so pronounced. However, Bailey[54] incorporates both cultural and structural dimensions in the definition of caste. Class as an analytic notion is used by Beteille, Bhatt and Aggrawal as they draw a distinct line of demarcation between caste, class and power.[55] Methodological device is the main concern of these and other sociologists in drawing a distinction between caste and class.[56] Emergence of grades within a caste has also been referred as class-like change within caste. Hypergamy within caste endogamy always refers to status distinctions based on economic position and parental heritage, and therefore, class grades have always been there as part of the caste system itself. Class is not a result of the new forces of change which have affected the caste system. Changes are in the traditional caste and class relations and not in caste alone paving way to emergence of class relations. Thus, classes are found as part of a system of social stratification in the same way as castes are rooted in the Indian society. There is no universal and monolithic nature of class, class relations and class conflict. There are certainly objective criteria of class identification and determination of class position. A class is certainly a concrete unit of interaction with other units.

Caste in India is mistakenly projected as a system of harmonic relations. Caste inheres numerous problems related to economic domination and subjugation, privileges and deprivations, and 'conspicuous waste' and bare survival. Class relationships are treated as domain assumption in the treatment of caste and kinship in India. *Jajmani* system can be explained in terms of class relations and the mode of production. Klass[57] hypothesizes that class exchanges women, whereas caste system exchanges goods without exchanging women. According to Klass, India has ecosystems in which people have different modes of life and within these systems caste adapts itself to nature and economic conditions.

Some empirical studies reveal a high concentration of socially backward castes among tenant cultivators. The study by Reddy and Murthy[58] shows that as many as 73 per cent of the pure tenant-cultivators belong to the backward castes, and of the owner-cum-tenant cultivators 70 per cent belong to these backward castes. The backward castes tenant-cultivators are predominant in the small and medium size groups. The socially backward castes in Andhra Pradesh consist of Settibaliji and Harijan, and the socially advanced castes consist of Brahmin, Kapu, Devanga and others. Thus, most of the tenants of small and medium size belong to economically and socially depressed castes and pure rent-receivers except 12 per cent belong to the dominant castes. Mukherjee cites the example of caste riots to explain the unidimensionality of caste, class and religion. He writes: "Caste riots are frequent in those areas where the castewise 'social' deprivations are manifestly correlated with the classwise economic deprivations, such as in Bihar, Maharashtra, Tamil Nadu, etc."[59] According to Mukherjee, these caste contradictions are due to inherent class contradictions in the caste system. Vagiswari[60] observes that the Harijans have proletarianized between 1950 and 1970, while the non-Harijans have improved their economic standing during the same period.

The *dalits* have been attacked, murdered, their women-folk raped and put to indignities. Sinha[61] observes that it is 'class war' against Harijans, and not atrocities. In another despatch to *Economic and Political Weekly*, Sinha observes that "in the villages of Bihar, the rise of a rich peasant class has driven agricultural labourers of all castes—Chamars, Dusadhs, Kurmis, Yadavas, Bhumihars, and so on, to forsake their caste organizations and fight along trade union lines."[62] This shows that 'class war' cuts across caste lines. But the fact that a Harijan or Chamar agricultural labourer cannot simply be equated with his Brahmin or Bhumihar counterpart because the two have the same position in the class structure. The real situation in post-independent India is that a class of rich peasants from the backward castes is at the top of class hierarchy. This class is struggling against the social and political domination of the upper castes. The backward classes received encouragement for accelerating their struggle against the upper castes during the

Janata government regime in Bihar. The upper castes are upper class in overall sense of the term and the lower castes are lower class. The backward classes are at intermediate level in the caste hierarchy and so is their position in class structure. The Janata rule brought about a shift in the structure of dominance in Bihar having implication for the political economy of the state. Brahmins lost heavily their political dominance. A study of a village in Andhra Pradesh as mentioned earlier shows that the four tenurial categories, namely, pure tenants, owner-cum-tenants, pure rent receivers and owner-cum-rent receivers are concomitant with caste divisions. Most of the tenants of small and medium sizes belong to economically and socially depressed castes, viz., Settibaliji and Harijan, whereas the dominant sections (big size) of all the tenurial categories belong to socially advanced castes, viz., Kapu, Brahmin and Devanga.

The incidents of massacre, loot and rape of scheduled castes in Belchi, Agra, Pantnagar, Marathwada and Bajitpur, among other places, show the role of the caste system *vis-a-vis* class struggle and class organization as reported by Atyachar Virodhi Samiti.[63] The Samiti investigated the nature and extent of repression of scheduled castes in Marathwada in Maharashtra. The SCs were also poor peasants and agricultural labourers. The specific oppression and exploitation of women among the rural poor both sexually and as a class, particularly of the *dalit* women, have been highlighted in the report by the Samiti. The findings and observations of the Samiti on caste are quite meaningful as caste is seen as a relation of production. The following points may be noted:

(1) The caste system functions as an extremely effective method of economic exploitation. The dominant class also acquires political power and social prestige which further perpetuates and consolidates caste hierarchy. Thus, caste hierarchy reflects ownership of land, and economic hierarchy is closely linked with social hierarchy.

(2) Caste determines a definite relation to the means of production and subsistence specially in rural areas. Caste riots reflect conflict of class-interests.

(3) Caste also refers to the relations of production as it controls

the access of groups and individuals to the conditions of production and to resources and provides the social framework for politico-ritual activity.

(4) Ambedkar rightly observed that "the caste system was not merely division of labour, but also a division of labourers." However, caste prevents labourers from being a class-for-itself, hence caste as an ideology.

(5) Caste and religion are used to perpetuate a particular class structure.

(6) Caste persists as a part of feudal ideology.

The view of the Samiti seems to be apt for our discussion on the caste and class nexus, its continuity and change: "Caste is one of the most important aspects of Indian society. It represents a specific form of oppression at the level of relations of production. To say that there are only class issues, nothing like questions pertaining to caste, is totally absurd, because of the material reality that caste divisions beyond purely 'economic' classes yet persist. So issues around specific caste questions must be taken by all the progressives and leftists, *dalits* and non-*dalits* and organizations..."[64] The reality today is of caste oppression and class exploitation in India and particularly in villages. A report from a village in Punjab by Singh[65] shows that farm workers are Harijans and rich farmers are Jat Sikhs. The principal demand of the village workers is an increase in the wage rates. The big and middle peasants are united in opposition to the agricultural labourers. Thus, both class and caste are found inseparably in the tense situation. Convergence of caste and class has been reported in Gujarat by Bose[66] against reservation of seats for post-graduate medical courses, and in Bihar against for reserving 44 per cent of government jobs for the backward classes. Scarce resources and employment opportunities are the main cause of caste-class convergence. The Mandal Commission for Backward Classes was faced with the problem of caste and class convergence. It thought that caste and class hierarchies went together, and therefore, caste was considered as the basis of determining backwardness of a given member of society. Again, in the context of Bihar, Das[67] observes that apparently the phenomenon of caste is found in its virulent form, but to ignore the concept of class is to undermine the concrete conditions of the state. Caste is not a simplified entity as it would have only non-class social elements. Class is not an abstract, mechanical construct; it is a politico-economic concept, it refers to an active process and not to a catalogue category. A 'class analysis' of Bihar situation even in terms of expressions through caste idioms is essential."

Classes are found in India in caste idiom. A Marxist explanation of this statement is quite relevant here. Caste should be analyzed in regard to its nature, its material basis in history and in the present, and its role in politics. Which castes are the ruling ones, and which ones own land and capital, employ wage-labourers and extract surplus. Caste divisions hamper progress and unity among the oppressed classes. According to this view, all classes are defined by the relations in which the various sections of society are found related to the means of production, and castes are a carry-over of feudal class divisions. The Annual Number of *Economic and Political Weekly* of 1979 is specially devoted to "class and caste in India" employing a 'class view' of caste and not *vice-versa*. The titles in this volume include "Dialectics of Caste and Class Conflicts", "Caste and Class: An Interlinked View", "Caste Conflicts versus Growing Unity of Popular Democratic Forces", "Caste, Class and Property Relations", "Caste and Class in Maharashtra", "Class and Caste in Tribal Movement", "Caste, Class and Economic Opportunity in Kerala: An Empirical Analysis", "Caste and Class in Bihar", and "Class and Jati at Asthapuram and Kanthapuram." All these studies report caste and class nexus, use of caste, class and religion for gaining political power, emergence of an elite class in every caste, an interlinked view of caste and class, realization of caste idioms in power game, role of caste in agrarian and social movements, etc.

V

Extreme viewpoints have been expressed about caste and class. One such view is that the two are polar opposites and antithetical to each other. The other view is that caste represents ideational and normative aspect whereas class refers to basic economic relations.

We have discussed in the present paper the nexus between these two systems of social stratification in terms of their continuity and change. Our analysis shows that there is a caste basis of class and a class basis of caste. A given caste association, for example, is not simply an organization of the members of that caste group, but it is also an organization of unskilled workers or potters or traders etc.

Structural aspects of caste, namely, economic and political dimensions, etc. have remained underestimated, whereas the cultural aspects such as pollution-purity and rules of marriage, etc., have been over-emphasized. We have stated that a wholesome treatment of both structural and cultural aspects of social stratification could provide a deeper understanding of India's social formation as the two are, in fact, inseparable from each other. Both are conceptual constructs as well as empiric phenomena. Thus caste and class represent to a large extent though from different angles the same social reality. Classes function within the contexts of castes. Caste conflicts are also class or agrarian conflicts. The rifts between the upper and the lower castes to a large extent correspond with the conflicts between the landowners and the sharecroppers or agricultural labourers. Hence, an over-emphasis on either ideological or on structural aspect would provide an incomplete view of social reality.

Notes

1. Dumont, L., *Homo Hierarchicus*, London: Paladin Granada Publishing Ltd., 1970.
2. Madan, T.N., "On Understanding Caste", *Economic and Political Weekly*, Vol. VI, No. 34, 1971, pp. 1806-1808.
3. Barth, F., "The System of Social Stratification in Swat, North-West Pakistan", in, E.R. Leach (ed.), *Aspects of Caste in South India, Ceylon and North-West Pakistan*, Cambridge: Cambridge University Press, 1960, pp. 113-46; and Berreman, G.D., "Stratification, Pluralism and Interaction: A Comparative Analysis of Caste", in Anthony de Reuck and J. Knight (eds.), *Caste and Race: Comparative Approaches*, J & A Churchil Ltd., 1967 pp. 45-73.
4. Dumont, L., op.cit., 1970; and Leach, E.R., "What Should We Mean by Caste", in, E.R. Leach (ed.), op.cit., 1960, pp. 1-10.

5. Bailey, F.G., "Closed Social Stratification in India", *European Journal of Sociology*, Vol. IV, No. 1, 1963, pp. 107-24.
6. Beteille, A., "Closed and Open Social Stratification in India", *European Journal of Sociology*, Vol. VII, 1966, pp. 224-46.
7. Sharma, K.L., "New Introduction", in J. Murdoch, *Review of Caste in India*, Jaipur: Rawat Publications, 1977, p. vii.
8. Risley, H.H., *The Peoples of India* (2nd ed.), Delhi: Orient Books, 1969, p. 47; Ketkar, S.V., *The History of Caste in India*, Ithaca, New York: Cornell University Press, 1909, p. 15; Senart, E., *Caste in India: The Facts and the System*, London: Methew & Co., 1930, p. 35; Hutton, J.H., *The Caste in India*, Oxford: Oxford University Press, 1946: Furnivall, J.S., Netherlands, *India: A Study of Plural Economy*, Cambridge: Cambridge University Press, 1909; Sherring, M.A., *Hindu Castes and Tribes*, Delhi: Cosmo Publications, 1974, p. 214; and Ghurye, G.S., *Caste and Class in India*, Bombay: Popular Book Depot, 1950, p. 18.
9. Srinivas, M.N., "The Future of Indian Caste", *Economic and Political Weekly*, Vol. XIV, Nos. 7 and 8, 1979, pp. 237-42.
10. Marx, K., *Articles on India*, Bombay: Asia Publishing House, 1951; and Marx, K., "Pre-Capitalist Economic Formations", Translated by Jack Cohen with an Introduction by E. Hobsbawn, New York: International Publishers, 1965.
11. Maine, H.J.S., *Village Communities in the East and the West*, London: 1890.
12. Dumont, Louis, 1970, op.cit.; and Bougle, C., *Essays on the Caste System*, Cambridge: Cambridge University press, 1971.
13. Hocart, A.M., *Caste*, London: Mathew & Co., 1950.
14. Weber, M., *From Max Weber: Essays in Sociology*, London: Routledge & Kegan Paul, 1948.
15. Beteille, A., "Ideas and Interests: Some Conceptual Problems in the study of Social Stratification in India", *International Social Science Journal*, Vol.21, No. 7, 1969, pp. 17-31.
16. Dumont, L., and Pocock, D.F., "Pure and Impure", *Contributions to Indian Sociology*, Vol. III, 1959.
17. Srinivas, M.N., "The Dominant Caste in Rampura", *American Anthropologist*, Vol. LXI, No. 1, 1959.
18. Srinivas, M.N., *Caste in India and other Essays*, Bombay: Asia Publishing House, 1962.
19. Mathur, K.S., *Caste and Ritual in a Malwa Village*, Bombay: Asia Publishing House, 1964.

20. Marriott, M., *Caste Ranking and Community Structure in Five Regions of India and Pakistan*, Poona: Deccan College, Poona, 1965; Marriott, M., "Interactional and Attributional Theories of Caste Ranking", *Man in India*, Vol. 34, No. 2, 1959; Marriott, M., "Caste Ranking and Food Transactions: A Matrix Analysis," in M. Singer and B.S. Cohn (eds.), *Structure and Change in Indian Society*, Chicago: Aldine Publishing Company, 1968a; and Marriott, M., "Multiple Reference in Indian Caste System", in J. Silverberg (ed.), *Social Mobility in the Caste System in India*, The Hague: Mouton Publishers, 1968 b.
21. Kothari, R., *Caste in Indian Politics*, New Delhi: Orient Longman Ltd., 1970a; and Kothari, R., *Politics in India*, New Delhi: Orient Longman Ltd., 1970b.
22. Hazlehurst, L.W., "Multiple Status Hierarchies in Northern India", *Contributions to Indian Sociology*, New Series, No. II, 1968, pp. 38-57.
23. Dube, S.C., "Caste Dominance and Factionalism", *Contributions to Indian Sociology*, New Series No. II, 1968, pp. 83-97.
24. Sharma, K.L., "Stresses in Caste Stratification", *Economic and Political Weekly*, Vol, IV, No. 3, 1969; Sharma, K.L., *The Changing Rural Stratification System*, New Delhi: Orient Longman Ltd., 1974; Sharma, K.L., op.cit., 1977; Sharma, K.L., *Essays on Social Stratification*, Jaipur: Rawat Publications, 1980; and Sharma K.L., "Caste and Class: Factors Affecting Social Mobility Among the Scheduled Castes", *The Journal of Sociological Studies*, Vol. 2, 1983.
25. D'Souza, V.S., "Caste and Class: A Reinterpretation", *Journal of Asian and African Studies*, Vol. 2, Nos. 3-5, 1967, pp. 192-211.
26. Stein, B., "Soçial Mobility and Medieval South Indian Sects" in J. Silverberg (ed.), op.cit., 1968; and Panikkar, K.M., *Hindu Society at the Crossroads*, Bombay: Asia Publishing House, 1955.
27. Kosambi, D.D., *An Introduction to the Study of Indian History*, Bombay: Popular Prakashan, 1958, pp. 86-87.
28. Thapar, R., "Social Mobility in Ancient Indian Society", in R.S. Sharma (ed.), *Indian Society: Historical Probings*, New Delhi: Peoples Publishing House, 1974, pp. 95-123; Habib, I., "Social Distribution of Landed Property in the Pre-British India: A Historical Survey", in R.S. Sharma (ed.), op.cit., 1974, pp. 264-316; and Desai, A.R., *Social Background of Indian Nationalism*, Bombay: Popular Book Depot, 1948.

29. Lamb, H.B., "The Indian Merchant", in M. Singer (ed.), *Traditional India: Structure and Change*, Jaipur: Rawat Publications, 1975, pp. 25-34.
30. Gough, K.E., "Modes of Production in Southern India", *Economic and Political Weekly*, Vol. XV, Nos, 5, 6 & 7, Annual Number, 1980, pp. 337-64.
31. Namboodiripad, E.M.S., "Caste Conflicts vs. Growing Unity of Popular Democratic Forces", *Economic and Political Weekly*, Vol. XIV, Nos. 7 & 8, Annual Number, 1979, pp. 329-36; and Ranadive, B.T., "Caste, Class and Property Relations", *Economic and Political Weekly*, Vol. XIV, Nos. 7 & 8, Annual Number, 1979, pp. 337-48.
32. Meillassoux, C., "Are there Castes in India?" *Economy and Society*, February, 1973, pp. 89-111.
33. Goran, D. and Lindberg, J., *Behind Poverty: The Social Formation of a Tamil Village*, London: Curzon Press, 1975; Singh, H., "Kin, Caste and Kisan Movement in Marwar: Some Questions to the Conventional Sociology of Kin and Caste", *Journal of Peasant Studies*, Vol. 7, No. 2, 1979; Thorner, D., *Land and Labour in India*, Bombay: Asia Publishing House, 1974; Saith, A. and Tanakha, A., "Agrarian Transition and the Differentiation of the Peasantry—A Study of a West U.P. Village", *Economic and Political Weekly*, Vol VII, No. 14, 1972, pp. 712-23; and Bhardwaj, K. and Das, P.K., "Tenurial Conditions and Mode of Exploitation", *Economic and Political Weekly*, Vol. X, Nos. 5-7, 1975, pp. 222-33.
34. Singh, Y., "Caste and Class: Some Aspects of Continuity and Change", *Sociological Bulletin*, Vol. XVII, No. 2, 1968, p. 171.
35. Mencher, J.P., "The Caste System Upside Down, the Not-So Mysterious East", *Current Anthropology*, Vol. 15, No. 4, p. 469.
36. Kurian, K.M., "Class Analysis and its Relevance to the Study of Indian Society", *State and Society*, 1980, pp. 96-106.
37. Rudra, A., "Class Relations in Indian Agriculture—I", *Economic and Political Weekly*, Vol. XII, No. 22, 1978, pp. 916-23.
38. Desai, A.R., op.cit., 1948; *State and Society in India: Essays in Dissent*, Bombay: Popular Prakashan, 1975.
39. Sharma, K.L., "Agrarian Stratification: Old Issues, New Explanations and New Issues, Old Explanations", *Economic and Political Weekly*, Vol. XVIII, Nos. 42 & 43, 1983b.
40. Kosambi, D.D., op.cit., 1958.

41. Mukerji, D.P., *Diversities*, New Delhi: People's Publishing House, 1958; and Thorner, D., op.cit., 1974.
42. Patnaik, U., op.cit, 1972; and "Class Differentiation within the Peasantry: An Approach to Analysis of Indian Agriculture", *Economic and Political Weekly*, Vol. XI, No. 39, 1976, pp. A 82-A 101.
43. Lin, S.G., "Theory of a Dual Mode of Production in Post-Colonial India", Economic and Political Weekly, Vol. XV, Nos. 10 & 11, 1980.
44. Dandekar, V.M., "Nature of Class Conflict in the Indian Society", *Artha Vijnana*, Vol. 20, No. 2, 1978, pp. 102-24.
45. Gough, K.E., "Caste in a Tanjore village", in E.R. Leach (ed.), op.cit., 1960, pp. 11-60.
46. Mukherjee, R.K., *Dynamics of a Rural Society*, Berlin: Akademie Verlag, 1957.
47. Bose, N.K., *Culture and Society in India*, Bombay: Asia Publishing House, 1967.
48. Misra, B.B., *The Indian Middle Classes*, Oxford: Oxford University Press, 1964; Beteille, A., op.cit, 1969; Miller, D.B., *From Hierarchy to Stratification: Changing Patterns of Social Inequality in a North Indian Village*, Delhi: Oxford University Press, 1975; and Kolenda, P., *Caste in Contemporary India: Beyond Organic Solidarity*, California: Benjamin Cummings Publishing Co., 1978.
49. Desai, A.R., op.cit., 1948; op.cit., 1975; and "Relevance of the Marxist approach to the Study of Indian Society", Presidential Address, 15th Indian Sociological Conference, 2nd November, 1980; and Bettelheim, C., *India Independent*, London: Mac-Gibbon and Kee Ltd., 1968.
50. Harris, J., *Capitalism and Peasant Farming*, Bombay: Oxford University Press, 1982; and Omvedt, G. (ed.), *Land, Caste and Politics in Indian States*, Delhi: University of Delhi, 1982.
51. Srinivas, M.N., *Religion and Society among the Coorgs of South India*, Oxford: Clarendon Press, 1952; and, Srinivas, M.N., *The Remembered Village*, New Delhi: Oxford University press, 1976.
52. Dumont, L., op.cit., 1970.
53. Parvathamma, C., "The Remembered Village: A Brahminical Odyssey", *Contributions to Indian Sociology*, New Series, Vol. 12, No. 1, 1978, p. 91.
54. Bailey, F.G., op.cit., pp. 107-24.
55. Beteille, A., *Caste, Class and Power*, Bombay: Oxford University Press, 1965; Bhatt, A., *Caste, Class and Politics*, Delhi: Manohar

Book Service, 1975; and Aggarwal, P.C., *Caste, Religion and Power*, New Delhi: Shri Ram Centre for Industrial Relations, 1971.

56. D'Souza, V.S., op.cit., pp. 192-211.
57. Klass, M., *Caste: The Emergence of the System in South Asia*, Philadelphia: Institute for the Study of Human Issues, 1980.
58. Reddy, V.N., and Murthy, C.S., "Backward Castes and Tenancy: A Village Study", *Economic and Political Weekly*, Vol. XIII, No. 26, 1978, pp. 1061-76.
59. Mukherjee, R., "Realities of Agrarian Relations in India", *Economic and Political Weekly*, Vol XVI, No. 4, 1981, p. 112.
60. Vagiswari, A., *Income Earning Trends and Social Status of Harijan Community in Tamil Nadu*, Madras: Institute of Development Studies, 1972.
61. Sinha, A., "Bihar violence Against the Poor", *Economic and Political Weekly*, Vol. XII, No. 15, 1977, pp. 2037-40.
62. Sinha, A., "Bihar's Advancing Class Interests in the Name of Caste", *Economic and Political Weekly*, vol. XIII, No. 16, 1978, pp. 675-76.
63. Samiti, Atyachar Virodhi, "The Marathwada Riots: A Report", *Economic and Political Weekly*, Vol. XIV, No. 19, 1979, pp. 845-52.
64. Ibid., p. 852.
65. Singh, A.P., "Farm Workers vs. Rich Peasants: Class and Caste in a Punjab Village", *Economic and Political Weekly*, Vol. XIV, Nos. 42 & 43, 1979, pp. 1753-54.
66. Bose, P.K., "Social Mobility and Caste violence: A Study of Gujarat riots", *Economic and Political Weekly*, Vol. XVI, No. 16, 1981, pp. 713-16.
67. Das, A.N., "Class in Itself, Caste for Itself: Social Articulation in Bihar", *Economic and Political Weekly*, Vol. XIX, No. 37, 1984, pp. 1616-19.

5

A Note on Louis Dumont's *Homo Hierarchicus*

Louis Dumont, a French scholar, is an expert in the domains of sociology, social anthropology and indology. He has written on Hinduism, caste, kinship, kingship in ancient India, and social and political movements in modern India. Dumont's writings are rooted into French tradition, and he has written his magnum opus—*Homo Hierarchicus* for the French-speaking people. *Homo Hierarchicus* is a study of the caste sysiem and its implications for Hindu society and allied groups. Its French edition was published in 1966, and the English edition appeared in 1970.[1] *Homo Hierarchicus* is, literally speaking, opposite of *Homo Acqualis*, in other words, 'homo hierarchicus' is opposite of 'equality'. A commentator observes: "By taking this approach, Dumont rejects the ethnocentrism of western sociology, which has usually viewed caste as the ultimate form of social distinctions found in egalitarian societies. He insists instead on viewing India on her own terms, as a society based on different principles for which new sociological concepts are needed." Dumont has been praised for making most profound and important contributions to the study of Indian society. He has the clarity of thought, erudity of scholarship and lucidity in writing. Leach states that Dumont is possibly one of the most important sociological thinkers of his generation.[2] Dumont's book is the most important theoretical treatise on caste. A discussion on hierarchy, ideology and observation, problem of comparison, change, ideology of caste, pure and impure, division of labour and egalitarian society, etc. is given in a highly scholastic manner. Madan writes: "*Homo Hierarchicus* is an unusual work in its conception, design and execution."[3]

Defining Caste

The first question that Madan asks is: How does Dumont define caste? Dumont observes that the western scholar's definition of caste as a type of social stratification is socio-centric. He makes it clear that caste cannot be interpreted and understood from the point of western ideas of egalitarianism, individualism, and pre-eminence of politics and economics in society. Dumont is an Indianist at the core. Caste stands for inequality in theory and practice both, but it is not simply an opposite of 'equality'. The inequality of the caste system is a special type of inequality. Dumont admits that the idealist or intellectualist orientation of the French tradition is dominant in his understanding of sociology, hence the study of ideas and values. Dumont writes: "The ideas which they (the people) express are related to each other by more fundamental ideas even though these are unexpressed... The caste system, for example, appears as a perfectly coherent theory once one adds the necessary but implicit links to the principles that the people themselves give."[4] Thus, Dumont adopts the methodology of structuralism in his analysis of the caste system.

One finds stress on the role of ideology in moulding human behaviour, hence a close tie between sociology and indology in Dumont's works. The notion of the fundamental opposition between the pure and the impure like Bougle is the hallmark of Dumont's analysis of the caste system. Bougle defined caste system much before Dumont in terms of hierarchically arranged hereditary groups, segregation, and interdependence. Dumont recognizes significance of these three mutually entailed 'principles', but they are based on the fundamental principle of the opposition between the pure and the impure. Dumont calls it 'a single true principle'. "This opposition underlies hierarchy, which is the superiority of the pure to the impure, underlies separation because the pure and the impure must be kept separate, and underlies the division of labour because pure and impure occupations must likewise be kept separate. *The whole is founded on the necessary and hierarchical coexistence of the two opposites.*"[5]

Thus, hierarchy, as defined by Dumont in terms of the superiority of the pure over the impure, is the most important notion in Dumont's approach to the caste system. As such hierarchy is independent of other biological inequalities and the distribution of power.[6] Hierarchy is, in fact, the principle by which the elements of a whole (society) are ranked in relation to the whole.[7] Here Dumont becomes a sort of 'functionalist' like Talcott Parsons and Kingsley Davis. Since religion provides a view of the whole, caste hierarchy tends to become religious in essence. According to Dumont, hierarchy is the relationship between "that which encompasses and that which is encompassed."[8] Madan remarks that "such a perspective helps us to obtain a holistic view of the system and to overcome the dualism of opposition."[9]

Method of Study

Dumont analyzes "the traditional social organization of India from the point of view of theoretical comparison."[10] Dumont's approach seems to be the construction of a model of the traditional caste system in an ideal form. He does not concern himself much with the social formation of present-day India. Dumont does not provide a history of the caste system. However, he uses historical data and indological sources in the formulation of his model for the understanding of the caste system. According to Madan, Dumont's method is of a theorist. His analysis is both deductive and dialectical. He calls his method as an 'experiment'.[11]

Use of ethnographic materials is found in abundance in Dumont's method. He uses it in two ways or at two levels. Firstly, his major concern is undoubtedly with ideology, that is, with a system of 'values and ideas', but Dumont realizes that ideology is not everything. Ideology encompasses the whole of social reality, but cannot explain everything. Likewise, observation of actual behaviour can reveal everything. To understand this 'residue', ethnographic materials have been used to confirm nexus between ideology and observation. Secondly, Dumont uses ethnographic materials to elucidate or qualify various aspects of the main thrust of the book.

Hierarchy

Dumont writes that the castes teach us a fundamental social principle, namely, hierarchy. The opposite of equality is hierarchy and not inequality. According to Dumont, hierarchy is an indispensable element of social life everywhere, but it is more so in case of India as it is very well affirmed. The caste system is a system of ideas and values, a formal, comprehensive rational system, a system in the intellectual sense of the term. The foremost aim is to understand this intellectual system, this ideology. Castes are related through a system of oppositions, a structure, in terms of the opposition between the pure and the impure. Thus, Dumont introduces the notions of 'system' and 'structure' in terms of ideology of/and relations between the pure and the impure castes. Dumont discuss these points in the first two chapters.

Chapter 3 deals with hierarchy—the theory of *varna*. Upholding his view about primacy of 'values and ideas', Dumont focuses on *the differentiation between status and power, and the subordination of the king to the priest*, in Hindu society. Hierarchy involves gradation, but it is distinct from both power and authority. Dumont states that hierarchy refers to 'religious ranking' and classifies 'things' and 'beings' based on their dignity. Therefore, hierarchy is an all-embracing, comprehensive concept. Hierarchy and *varna* are found to be in consonance like *varna* and *jati*. Hierarchy, in fact, encompasses both *varna* divisions and caste system. However, the connection between hierarchy and power remains problematic. Hierarchy cannot give a place to power without contradicting its own principle. Realizing the tie between purity and power in 'actual situations', Dumont gives a place to power without compromising with his main argument. Both 'interaction' and 'attribution' are present in a situation where ideology and power coexist. Based on his main plank of thought, Dumont analyzes *ja-*

jmani system and regulation of marriage, and commensality, untouchability and vegetarianism, etc. in Chapters 4,5 and 6, respectively.

Ideology and Observation

Chapters 7 and 8 are very significant as they deal with power and territory, and justice and authority, respectively. Dumont discusses the confrontation of ideology and observation as most important aspects of his method of study. In regard to actuality of caste, Dumont analyzes territory, power, village dominance, and ownership of wealth, and their mutual relationship. These are referents of fact and not of theory or ideology. Realizing the ontological basis of caste, Dumont discusses dominant caste, factions and economics. He concludes that just as religion encompasses politics, so politics encompasses economics within itself. However, Dumont clearly states that religion is supreme, and politico-economic domain is subordinate, and further economics remains undifferentiated within politics. This clearly shows Dumont's preference for culturological determinism.

Let me quote from my earlier work about the essence of Dumont's approach to the caste system. The following points are important[12]:

1. In the caste system we have to do pre-eminently with religious ideas connected with purity.
2. The caste system can be understood when we realize that it is permeated by essentially religious conceptions and further that these religious conceptions are based upon a social apprehension of the pure and the impure.
3. In order to understand the distribution of occupations in India we have to go to beliefs of a religious nature.
4. It is above all religious ideas rather than economic values which establish the rank of each group.
5. These religious values commingle with elements of power and form a composite system of social stratification, which Dumont calls 'Kingly model'. The Kingly model, according to Dumont, rests upon the mutuality and interdomination be-

tween the principles of *Kshtra* or power and *Brahman* or the priestly normative order. Both are, however, rooted in the religico-ritualistic order of the caste system.

However, this does not mean that Dumont is immune to empiricism. He discusses ethnographic data on caste from Uttar Pradesh in Chapter 8. The source of authority such as the village panchayat, caste panchayat, caste jurisdiction, and ex-communication are discussed in this chapter. Clearly Dumont gives premium to ethnographical evidence as against ideology. But the basic principle is that of hierarchy to understand authority and dominance. Dumont is not able to resolve the dilemma whether caste encompasses power or power encompasses caste. If the latter is right, *dharma* (ideology) becomes subordinate to *artha* (power), and if the former is upheld as superordinate, the ruler becomes subservient to priestly order. However, in the final analysis, Dumont upholds ritual or religious power (hierarchy) superordinate to politico-economic power.

Problem of Comparison

Dumont considers Indian and western societies as logically opposite cultural types. But this does not mean that in the western society there was nothing but the individual, and in the Indian society nothing but the collective man (caste). More important is to see whether the caste system could have existed and survived independent of its contradictions. In fact, both collectivity and man were operative in Indian society in a particular way, and hence adaptability of the caste system. Dumont discusses these points in Chapter 9. However, Dumont is unable to come out of his ideological leanings. He says in Chapter 10 that caste should be deemed to be present only where the disjunction between status and power is present and where castes exhaust the entire society.

Dynamics

Dumont poses the question: What is the caste system becoming now-a-days.[13] Dumont answers that contemporary literature on caste overestimates and exaggerates changes. The overall frame of society has not changed. There has been change *in* the society and not *of* the society.[14] The only significant change, according to Dumont, is in the organic (traditional) interdependence between castes; now different castes have become segmentary competitive groups. Dumont calls this process 'the substantialization of caste'. Most noticeable changes in the caste system are juridical and political, socio-religious reform, westernization, growth of modern professions, urbanization, spatial mobility, and the growth of market economy. Dumont admits that change does not mean replacement, it means a 'mixture' or a 'combination' of traditional and modern features.

Why *Homo Hierarchicus*

Madan holds the view that *Homo Hierarchicus* is a most impressive achievement and shall long remain a basic work for Indianists.[15] Dumont, unlike Maine, does not consider caste as "the most dangerous and blighting of all human institutions." Dumont also does not defend caste like Bougle, Hocart, Senart, Hutton etc., but his treatment of caste amounts to its defence and perpetuation. Dumont considers caste as worthy of serious study. *Homo Hierarchicus* is neither a historical work nor a stock of available ethnographical information. Madan writes: "His is essentially an essay in methodology. He seeks to construct a model to help us understand the caste system." Further, Madan praisingly writes: "What I find most valuable in Dumont's approach to the understanding of caste is his attempt to seize its specificity: he preserves it by 'typifying' it and does not dissolve it by 'classifying' it."[17]

To me it seems that nothing is more important to Dumont than the ideology of caste itself. Nothing can be studied without ideas and values. All aspects of caste and even of entire gamut of social relations can be studied only from the ideational point of view. Therefore, Madan's view that *Homo Hierarchicus* is an essay in methodology is not quite tenable. His (Dumont's) method of study follows from the ideology of caste itself, and so is in the case of ethnographic data he pours into *Homo Hierarchicus*.

Some Criticisms

A sociology of knowledge perspective would ask clearly for (i) the 'fit' between theory, method and data; (ii) the ideologizing influences on the understanding of Indian society; (iii) the construction of reality in Indian context; and (iv) the specificity of Indian sociology different from that of the western countries.[18] These questions have not been clearly formulated by Dumont as he has been overwhelmed by the nostalgia of French tradition in sociology, and the uniqueness of Indian society. Dumont thus equates indology or culturology 'for a sociology of India'. Two questions follow from this position of Dumont: (1) Is it not an attempt toward academic indoctrination of scholars interested in the study of Indian society?, (2) Is it not Dumont brings in the ideas which would reinforce and relegitimize India's caste system?

While commenting on Iravati Karve's book—*Kinship Organisation in India*, Dumont and Pocock have suggested that Karve should choose between sociology and culturology.[19] Why Dumont ignores this suggestion in his own case? He projects his eclectic indology and part-ethnography as sociology proper in India's case.[20] Bailey rightly observes that Dumont and Pocock's is a "very odd kind of inverted ethnocentrism."[21] Their view is more of an assertion than an evidence.[22] Saran's view is no less culturological than that of Dumont[23], but Dumont calls Saran's view as 'cultural solipsism', a Hindu sociology.[24] Dumont is also disdainful of the Marxist approach. While commenting on Desai's book—*Social Background of Indian Nationalism*[25], Dumont writes: "More than university thesis, it is an overgrown political pamphlet clad in a university gown."[26] Thus, Dumont is critical of both culturological and Marxist approaches except his own approach which he considers very specific and unique one. Dumont can blame Saran for wrong 'hypothetical deductive reasoning', 'irrelevant quotations', and for his 'neo-Hindu creed', to Desai for his 'doctrinaire dogmatic Marxism', but why he (Dumont) gives such an enormous premium to culturology and caste system and its allied institutions—remains an open secret.[27] Why India's caste system becomes a datum for Dumont to develop a global sociology? Dumont is too naive a scholar if he thinks that India does not have differences, differential interests, conflicts, exploitations, etc. He lacks in elementary education about India. To think that they are prevalent but do not become the data for sociological enquiry compounds Dumont's scholastic ignorance. Dumont's polemics would not really provide a clear frame of reference, a method of study, and relevant data for understanding the fast changing character of India's caste system.

Even Madan, an ardent admirer of Dumont, raises a few questions about Dumont's model of traditional Hindu society. For example, it is not clear at what point of time the caste system as portrayed by Dumont crytallized. His (Dumont's) manner of citing literature is not very helpful in this respect. It seems after the crystallization of the caste system, all further change was ruled out.[28] Madan pointedly asks: (1) Is it not Dumont's method, then which makes him play down the element of change? (2) Is he (Dumont) not setting up too narrow a definition of change?[29] Dumont writes: "A form of organization does not change, it is replaced by another; a structure is present or absent, it does not change."[30] Most of the changes in India take place in politico-economic domain and since this occupies a secondary place in Dumont's scheme, they remain generally unnoticed to Dumont.

Now a few more criticisms of *Homo Hierarchicus*. Berreman accuses Dumont of presenting a 'distorted image' of the caste system based upon 'limited, biased, albeit scholarly, sources of evidence.'[31] Dumont, in fact, puts forth his model independent of the body of indological and ethnographic literature. Leach points out that to assess the value of a model in view of 'facts' is wholly erroneous. No model is a replica of reality. Dumont's model has explanatory power through its principle of *hierarchy*. Other commentators have suggested instead of the dichotomy of pure-impure the more inclusive dichotomy of the sacred and the non-sacred. Along with the notion of hierarchy, the notions of reciprocity and equality, and contradiction can be useful in understanding of the caste system. Dumont's use of the structuralist approach, his emphasis upon the *specificity* of the caste system, and 'typification' have come under severe attack.

The value of *Homo Hierarchicus* remains immense in spite of the criticisms we have listed above. The wide acclaim it has received and the controversy it has created speak volumes for Dumont's scholarship and involvement in understanding of the caste system. Madan writes: "*Homo Hierarchicus* is a work complete in itself and must be judged as such."[32] "What distinguishes this work from the usual social anthropological discussions of caste is that it does not proceed from field-work to a model of how the system works. Instead it begins with a cardinal explanatory principle—hierarchy—and boldly sets out to build a model thereon, throughout maintaining the position that theory or ideology overrides and encompasses ethnography. A conscious and single-minded preoccupation with the ideology of complementarity and separation leads Dumont to ask fundamental questions about Hindu society and about the structuralist method."[33]

Notes

Besides *Homo Hierarchicus*, I have largely depended upon the following sources: (1) *Contributions to Indian Sociology*, New Series, No. V, December 1971; (2) "On Understanding Caste", a review article by T.N. Madan, *Economic and Political Weekly*, Vol. VI, No. 34, August 21, 1971; (3) *Homo Hierarchicus* essai sur le systeme des castes, a book reviewed by J.Boel, *Sociological Bulletin*, Vol. XVII, No. 1, March, 1968; and (4) *Sociology in India:A Perspective from Sociology of Knowledge*, by Surendra Sharma, M.Phil. dissertation (mimeographed), 1983, Jawaharlal Nehru University, New Delhi. I gratefully acknowledge these sources, particularly T.N. Madan's two articles.

1. Dumont, Louis, *Homo Hierarchicus: The Caste System and Its Implications*, London: Paladin, 1970.
2. Leach, Edmund, "Espirit' in Homo Hierarchicus", *Contributions to Indian Sociology*, No. VI, December, 1971.
3. Madan, T.N., "Introduction", *Contributions to Indian Sociology*, No. V, December 1971a, pp. 1-2. This includes a review symposium on Louis Dumont's *Homo Hierarchicus*—a discussion on the nature of caste in India. Besides T.N. Madan, other contributors are Edmund Leach, Gerald D. Berreman, C.Von Furer-Haimendorf, R.S. Khare, Veena Das and Jit Singh Uberoi, J.C. heesterman, Detlef Kantowsky, Milton Singer and Louis Dumont.

4. Dumont, Louis, *Religion, Politics and Society*, Paris and the Hague: Mouton, 1970, p.7.
5. Dumont, Louis, op., coit., 1970a, p. 43.
6. Ibid., p. 20.
7. Ibid., p. 66.
8. Ibid., pp. XII.
9. Dumont, Louis, op.cit., 1970b, pp. 3-4.
10. Dumont, Louis, op.cit., 1970a, pp. xx.
11. Madan, T.N., op.cit., p. 4.
12. Sharma, K.L., *The Changing Rural Stratification System*, New Delhi:Orient Longman, 1974, pp. 16-17.
13. Dumont, Louis, op.cit., 1971a, pp. 207.
14. Ibid., p. 218.
15. Madan, T.N., "On Understanding Caste", *Economic and Political Weekly*, Vol. VI, No. 34, 1971b, p. 1807.
16. Ibid. p., 1807.
17. Ibid.
18. Sharma, Surendra, *Sociology in India:A Perspective From Sociology of Knowledge*, M.Phil dissertation, JNU, New Delhi, 1983, p. 40.
19. Dumont, Louis and Pocock, D.F., "Kinship" (a review of Iravati Karve's *Kinship Organisation in India*), *Contributions to Indian Sociology*, Vol. I.
20. Dumont, Louis and Pocock, D.F., "For a Sociology of India", *Contributions to Indian Sociology*, No. I, 1957.
21. Bailey, F.G., "For a Sociology of India", *Contributions to Indian Sociology*, No. III, 1959, pp. 88-101.
22. Ibid.
23. Saran, A.K., "A review of Contributions to Indian Sociology, No. IV", *Eastern Anthropologist*, Vol. XV, No. 1, 1962.
24. Dumont, Louis, "Nationalism and Communalism", *Contributions to Indian Sociology*, No. VII, 1964, p. 32.
25. Desai, A.R., *Social Background of Indian Nationalism*, Bombay: Popular Prakashan, 1948.
26. Dumont, Louis, op.cit., 1964, p. 32.
27. Dumont, Louis, "A Fundamental Problem in the Sociology of Caste", *Contributions to Indian Sociology*, No. IX, 1966, pp. 25-26.
28. Madan, T.N., op.cit., 1971b, pp. 1807-8.
29. Ibid. p., 1808.
30. Ibid.

31. Berreman, Gerald, D., "The Brahminical View of Caste", *Contributions to Indian Sociology*, No. V, 1971, pp. 16-23.
32. Madan, T.N. op., cit., 1971b, p. 8.
33. Ibid., pp. 8-9.

6

Social Stratification in Urban-Industrial Setting in India

Several criteria have been used to understand urban-industrial social structure and stratification. These include the extent of closure or openness and the nature of deprivations and gratifications. Other criteria are: (i) the motivational structure, (ii) the opportunity structure, and (iii) the communication structure or the extent of 'visibility' of opportunity. Based on these sets of criteria of understanding urban-industrial social life, there are multiple references for an individual in urban-industrial milieu because a person is evaluated in terms of his/her attributes like education, income, occupation, style of life, etc. All these criteria are juxtaposed keeping in view the rural-agrarian social structure and stratification as opposite of the urban-industrial world.

'Rural' and 'urban' are certainly two distinct patterns of life because of the distinction between population living in these two settings, but these do not imply two different principles of social stratification. It becomes difficult to draw a strict line of demarcation between 'rural' and 'urban', and 'individual' and 'corporate' rankings. The rich and the poor are the same to a large extent in both the settings; the difference is mainly a contextual one. An individual is a part of his family, and a family is linked with a group, hence individual exists as a corporate entity to a considerable extent. Similarly, a village is part of its region, and the region is linked with civilization, hence village is part of a wider society and civilization.

A lot of changes are taking place in the countryside particularly in the caste stratification, agrarian relations and power structure, but rural social stratification has not transformed itself into urban stratification system. There are several common features of social stratification in the rural-agrarian and the urban-industrial settings as the same principles determine social relations in the two. The main difference is in terms of the extent of operation of a particular principle or a set of criteria/attributes. Caste, class and power are common to both the settings, but they differ in social life operationally because of the structural differences between the village and the town.

Defining Urban-Industrial Stratification

Urban industrial social stratification is characterized by 'professional' and 'working' classes to a large extent. Professionalism requires training to acquire skills for performing specific roles. It imparts values of rationality, objectivity and pragmatism. Professional classes reflect social and structural differentiation or changes from tradition to modernity in the fields of occupation, industry and economy. Emergence of professional classes becomes a measure of social mobility in the persisting social stratification. Navalkha (1971) reports that as compared to other Asian countries the professional classes in India constitute a less significant proportion of all workers. Navalkha also highlights the uneven growth of professions revealing the pattern of recruitment process heavily biased in favour of the upper castes, urban dwelling groups and the metropolitan population. It is evident from several other accounts as well that caste is not a rural phenomenon alone and class is not simply found in urban India. Both have coexisted in rural and urban-industrial formations though in different forms and proportions.

Urban-industrial social stratification consists of the following classes:

(i) upper class,
(ii) upper middle class,

(iii) lower middle class, and
(iv) working class,

These classes are generally formed on the basis of 'income' and 'occupation'. However, it may be quite difficult to know the 'real income' from the apparent occupational status. D'Souza (1968) analyzes the 'bases of social organization' in the city of Chandigarh taking into consideration kinship, caste, class, religion and displaced or non-placed condition of the inhabitants. D'Souza finds that the educational, occupational and income hierarchies are significantly correlated with each other. But the correlation of each of them with the operational caste hierarchy is not significant. In a recent study, Mishra (1991) observes that the local institutions such as caste and kinship play a significant role in recasting the relationship between man and machine without dislocating the traditional social structure and also without affecting adversely the process of industrialization.

Theoretically, an industrial society is characterized by a very open view of status, role and power allocation. Open relationship, competition, radicalism, innovation and utilitarianism-rationalism are the main features of an industrial society. Relevant points regarding social stratification in industrial society are as follows:

1. What is the social background of the entrepreneurs and managers?
2. Does the hierarchy of the industrial elite correspond with the caste hierarchy?
3. Do the values of the pre-industrial society coexist with those of the industrial society?
4. What is the relationship between the internal structure of the factories and the caste and class structure of the workers?
5. Do the industrial employers, municipal councillors, the benefactors and controllers of educational and religious institutions belong to the families which have become prominent in recent decades?

Studies of urban-industrial social stratification in India have come up mainly as a reaction to the studies of rural-agrarian relations, migration from rural to urban areas, social mobility and increasing number of urban-industrial towns. The studies by

D'Souza (1968), Navalkha (1971), Sheth (1968), Saberwal (1976), Lambert (1963), Berna (1960), Sharma (1986), Sheth and Patel (1979), Raj Bala (1986), Sheobahal Singh (1985), Krishan Lal Sharma (1981), Singer (1972), Akbar (1990), and Philips (1990) impress upon the need to go 'beyond the village', and show how urban-industrial society and its components are constituted. Studies of urban-industrial social stratification have concentrated mainly on class and caste, occupation, income, education and class, social mobility and elite formation, professionals and working classes, middle classes, processes of social change and status-crystallization, dissonance and inconsistency, professional associations and trade unions.

A detailed annotated bibliography and analysis of trends in industrial sociology in India by Sheth and Patel (1979) and Patel (1985) examine the impact of society on industrialization and the effects of industrialization on society. Sociology of industrialization incorporates workers, supervisors and managers as the major human components along with trade unions, informal groups and owners of industry. Industrialization has fragmented the Indian society into 'classes' by weakening the caste system. The economic fragmentation created by industrialization has brought about both vertical and horizontal change, thereby a change is being registered in the persisting criteria of status-evaluation (Panini,1986). Industrialization can transform life of the people, means of production, surplus labour, etc. Rubin (1986) writes: "And industrialization can produce the professional employments and affluent style of life to which urban middle and upper classes aspire."

Historicity of Urban-Industrial Stratification System

The process of urbanization and industrialization though not necessarily unrelated are also not essentially concomitant in entirety. In the pre-industrial period, urbanization existed not only as an exclusive phenomenon, it was quite pronounced and was an ideal reference for a desired living. Based on the study of *Arthashastra* (C300-200 BC) and *Varna Ratnakara* (early 14th century AD), Jha (1988) finds 'urbanism' as a way of life in ancient Bihar. Besides provisions for water, roads, grounds, defence and other civic amenities, according to *Arthashastra*, there was a developed system of social ranking. The head of the city was called *nagarka* (mayor). Below the *nagarka* were *sthanikas* and the latter had *gopas* as their subordinates. There were also other functionaries and officials to look after various essential services. The administrative hierarchy was constituted independent of *varna*/caste ranking. Non-agricultural occupations, formal groups and impersonal relationship were the main features of urban social life. *Varna Ratnakara* provides, however, a vivid account of the lower castes, market activities, and artistic endeavours, ascetics along with a description of predominance of non-agricultural occupations, complexity and heterogeneity of population and preference for personalized relationship. These two valuable classical sources speak not only of the dynamics of urbanization, but also explain structural and cultural indices of urban life.

One can name several towns which had acquired a place of cultural and religious significance in ancient India (Rao, 1991). Many of these towns became known as centres of administrative and political activities. Naqvi (1968) classifies towns in medieval India into four categories: (i) capital cities (centres of administration, industry and trade), (ii) administrative centres with trading activities, (iii) pilgrimage centres, and (iv) specific-economy towns. However, our main concern here is to know about the people and the criteria on the basis of which they were ranked 'high' and 'low'. A subaltern study of a north Indian *Oasba* (small town) in the nineteenth century by Pandey (1984) shows that the community consciousness centered around the religious fraternity, class, *qasba*, and *mohalla*, and this cannot be explained in terms of today's social science vocabulary such as Muslim/Hindu, working class/rentier, urban/rural, etc. Self-respect and human dignity were the main determinants of the community consciousness.

Despite the community consciousness rooted into a certain perception of honour and dignity people were *socially* differentiated into the following classes:

1. Zamindars
2. Weavers

3. Trader-moneylenders
4. Cultivating tenants
5. Labourers
6. Others (*halwais*, *pansaris*, beggars, etc.).

A comparative study of Bombay and Poona (1650-1900) by Meera Kosambi (1991) provides details regarding occupational structure, ethnic composition, languages, religious composition, age-sex structure, etc. However, Kosambi's study focuses mainly on the 'functions' performed by the two cities rather than on the system of social stratification.

Lipton (1982) argues: "Inequalities *within* rural areas also owe much to the urban-biased nature of the development policy." Rural-born doctors, teachers, engineers and administrators serve the urban population. Surpluses from rural areas are extracted out for the urban populace. But, in case of India, the urban-rural balance is not as disappointing as it is implied in Lipton's formulation. Green revolution has brought about a considerable change in agrarian stratification having implications for urban social structure. Urban social stratification in terms of capital/labour relation can be characterized by capitalists, administrators, professionals, labour aristocracy and large landowners. On the contrary, there are small farmers and tenants, landless agricultural workers and members of the informal sector in the countryside (Griffin,1977). Byres (1981), however, finds 'rural bias' as the main hindrance in industrialization.

Two recent studies of sugar industry by Simon Commander and Ignatus Chithelen have thrown up enough evidence to show the emergence of a new pattern of social stratification. Commander (1985) writes about the sugar industry in North India: "The hub of the system was clearly agricultural and the divorce from the means of production characteristic of the factory system proper was never wholly engendered. Instead, the controls exercised by the *zamindar-khandasari* over labour, land and credit, which provided the basis of the system were, in many respects, antagonistic to a model of pure capitalism."

The assimilability of the non-capitalist features of economy with the capitalist system of production has produced a system of social stratification different from both the agrarian and the urban-industrial. The growth of regional markets and the development of modern transportation networks initially provided the requisite stimulus for the development of sugar industry. But the main factors were the ample reservoir of cheap, unorganized labour and money-lending-debt-linkages which generated significantly high profit margins. However, the emergence of a rich peasant stratum in the early 1900s, and the spread of canal irrigation, coupled with financial support from a co-operative credit infrastructure, enabled the rich peasants to cultivate sugarcane in the Ahmednagar district of Maharashtra (Chithelen, 1985).

Stratification within Deccan peasantry in early 1900s contributed to the emergence of a rich peasant stratum placing them in a commanding position. By the mid-1900s, the distinction between the rich peasants and the mass of poor peasants had become distinctly clear. A rich peasant was one who had control and ownership of land as well as ownership and mastery of agricultural implements and techniques. The rich peasants also enjoyed independence and autonomy in the credit relationship. They were themselves lenders of money and suppliers of credit to others. By having control over debtors's crop as wells as lands, the rich peasants expanded their commercial links. These rich peasants belonged to the non-Brahmin upper castes of Maharashtra. They were earlier traditional cultivating elites or members of former royal families or *Inamdars* and other office-holders. A few low status caste groups like *malis* also rose to become rich peasants. Several factors including the spread of canal irrigation, co-operatives, legislations, favourable political milieu, etc. brought about socio-economic and political transformation of the peasantry having implications for change in the rural as well as the urban social stratification (Chithelen, 1985).

The Indian Bourgeoisie/Capitalist Class

The bourgeoisie/capitalist class is characterized by the following features (Hamilton and Hirszowicz, 1987):

(i) concentration and private ownership of the means of production;
(ii) a free market for the sale and purchase of commodities and services;
(iii) formally free labour sold in the market as a commodity;
(iv) the pursuit of profits by entrepreneurs for wages; and
(v) the division of society into two opposed and antagonistic classes as a consequence of the exploitation and alienation of the labour from the means of production.

The property-owning, entrepreneurial, capitalist-employer has emerged from a variety of sources including the decline of the feudal system. Along with the bourgeoisie the capitalist system has produced a *working class*. Marx's theory of the capitalist society is the theory of the commodity-producing society. Worker is treated as a *commodity* (Bottomore,1985). Though Marx refers to bourgeoisie and the proletariat as the main antagonistic classes, he realizes the transition of society and the emergent role of the intermediate stratum situated between the workers and the industrial capitalists. He also realizes the increasing role of the managerial and ministerial classes and trade unions as a result of the transition from capitalism to socialism.

There is differentiation between and within the bourgeoisie, the petty-bourgeoisie and the working class. Class inequality is not simply 'economistic'. However, economic groupings in the form of classes and domination of one class over the other are found in all societies whether they are industrially more advanced or less advanced (Giddens,1987; Godelier, 1978). Capitalist society has undergone the following changes over a period of its long journey (Hamilton and Hirszowicz, 1987):

1. Capital and industry are today controlled by professional salaried management due to growth of large joint-stock enterprises.
2. The class structure has diversified. Middle classes have grown enormously, particularly in the developing countries like India due to the new state apparatus.
3. The material standards of workers have improved considerably all over the world.

4. Power of the working class has enhanced greatly due to trade unions, civil liberty movements and democratization.

Planning in India, prior to her independence, aimed at overthrow of the colonial state structure and its replacement by an independent indigenous capitalist state structure (Mukherjee, 1978). The big capitalists, a large number of small traders and merchants actively supported the national movement opposing thereby the colonialist mercantilism and capitalism (Chandra et al., 1988). The Indian capitalist class had the following features:

1. The Indian capitalists had largely an independent capital base and did not act as junior partners of foreign capital or as compradors.
2. The capitalist class on the whole was not tied up in a subservient position with pro-imperialist feudal interests, either economically or politically.
3. It grew rapidly between 1914 and 1947, a period close to India's independence.

Rudolph and Rudolph (1987), among other features of the Indian State, list 'the marginality of class politics' as a major development in the post-1947 period. Capital and labour play a marginal role in Indian politics and policy because of the centrality of a third factor—the State. The Indian State has acquired the role of a defender and protector of the interests of the poor and the working class. There are also strong unions and organizations of the white-collar groups which in turn weaken both the bourgeoisie and the proletariat. Business has exercised some influence on the government but it has not been able to control it directly or indirectly.

The Industrial Policy Resolution of 1956 though reasserts the constitutional position that the 'common good' of the people and 'distributive justice' would remain the central concerns; the role of larger industrial houses and multinationals remains unaffected to a large extent (Siddharthan,1979). Associations formed by the capitalists have been used to promote economic as well as political interests (Mukherjee, 1978; Sharma, 1981). However, Desai (1984) considers the Indian State as an agent of the bourgeoisie pursuing the capitalist path of development. The state has been 'repressive' and 'oppressive' in nature.

Whether the Indian big bourgeoisie like the big landlords were a product of colonial rule or not is not a much relevant question for us. What is important here is that the Indian bourgeoisie was never a monolith, and its character was partly determined by the colonial rule and partly by the class character of the Indian National Congress, the movements launched by it and the fact of India's freedom and partition. The bourgeoisie is divided as it comprises two categories: (i) big comprador, and (ii) the small and medium national bourgeoisie (Ghosh, 1985). Because of the comprador character of the big bourgeoisie and latent tendency in the national bourgeoisie to follow suit have resulted into 'guided industrialization'. A similar historical account of the Parsi Seths regarding their roots, entrepreneurship, and comprador role is provided by Guha (1984).

The Entrepreneurs and Entrepreneurship

Let us now take a note of the entrepreneurs and entrepreneurship. In a situation of new social dynamics new opportunities for economic activities are perceived for enhancement of one's economic and social standing. While presenting an integrated view of entrepreneurship, Tripathi (1985) deliberates on the entrepreneurial process taking into account constellation of forces, entrepreneurial initiative, and change in constellation of forces. An entrepreneur is a person who finds a constellation of socio-political and economic forces favourable for venturing into one or other enterprise, and if he succeeds, he becomes socially and economically distinct from those who remain out of such activities and from those who prove to be a failure.

Recent studies have shown that money-lending and trading were taken even by the landlords and substantial cultivating families in many parts of the country prior to independence. Today, entrepreneurial area is wide open for castes and communities which were earlier engaged in non-merchantile pursuits. There were 'peasant entrepreneurs', and there were upper caste manual and agricultural workers. Moreover, entrepreneurship is not confined to agriculture, business and industry alone. It has spread to the domains of medicine, science, government service, teaching, etc.

Interest in the study of entrepreneurs as a significant stratum in the scheme of social stratification is evident in some of the recent studies (Singh,1985; Trivedi,1991; Akbar,1990). Singh's study shows that 39 per cent of the total entrepreneurs in an eastern Uttar Pradesh carpet manufacturing town were Muslims, whereas 56 per cent were Hindus, 3 per cent Jains and 2 per cent Sikhs. Banias, Muslims and to some extent Rajputs dominate carpet industry. A close tie is found between landownership, leadership and entrepreneurs by R.S. Singh (1985). However, about 75 per cent of the rural entrepreneurs belong to three upper castes, namely, Brahmins, Rajputs and Bhumihars. In the city of Calcutta, Mahisyas, a peasant caste, have dominated the engineering industry surpassing both Brahmins and Kayasthas, mainly due to historically contingent factors after the Second World War (Owens, 1973). Trivedi's study of 250 tribal entrepreneurs explains emergence of new criteria of status-determination. Muslim entrepreneurs find no social values obstructing entrepreneurial growth (Akbar, 1990).

Middle Classes and Professional Elites

The pre-British middle classes comprised of the merchant, the artisan and the landed aristocracy having their roots in 'authoritarianism'. During the British period, the structure and complexion of the middle classes transformed due to a variety of factors and policy changes. The new middle classes included the businessmen and entrepreneurs, industrialists, landed people, educated groups, professionals, etc. The middle classes are basically trained 'service groups', and therefore, serve both the upper and the lower classes, though not making available their services in equal measure. The structure of the middle classes after independence has undergone a considerable change in terms of their size, functions and role mainly due to the nature and character of the Indian State. A brief sketch of some selected studies is provided below.

In the context of anti-reservation agitations in Gujarat, Shah (1987) writes: "The middle class has grown in size disproportionately with economic growth in Gujarat. While their aspirations have risen, they are unable to satisfy their needs and maintain the traditional status, and therefore, experience a strong sense of deprivation. This is specially true of the upper and middle caste members who are jealous of the new entrants from the traditionally low castes." For Shah, the middle class is a class between labour and capital.

The middle classes in India are a product of both capitalist development and the state. The anti-reservation agitations in Gujarat as understood by Shah imply a conflict-situation between the *entrenched* middle classes and the lower classes aspiring for the middle classes status by having access to lucrative white-collar occupations.

Elite formation in India (Navlakha, 1989) is largely determined by the traditional social structure (particularly caste), religion, language, networks, income, occupational background, education, family background, etc. The findings of this study show that select social positions are usually taken by persons from select social strata. This select group controls the positions of prestige, power and responsibility. Higher education is still under the grip of upper castes, hence it is 'status-stabilizer' (Jayaram, 1977) rather than an invader on status-rigidities. In four most prestigious institutions in Bangalore, despite a long history of reservations, 60 per cent Brahmin and 34 per cent Lingayat and Vokkaliga students were admitted to prepare them for higher professional and administrative careers, whereas only 4 per cent lower caste students found placement for this programme.

Navalkha's findings (1989) are quite revealing. As many as 81.3 per cent of the Hindu respondents hailed from upper caste groups (Brahmin, Kayastha, Vaishya and Kshtriya), 6.8 per cent came from the higher cultivating and other intermediate castes, and only 4.6 per cent belonged to lower castes. Further, 86.5 per cent of the respondents were of urban origin, 89.3 per cent were educated in modern educational institutions and 79 per cent of the respondents came from the highest advantaged stratum of the society.

Let us now take up a few studies of professions. A study of lawyers and law students in Pune, conducted by S.P. Sathe, Shaila

Kunchur and Smita Kahikar (1982) and commented upon by H.K. Pranjape (1983) shows that the Brahmins dominate the profession both in terms of quantity and professional success. The proportion of lawyers from the backward classes is quite small, and most of them are recent entrants to the system. They also earn much less. However, women lawyers from among the backward classes are more as compared to Brahmin and other Hindus. The main reason given in the study is that it is easier to accept a backward woman lawyer as junior practitioner. Several studies in the field of sociology of law and legal profession have been conducted in the recent past. Notable among these are by J.S. Gandhi (1982), K.L. Sharma (1982, 1984, 1988), Upendra Baxi (1982), S.L. Sharma (1985), S.K. Lal (1988), Yogendra Singh (1989), and T.K. Oommen (1983). These studies provide sketches of stratification among lawyers and relations between lawyers, judges, *munshis*, touts and clients.

There are not many studies of technocrats, scientists and managers partly because of their considerable distance from administrative-political set-up and partly because of their style of work and way of life. Technocrat/engineer today combines management expertise with scientific know-how. An engineer with a degree of Master of Business Administration (MBA) has made a place of 'high status' in Indian society. Even an MBA without an engineering degree has much more job opportunity than those having skills in several other fields. Higher technical education provides a passport for a high-status lucrative job. The graduates of the Indian Institutes of Technology (IIT) enjoy more prestige, and they are more in demand than the graduates of ordinary engineering colleges. A large number of graduates of IIT, Bombay have gone abroad for better career prospects and work conditions (Sukhatme and Mahadevan, 1988).

The industrialists, technocrats and managers have to work in India under the politicians in particular, and to a considerable extent under the administrators (Bhattacharya, 1984). Managers and officers are organizing themselves through trade unions and associations (Ramaswamy, 1985). Hardly any literature is available on Indian scientists. Three articles in Lal et al. (1988), namely, by Sri

Chandra (1988), Ramanama and Bambawale (1978) and Srivastava and Toha (1988) on India's scientists as professionals do not list any notable studies of scientists in India. Articles by Sri Chandra and Srivastava and Toha are in the form of preliminary notes without having any empirical bearing. However, Ramanama and Bambawale, based on their study of 780 scientists working in thirteen organisations, including universities, public sector and private sector undertakings in Bombay and Pune, report ambivalence and role-conflict as the main problems of the scientists working in all the three sectors.

The initial studies of medical profession have particularly emphasized social-structural and organizational aspects of the profession. Some of the recent studies too put more emphasis on the pattern of relationship between different segments of hospital as a social organization. Advani (1980), Chandani (1985,1988), Mehta (1988) and Nagla (1988) have substantiated the exercise conducted in the earlier studies.

In the studies of managers, technocrats, scientists and medical doctors, high status of these professionals is taken for granted, and therefore, instead of knowing the actual social status, emphasis is put more on the formal criteria of social status.

In evaluation of formal positions like professor, reader and lecturer, non-formal criteria such as academic achievements, reputation as a teacher and scholar, cultural style of life, family background, etc. matter a lot. Since academic profession is accredited with a high degree of autonomy like the legal profession, informal criteria of status evaluation are valued in good measure along with the formal criteria like rank, income and office. The recent studies by Khanna (1988) and Bhoite (1987) only casually stress upon the stratificational aspect of academic community.

Rudra (1989) considers the emergence of the intelligentia as a ruling class in India in addition to the already existing two ruling classes: one with base in agriculture, and the other with base in large industry. The intelligentia have become a member of the ruling coalition. The two traditional ruling classes have co-opted the intelligentia as a member of their fraternity. The intelligentia include the following:

1. All white-collar workers in the organized private sector, from managers and top executives down up to clerical workers.
2. All office workers in administrative services from top bureaucrats right up to lower division clerks.
3. Teachers (from the school to the university levels), doctors and nurses, lawyers and judges, engineers and architects in both private and public sectors.
4. Writers, journalists, artists and other skilled workers.
5. Professionals, politicians, trade union leaders, etc.

One common feature of all these middle classes is that "they do not themselves produce any values in the material product sense of value" (Ibid.). "Members of this (middle) class therefore depend for their economic gains on the largesse of the other two ruling classes as well as the state" (Ibid.). However, there is no homogeneity among its members in terms of income, wealth and level of living. Very high inequality exists within the classes in respect of these criteria. Another commonalty is of 'social' nature, that is, they all can be regarded as a 'babu class', 'salaried people' or the class of people earning equivalent to the salaried class. One more point of commonalty among them is found in terms of 'culture and ideology'. The intelligentsia as a class have contradictions and conflict of interests with other classes, while the intelligentia are considered as an ally and not as an adversary by the traditional ruling class.

Beteille (1989), while generally accepting Rudra's hypothesis regarding intelligentia as a third co-opted ruling class in India, observes that intellectuals in India would not like to associate themselves with the exploiters of the masses—the workers and the peasants. Beteille suggests for seeking more empirical evidence before we arrive at some conclusion on the status and role of the intelligentia (Ibid.). Main disagreement is expressed by Beteille about the concepts of 'class' and 'contradiction'. Beteille writes: "I maintain that contradiction is an inherent feature of all human societies whereas others believe that it is a feature of some or even most societies, but not necessarily all" (Ibid.).

Pranab Bardhan (1984) is also critical of Ashok Rudra's understanding of India's 'middle classes'. He writes: "Ashok Rudra underestimates the power of the professional class *vis-a-vis* the other two dominant classes. Compared to most western countries, the state is considerably more autonomous in India not merely in the political spheres but as a predominant *economic actor*. In some sense the state has captured the commanding heights of the economy, and sections of the professional class which run this gigantic machinery have thereby acquired powers which are not just of a junior partner in the ruling coalition. Further, because of the increasing social and economic interpretation among these classes, the conflicts among the classes in the dominant coalition are likely to decline" (1989). The public sector professionals benefit directly from all kinds of state subsidies and indirectly from the rental income earned by the state (Bardhan,1984).

Middle classes are not direct rulers nor are they economic producers like the industrialists, workers and peasants. There is a marked lack of homogeneity among different middle classes. In fact, structural distinctions are quite marked even between the apparently equal/homogeneous classes. Some classes are not so important in people's eyes, yet they enjoy high prestige because of the autonomy of their professions and the networks which they develop simply as a by-product of their professional obligations. These points require further probing.

Indian Working Class

For Marx the central issue was the understanding of the productive system in which the interests of the owners of the means of production and the wage-earning working class clashed. Marx always thought of ways and means for organizing the working class into a collective force to transform the capitalist system into a socialist society. Connections between social relations of production, social organization of the exploited classes and the state power formed the main basis of Marxian analysis. The growing social power of the organized working class was taken as a challenge to the authority of the state. Weber always emphasized on the problem of authority and legitimacy. 'Rational authority' was considered as key to the smooth functioning of bureaucracy and modern state.

Petras (1980), however, considers the notion of 'political legitimacy' as irrelevant issue or at best a derivative or subsidiary concern. "Different electoral regimes derive their legitimacy from different class reference groups and different balance of class forces." Power creates its own legitimacy. The organized working class itself becomes a power to reckon with, as it is embodiment of the class interests of the poor and the less privileged sections of society. An organized group representing its class interests becomes a 'political class' in its own right.

Studies of the Indian working class (Das,1983) consider labour as a commodity, and the value of labour power as the basis of understanding the capitalist appropriation and exploitation of the surplus generated by the proletariat. According to Dev Nathan (1987), the working class can be divided into four broad sections:

(1) that which gets more than a family, i.e., more than the value of labour power;
(2) that which gets a wage about equal to the family wage, and can thus at a reasonable standard, cover the full cost of production and reproduction of labour power;
(3) that which is more or less able to cover the immediate costs of production of labour power, but has to depend on the non-capitalist sector in order to reproduce itself/or has to depress its standard of living in order to reproduce itself; and
(4) the pauperized section that is not even able to meet the immediate cost of production of labour power.

The composition of the working class is affected by two factors: (i) the caste, tribal or ethnic origin of the worker in the pre-capitalist sector; and (ii) the gender-based division of labour between male and female and the associated patriarchy. Thus, the working class is highly stratified within and in relation to the capitalist and the middle classes. The factors such as caste, ethnicity and gender create inequalities within the working class structure and therefore obstruct smooth sailing of the working class movement. The distinctions found within the working class structure ranging from the 'labour aristocracy' on the one hand and the 'pauperized labour' on the other explain the nature of economic stratification and its socio-cultural consequences on the workers.

Lieten's study (1987) of workers in multinational companies shows that a segment of the working class is able to command higher wages and can thus divide the class in a distinct manner. Such a structural divide within the working class hampers uniform class consciousness. The consciousness of the jute mill workers of Bengal (Chakrabarty, 1984) could not transcend their identification as a Hindu or a Muslim to have identification as a solid working class. Thus, all collective public actions of the workers were marked by inherent duality. The working class in terms of its socio-cultural composition is constituted of the urban poor living in slums and hutments, industrial workers (both men and women), textile workers, sugar industry workers, plantation workers, railway workers, cottage industry and informal sector workers, etc. The working class, despite these differences, is comprised of urban and rural poor both in organized and informal sectors of economy. This would mean that the poor are just poor, and therefore, it would be better if we understand them as such without undermining this fact by using rural/urban, caste/class and caste/caste criteria (Joshi, 1979). Caste is not found as a major principle of social organization among industrial workers (Ramaswamy, 1979).

The Special Number of *Economic and Political Weekly* (1981) on "Indian Working Class: Some Historical Perspectives" contains papers on the following themes:

(1) Structure of the labour market in colonial India by Ratan Das Gupta.
(2) Labour legislation and working class movement: The case of the Bombay Labour Officer, 1934-37 by Dick Kooiman.
(3) Kanpur textile labour: Some structural features of formative years by Chitra Joshi.
(4) Growth of trade union consciousness among jute mill workers, 1020-40 by Ira Mitra.
(5) Industrial unrest and growth of labour unions in Bengal, 1920-24 by Sanat Bose.
(6) Tea labour in Assam: Recruitment and government policy-1840-80 by Suranjan Chatterjee and Ratan Das Gupta.

Labour market, labour legislation, caste and class background of workers, class consciousness, working class movements and their leadership are some of the issues taken up in these studies of the working class in India.

Concluding Remarks

The 'industrial man' is not a monolith. Holmstrom (1984) discusses at length that 'industry' is primarily an inequalitarian system in terms of organized and unorganized labour sector, contract labour, labour markets, the working class conditions, workers' social worlds, the domineering role of owners, managers, superiors and leadership of trade unions. These distinctions based on gender (Mies, 1981) and nature of industrial or semi-industrial work (Bhowmik, 1980; Prasanneswari, 1984; Behal, 1985; Thomas Issac, 1982) have been taken as the main criteria of socio-cultural and economic heterogeneity of the working class, particularly in the analysis of working class consciousness, intra and inter-working class relations and relations of the working class with the owners and managerial and supervisory cadres of industry.

References

Advani, Mohan, 1980, *Doctor-Patient Relationship in Indian Hospitals*, Jaipur, Sanghi Prakashan.

Akbar, M., 1990, *Entrepreneurship and Indian Muslims*, New Delhi, Manak Publications.

Bala, Raj, 1986, *Trends in Urbanization in India*, Jaipur, Rawat Publications.

Bardhan, Pranab, 1984, Land, *Labour and Rural Poverty: Essays in Development Economics*, New York, Columbia University Press.

Bardhan, Kalpana, 1989, 'Poverty, Growth and Rural Labour Markets in India, *EPW*, Review of Agriculture, March 25.

Baxi, Upendra, 1982, *The Crisis of the Indian Legal System*, New Delhi, Vikas Publishing House.

Behal, Rana Pratap, 1985, 'Forms of Labour Protest in Assam Valley Tea Plantations, 1900-1930', *EPW*, Review of Political Economy, Vol. XX, No.4.

Berna James J., 1960, *Industrial Entrepreneurship in Madras State*, London, Asia Publishing House.

Beteille, Andre, 1989, 'Are the Intelligentia a Ruling Class?', *EPW*, Vol. XXIV, No. 3.

Bhattacharya, S.K., 1984, 'Managers and Technocrats Role in the Political Administrative World: Some Current Issues,' *EPW*, Review of Management, Vol. XIX, No. 8.

Bhowmik, Sharit K., 1980, "The Plantation as a Social System," *EPW*, Vol. XV, No. 36.

Bhoite, U.B., 1987, *Sociology of Indian Intellectuals*, Jaipur, Rawat Publications.

Bhoite, U.B., 1988, 'Academic Profession and Social Development,' in Sheo Kumar Lal et.al. (eds.), *Readings in the Sociology of Professions*, Delhi, Gian Publishing House, 1988.

Bose, Sanat, 1981, 'Industrial Unrest and Growth of Labour Unions in Bengal, 1920-1924, *EPW*, Vol. XIV, Nos. 44, 45 and 46.

Bottomore, T.B., 1985, *Theories of Modern Capitalism*, London, Geogre Allen and Unwin.

Byres, T.J., 1981, 'The New Technology, Class Formation and Class Action in the Indian Countryside,' *Journal of Peasant Studies*, Vol. 8, No. 3.

Chakrabarty, Dipesh, 1984, 'Trade Unions in a Hierarchical Culture: The Jute Workers of Calcutta 1920-50,' in Ranjit Guha (ed.), *Subaltern Studies III*, Delhi, OUP.

Chandani, Ambika, 1985, *The Medical Profession: A Sociological Exploration*, New Delhi, Jainsons.

Chandra, Bipen et.al., 1988, (ed.), *India's Struggle for Independence, 1857-1947*, Viking Penguin Books India Ltd.

Chandra, Sri, 1988, 'Indian Scientists and Social System,' in Sheo Kumar Lal et.al. (ed.), *Readings in the Sociology of the Professions*, Delhi, Gian Publishing House.

Chatterjee, Suranjan and Dasgupta, Ratan, 1981, 'Tea Labour in Assam: Recruitment and Government Policy 1840-80,' *EPW*, Vol. XVI, Nos. 44, 45 and 46.

Chithelen, Ignatius, 1985, 'Origins of Cooperative Sugar Industry in Maharashtra,' *EPW*, Vol. XX, No. 14.

Commander, Simon, 1985, 'Proto-industrial Production as a Barrier to Industrialization?—Case of North Indian Sugar Industry, 1850-1950,' *EPW*, Vol. XX, No. 12.

Das, Arvind N., 1983, *Agrarian Unrest and Socio-Economic Change in Bihar*, 1900-1980, Delhi, Manohar Publications.

Dasgupta, Ranjit, 1986, 'From Peasants and Tribesmen to Plantation Workers,' *EPW*, Vol. XXI, No. 4.

Desai, A.R., 1984, *India's Path of Development*, Bombay, Popular Prakashan.

D'Souza, V.S., 1968, *Social Structure of a Planned City—Chandigarh*, New Delhi, Orient Longman.

Gandhi, J.S., 1982, *Lawyers and Touts: A Study in the Sociology of the Legal Profession*, Delhi, Hindustan Publishing Corp.

Giddens, Anthony and Jumer, J.H., 1987 (eds.), *Social Theory Today*, Cambridge, Polity Press.

Godelier, Maurice, 1978, *Perspectives in Marxist Anthropology*, Cambridge, Cambridge University Press.

Griffin, K., 1977, 'Review of Lipton's Why Poor People Stay Poor,' *Journal of Development Studies*, Vol. 14., No. 1.

Guha, Amalendu, 1984, 'More About the Parsi Seths, Their Roots, Entrepreneurship and Comprador Role, 1650-1918,' *EPW*, Vol. XIX, No. 3.

Hamilton, Malcolm and Hirszowicz, Maria, 1987, *Class and Inequality in Pre-Industrial Capitalist and Communist Societies*, New York, St. Martins Press.

Holmstrom, Marc, 1984, *Industry and Inequality: The Social Anthropology of Indian Labour*, Cambridge, Cambridge University Press.

Issac, T.M., Thomas, 1982, 'Class Struggle and Structural Changes: Coirmat and Matting Industry in Kerala, 1950-80,' *EPW*, Review of Political Economy, Vol. XVIII, No. 31.

Jayaram, N., 1977, 'Higher Education as a Status Stabliger: Students in Bangalore,' *Contributions to Indian Sociology* (New Series), Vol. II (1).

Jha, Hetukar, 1988, 'Tradition of Urbanism in Bihar: A Sociological Probe,' *Explorations*, Vol. 2.

Joshi, Chitra, 1981, 'Kanpur Textile Labour: Some Structural Features of Formative Years,' *EPW*, Vol. XIV, Nos. 44, 45 & 46.

Joshi, P.C., 1979, 'Perspectives on Poverty and Social Change: The Emergence of the Poor as a Class,' *EPW*, Vol. XIV, Nos. 7 & 8.

Khanna, Kirti, 1988, 'Career Decision-Making: A Caste of University Teachers' in Sheo Kumar Lal et.al. (eds.), *Readings in the Sociology of Professions*, Delhi, Gian Publishing House.

Kooiman, Dick, 1981, 'Labour Legislation and Working Class Movement: The Case of the Bombay Labour Officer, 1934-37,' *EPW*, Vol. XVI, Nos. 44, 45 & 46.

Kosambi, Meera, 1991, 'A Socio-Ecological Study of Two Indian Cities: Bombay and Poona (1650-1900)' in M.S.A.Rao, C. Bhatt and L.N.

Khandekar (eds.), *A Reader in Urban Sociology*, Delhi, Orient Longman.

Lambert, R.D., 1963, *Workers, Factories and Social Change in India*, Bombay, Oxford University Press.

Lal, Sheo Kumar, 1988 (ed.), *Readings in the Sociology of Professions*, Delhi, Gian Publishing House.

Lieten, G.K., 1987, 'Indian Workers in Multinational Companies,' *EPW*, Vol. XXII, No. 18.

Lipton, Michael, 1977, *Why Poor People Stay Poor: A Study of Urban Bias in World Development*, New Delhi, Heritage, 1982.

Mehta, V.R., 1988, *Ideology, Modernization and Politics in India*, New Delhi, Manohar Publications.

Mies, Maria, 1981, 'Dynamics of Sexual Division of Labour and Capital Accumulation: Women lace-Workers of Narsapur,' *EPW*, Vol. XVI, Nos. 10, 11 & 12.

Mies, Maria, 1982, 'Rural women and the World Market' in Lourdes Beneria (ed.), *Women and Development: The Sexual Division of Labour in Rural Societies*, New York, Praeger.

Mishra, Sanjay, K., 1991, 'Industrialization and Social Structure: A Case Study of Hatia, Ranchi,' *Unpublished, Ph.D. Thesis*, Jawaharlal Nehru University, New Delhi.

Mitra, Ira, 1981, 'Growth of Trade Union Consciousness Among Jute Mill Workers, 1920-40,' *EPW*, Vol. XVI, Nos. 44, 45 & 46.

Mukherjee, Aditya, 1978, 'Indian Capitalist Class and Congress on National Planning and Public Sector, 1930-47,' *EPW*, Vol. XIII, No. 35.

Nagla, Madhu, 1988, *Medical Sociology: A Study of Professionals and their Clients*, Jaipur, Print-well Printers.

Nagla, Madhu, 1988, 'Professionals and their Clients: A Study of Doctor-Patient Relationship' in Sheo Kumar Lal et. al. (eds.), *Readings in the Sociology of the Professions*, Delhi, Gian Publishing House.

Naqvi, H.K., 1968, *Urban Centres and Industries in Urban India, 1506-1803*, Bombay, Asia Publishing House.

Nathan, Dev, 1987, 'Structure of Working Class in India,' *EPW*, Vol XXII, No. 18.

Navalkha, Suren, 1971, *Ethnic Divisiveness in the New States of Asia: A Model for Analysis,' in P.C. Joshi and R. Dutta (eds.), Studies in Asian Social Development*, No. 1, New Delhi, Tata-McGraw Hill.

Navalkha, Suren, 1989, *Elite and Social Change: A Study of Elite Formation in India*, New Delhi, Sage Publications.

Oommen, T.K., 1983, *Social Transformation in Rural India: Mobilization and State Intervention*, New Delhi, Vikas Publishing House.

Owens, Raymond L, 1973, 'Peasant Entrepreneurs in a North Indian Industrial City,' in Milton Singer (ed.), *Entrepreneurship and Modernization of Occupational Cultures in South Asia*, Durham, NC, Duke University Press.

Panini, M.N., 1986, 'Industrialization and Social Stratification in India,' in K.L. Sharma (ed.), *Social Stratification in India*, Delhi, Manohar Publications.

Pandey, Gyanendra, 1984, 'Encounters and Calamities: The History of a North Indian Qasba in the 19th Century,' in Ranjit Guha (ed.), *Subaltern Studies III*, Delhi, OUP.

Patel, P.J., 1985, 'Industrial Sociology,' in ICSSR, *A Survey of Research in Sociology and Social Anthropology*, Vol. III, New Delhi, Satvahan Publications.

Petras, James, 1989, 'Class Politics, State Power and Legitimacy,' *EPW*, Vol. XXIV, No. 31.

Philips, W.S.K., 1990, *Social Stratification and Mobility in Urban India*, Jaipur, Rawat Publications.

Pranjape, H.K., 1983, 'Legal Profession and Social Change,' Review of S.P. Sathe's *Legal Profession: Its Contributions to Social Change: A Survey of the Pune City Bar*, *EPW*, August 20.

Prasanneswari, 1984, 'Industrial Relation in Tea Plantations: The Deoars Scene,' *EPW*, Vol. XIX, Nos. 24 & 25.

Ramanamma, A and Bambawale, Usha, 1978, 'Occupational Attitudes of Physicians,' *Sociological Bulletin*, Vol. 27, No. 2.

Ramaswamy, Uma, 1979, 'Tradition and Change among Industrial Workers,' *EPW*, Vol. XIV, Nos. 7 & 8.

Ramaswamy, E.A., 1986, 'Managerial Trade Union,' *EPW*, Review of Management, Vol. XX, No. 21.

Rao, M.S.A., 1991, *A Reader in Urban Sociology*, Delhi, Orient Longman.

Rubin, Barnett R., 1986, 'Journey to the East: Industrialization in India and the Chinese Experience,' in Dilip K Basu and Richard Sisson (eds.), *Social and Economic Development in India: A Reassessment*, New Delhi, Sage Publications.

Rudolph, S.H., and Rudolph, L.I., 1987, *In Pursuit of Lakshmi: The Political Economy of the Indian State*, New Delhi, Orient Longman.

Rudra, Ashok, 1989, 'Emergence of the Intelligentia as a Ruling Class in India,' *EPW*, Vol. XXIV, No. 3.

Saberwal, Satish, 1976, *Mobile Men: Limits to Social Change in Urban Panjab*, New Delhi, Vikas Publishing House.

Shah, Ghanshyam, 1987, 'Middle Class Politics: Case of Anti-reservation Agitation in Gujarat,' *EPW*, Vol. XXII, Nos. 19, 20 & 21.

Seth, N.R., 1968, *The Social Framework of an Indian Factory*, Manchester, Manchester University.

Sathe, S.P., 1986, 'Elusive Pursuit of Equality,' *EPW*, Vol. XXI, No. 33.

Sharma, K.L., 'Caste and Class in India: Some Conceptual Problems.' A working paper presented at XVI All-India Sociological Conference (mimeo), 1982.

Sharma, K.L., 1984, *Sociology of Law and Legal Profession*, Jaipur, Rawat Publications.

Sharma, K.L., 1986, *Caste, Class and Social Movements*, Jaipur, Rawat Publications.

Sharma, K.L., 1988, 'Legal Profession and Society: A Caste Study of Lawyers and their Clients' in Sheo Kumar Lal et. al. (eds.) *Readings in the Sociology of the Professions*, Delhi, Gian Publishing.

Sharma, Krishan Lal, 1981, *Voluntary Business Associations in Organizational Frame*, Jaipur, Rawat Publications.

Sharma, S.L., 1985, 'Sociology of Professions in India,' in ICSSR, *Survey of Research in Sociology and Social Anthropology, 1969-1979*, Vol. II, New Delhi, Satvahan Publications.

Sheth, N.R. and Patel, P.J., 1979, *Industrial Sociology in India*, Jaipur, Rawat Publications.

Siddharthan, N.S., 1979, 'Industrial Houses, Multinationals and Industrial Policy,' *EPW*, Vol. XIV, No. 29.

Singer, Milton, 1972, *When a great tradition modernizes: An anthropological approach to Indian civilization*, New York, Praeger Publishers.

Singh, R.S., 1985, *Rural Elite, Entrepreneurship and Social Change*, Jaipur, Rawat Publications.

Singh, Sheobahal, 1985, *Entrepreneurship and Social Change*, Jaipur, Rawat Publications.

Singh, Yogendra, 1986, 'Some Emerging Issues in the Indian Sociology of Social Stratification,' in K.L. Sharma (ed.), *Social Stratification in India*, Delhi, Manohar Publications.

Srivastava, A.L. and Toha, M., 1988, 'Professional Obsolescence: A Needed Area of Research,' in Sheo Kumar Lal et.al. (eds.), *Readings in the Sociology of Professions*, Delhi, Gian Publishing House.

Sukhatme, S.P. and Mahadevan, I., 1988, 'Brain-Drain and the IIT Graduate,' *EPW*, Vol. XXIII, No. 25.

Tripathi, Dwijendra, 1985, 'An integrated view of entrepreneurship,' *EPW*, Vol. XX, No. 48.

Trivedi, Madhusudan, 1991, *Entrepreneurship Among Tribals*, Jaipur Printwell.

7

Structuring of Social Inequalities in Rural India

Social inequality is a perennial problem, and therefore, it is found universally in one form or other. Its prevalence is a part of human existence. On the origin of inequality among men the following questions posed by Dahrendorf remain pertinent: (1) Why is there inequality among men? (2) Where do its causes lie? (3) Can it be reduced, or even abolished altogether? (4) Or do we have to accept it as a necessary element in the structure of human society?[1] These questions are, no doubt, ubiquitous, yet specific societies have shown differential patterns and expressions of social inequality. However, before we take up the case of social inequality in rural India in particular, it would be proper to analyze in brief the concept and perspective of social inequality.

Dahrendorf distinguishes between inequalities of natural capabilities and those of social position; and between inequalities that do not involve evaluative rank-order and those that do. Of these two pairs of distinction, Dahrendorf works out four types of inequality: (a) natural differences of kind, (b) natural differences of rank, (c) social differentiation of positions, and (d) social stratification based on reputation and wealth.[2] In all the four types, 'individual' is evidently the focal point of status evaluation. Such a conception of social inequality, built on distribution of property, wealth, honour and power among individual members, would imply a certain ideological basis and a structural arrangement of people based upon those inegalitarian institutionalized norms. In the final analysis such a conception of inequality provides a logical legitimacy to social inequality, and to its functionality and inevitability. Based on such a plea social inequality is visibly found in the division of labour, differentiation of roles and, in fact, in differential evaluation of different tasks and roles assigned to or taken up by different members.

We start with a simple conception that social inequality is found in one form or other, but it is not necessarily functional and inevitable. Division of labour or differential expertise is functional, and it is this which is required too. One may reject this view by dubbing it 'idealistic' and 'imaginary', but all human societies have been striving for such a formation of social relations all through their existence. Another viewpoint is that social inequality is a multidimensional and dynamic aspect in the sense that its one pattern changes in part or full and another pattern emerges modifying or altering the previous one. There are two implicit points in this statement: (i) social inequality is not monolithic as wrongly conceived by some students particularly in the context of caste; and (ii) there has been a continuous (with variations in the magnitude) structuring and restructuring of social inequality.

In fact, it is erroneous to perceive inequality opposite of equality both in theoretical terms and empirical contexts. Inequality is a 'relational' phenomenon, that is, it is to be seen in terms of one another rather in an absolute sense. In a family its members are unequal in regard to their kinship—based statuses, but they are 'equal' as members of an intimate primary primordial unit. Family members are different from members of a formal organization. Even when there is 'unequal' distribution of work or assignment of duties and responsibilities, members of a family are treated as 'equal'. To evaluate social inequality in India from the point of organization of the western industrial society would certainly undermine the role of India's social structure, culture, history and dialectics.[3] Of these concepts, the first two refer to structural and normative aspects, and the latter two refer to change and contradictions.

We may also state that there is no opposition between a structural analysis and a processual approach in the study of Indian society. These two together could explain the pattern of structuring of social inequality in a wholesome way. The dichotomy between the western industrial society and the traditional/backward society is also futile, and it is irrelevant to accept the former as a reference model for studying the latter.

We have no hesitation in accepting Beteille's view that a placement of people in layers (higher and lower) is inadequate for analyzing social inequality. There is a need for understanding the ongoing relations between individuals occupying different positions. But we notice some serious implications in what Beteille writes: "The problem of social inequality is above all the problem of how people interact with each other, how they compete and contend, how some succeed in moving up while others are pushed down despite their resistance."[4] We are aware that this formulation about social inequality is not specifically meant as such for studying Indian society, but formulations like this have quite often been used for analyzing Indian social situation without realizing the fact that it has emanated from the experience of modern western society. For example, if interaction among people is preordained by structural-social ties to a large extent, then competition would not become a pivotal aspect of social relations. There is nothing like a 'success theme' in the Indian society the way it is reflected in the above quotation. There is an implicit theoretical viewpoint which can be accepted only with some precautions. 'Rational' aspect assumes the element of volition which again is not quite a fact in India's context.

Statements about acceptance of western industrial society as a model for analyzing Indian society abound in the contemporary literature. Competition for status and power is more in modern industrial societies than in traditional agrarian societies. Individuals are units of social ranking in the western societies whereas groups and collectivities are the main basis of status and power in Indian society. Likewise these contrasts, continuity, ascription and cultural norms are said to be predominant in the Indian society, and change, achievement and material values overwhelm the western world. It has very often been stated that social classes are a feature of modern industrial societies. Even Aron's dichotomy between the *nomi-*

nalist and the *realist* conceptions of class in terms of 'individual' and 'collectivity', respectively, as the basis of class identification seems to be inadequate.[5] The nominalist (psychological) basis is not independent of the realist (collective consciousness) in the Indian context as the two have been inseparable parts of India's social formation.

The question is: Is the notion of *Homo hierarchicus* synonym of India's caste system? Another question is: Are there no elements of *Homo aqualis* in India's system of social stratification? We do agree with Beteille that "the idea of hierarchy entails that of inequality...," but inequality does not necessarily mean 'hierarchy', that is, rigidity of high and low statuses.[6] Rigidity of caste-based statuses is not more than that based on apartheid, estatehood and feudalism. Students of Indian social history have amply shown discontinuities, breakdowns, changes and contradictions in India's caste system in particular and in Indian society in general. Multidimensionality not only of India's social fabric but also of the caste system has already weakened the monolith of *Homo hierarchicus*. To accept *Homo aqualis* as ideological basis and also a fact of life of modern western industrial society is simply a myth, and to take it as a reference model for *Homo hierarchicus* in Indian society is perhaps a very serious ignorance (conscious or inadvertent) on the part of the students of Indian society.

Notions of both inequality and equality are built into the ideology and practice of the caste system. The position of priest speaks of superiority of ritual status, but the notion and practice of 'contra-priest' indicate the role of secular duties and obligations certainly with ritual umbrella. Relations between *jajman* (patron) and *kamin* (client) are not simply of higher and lower, superordinate and subordinate positions, but they also define rights and obligations of the lower sections along with the dominant castes. Therefore, we propose to cast a fresh look at the explanations of social inequality in rural India.

Approaches to the Study of Social Inequality

There are a number of approaches to the study of hierarchy and inequality. Following the Hegelian view, we would say that the 'world of things' is dominated by the 'world of thoughts'. "Hierarchy is the domination of thought, the domination of the spirit."[7] Marx also considers hierarchy more in terms of an ideal form. Inequalitarian relations are determined by the existential conditions in a given society. The existential conditions as depicted by Marx are reflected in the following statement: "As individuals express their life, so they are. What they are, therefore, coincides with their production, both with what they produce and with how they produce. The nature of individuals thus depends on the material conditions determining the production."[8] Marx simply does not speak of 'structure' of existential conditions, but also analyzes the process of change in these conditions.

Tribal ownership, ancient and state ownership, feudal or estate property ownership and capitalism are not only evolutionary stages but also, when put together, form the core of Marx's method for studying society and history. In each stage, Marx makes a mention about division of labour and distinctions between town and country, and, in fact, about nature of a socio-economic differentiation. Antagonism and contradictions are the causes of differentiation and change. The notion of basic structural change is an inseparable part of Marx's understanding of society and history as it is evident in his analysis of stages and groups of people in these stages.

Structuring of social inequality is a continuous process. Marx's view in this regard is: "The social structure and the state are continually evolving out of the life process of definite individuals, but of individuals, not as they may appear in their own or other people's imagination, but as they really are, i.e., as they operate, produce materially, and hence as they work under definite material limits, presuppositions and conditions independent of their will."[9] Further, he writes: "Consciousness can never be anything else than conscious existence, and the existence of men is their actual life process."[10] "Life is not determined by consciousness, but consciousness by life."[11]

We consider these eclectically taken statements from the *German ideology* in the form of a method for studying social inequality. Men are seen by Marx (Engels) in their actual life process. The practical process of development of men is taken into consideration for understanding social reality. How social life is produced? What is its mode of production? What units are produced as a result of certain social conditions? What is the nature of social interaction between the groups produced through such an evolutionary process? We find a sort of answer to these questions in the following: "History is nothing but the succession of the separate generations, each of which exploits the materials, the capital funds, the productive forces handed down to it by preceding generations, and thus, on the one hand, continues the traditional activity in completely changed circumstances and, on the other, modifies the old circumstances with a completely changed activity." Thus, in fact, Marx visualizes continuity of tradition and emergence of modernity side by side. Structure of social relations is determined by the direction of change. Structure and process are, in fact, coexistent.

Another methodological perspective is given by Max Weber. Gerth and Mills write: "Much of Weber's own work is of course informed by a skillful application of Marx's historical method."[12] Weber criticizes Marx for an untenable monocausal theory, a segmental perspective and reducing the multiplicity of causal factors to a single factor theorem. However, Gerth and Mills comment that Weber's work may be seen as an attempt to 'round out' Marx's economic materialism by political and military materialism.[13] Despite ideological and methodological differences between Marx and Weber, the two are interested in grasping the interrelations, and in other words, the social structure itself. The principles of rationalization, depersonalization and routinization are key to Weber's thinking and understanding of society. The individual and his action as the basic unit are core of Weber's *interpretative sociology*. All forms of associations and institutions should be reduced to 'understandable' action. Thus, methodologically, Weber's theory of stratification is subjective. Gerth and Mills observe: "The nominalism of Weber's method may be understood in terms of his attempt to avoid a philosophical emphasis upon either material or ideal factors, or upon either structural or individual principles of explanation."[14]

Nadel works out a definition of 'structure' and based on that examines the relevance of the 'structural analysis'. "Structure indicates an ordered arrangement of parts, which can be treated as transposable, being relatively invariant, while the parts are themselves variable."[15] Nadel speaks implicitly of 'dynamic equilibrium'. The structure of a society in terms of 'network' or 'system' of relationships could be only a starting point for analyzing the process of change in the social relationships. Nadel writes: "It (structural analysis) enables us to present our data neatly, synoptically, and with some elegance."[16] 'Time', 'reality' and 'function' are three cornerstones of the structural analysis. Therefore, the structural analysis is not just confined to 'the continuity' of a social life, its persistence and invariance; it accommodates the elements of 'time', 'variance' and 'changes' and even 'volition', hence a 'dynamic analysis'. Nadel agrees with Forte's view about social structure as "a sum of processes in time". All societies, therefore, combine necessarily structure and process (change). Ordering and reordering, and distribution and redistribution, imply both structuring and restructuring of social relations. In fact, there is no contradiction between structure and process, and the two are built into each other, and hence put limits upon each other.

Bailey, no doubt, unlike other researchers, discusses problems and methods of his study of Baderi village in Orissa. In his analysis of structure and system,[17] Bailey seems to have made a claim for making a structural analysis of political change. He writes: "A structural analysis emphasizes the regularity, the continuity, the permanence of certain forms of social interaction, and of groups of persons. It also emphasizes system..."[18] For Bailey, the word 'structure' refers to a higher level of analysis of interconnections between various sub- structures. Compared to Nadel, Bailey puts more emphasis on coherence and continuity. For 'rationalizing' this view, Bailey states that at empirical level there is no antipathy between conflict and a structural analysis. But he also reiterates his 'structural-functionalist' stance by saying that the structure itself contains rules for the resolution of conflict, and conflict even plays a crucial part in maintaining the structure. Obviously, implication of such a view is that nothing transforms, replaces and displaces particularly in the Indian context. Caste, village community, its power structure and its linkages with higher levels are visualized as 'static'. Formulation of the structural analysis is guided more by the coloured colonial misconceptions rather than by the vigour and logic of the approach itself. If a society has not been 'static' or 'unchanging', or it has not been changing as per the perception of change of colonial rulers and some scholars (particularly the western ones), it is erroneous to start with a 'static analysis' of Indian society. Besides this, a 'dynamic analysis' is understood, again erroneously, as a result of some external factors which implies that all changes are from without and not from within. History of India's social formation is full of contradictions and changes emanating from within its structure and normative pattern. Therefore, Bailey's notion of structure as a higher level of analysis, in effect, is "a low level of generalization".

Historical and Social Contexts of Social Inequality in Rural India

Along with the development of the order of the four ranks, namely, Brahmins, Kshatriyas, Vaisyas and Shudras, the development of state, law, religion, science and philosophy also took place in ancient India. Ruben holds the view that the structure of ancient Indian society can be described in terms of agrarian production and relations of different social strata to property, especially the soil.[19] Thus, the rank-orders in the village community depended upon the quality of agricultural land and infrastructure for cultivating it. However, Ruben does not seem to be right in assuming that the village community was stationary and inflexible. Guild (*sreni*), caste (*jati*) and devotion (*bhakti*) were later developments. Ruben also, along with some historians, prefers to characterize the Indian society by the Asiatic mode of production. He writes: "Thus, we may like to characterize Indian history as that of a society based on the Indian variant of the Asiatic mode of production with strong elements of slavery in antiquity and of feudalism in the middle ages, succeeded by capitalism which mainly came to India in the form of British colonialism till capitalist India became independent in

1947."[20] Such a unilinear mode of change undermines variations within each of the elements of one stage into the next one. The hypothesis referring to replacement/displacement of social structure underlies such a process of evolutionary scheme.

Romila Thapar emphasizes two major aspects of the functioning of social groups and their mobility in the study of a society.[21] She refers to pastoralism, settled agrarian economy, and an emergent commercial urban economy as features of Vedic, Mauryan and Gupta periods, respectively. She also observes that changes at the level of elite groups were most obviously brought about by foreign invasions and migrations. The migrations affected status relationships and the rules of marriage. Thapar's view that ancient Indian society was not a rigidly structured society is based on the fact that a hierarchy of statuses was absent. The *varna* concept did not refer to an actual description of the social functioning, and therefore, Indian society was not a frozen one. There were periods of change which influenced social institutions and other domains of social life.

Thapar brings out a distinction between ritual status and actual status in terms of economic and political power.[21] Despite a hazy line of demarcation between the two and the ideology of *varnaashram dharma*, there were secular bases of social stratification. Rigidity of *varna* was weakened by the emergence of 'mixed castes'. Tribal identity and occupational identity paved a way for mixed castes. No doubt, ritual status was fixed, but change in its rigidity was brought about by improving it or by denying its importance. This was more of an ideological sort of change. There was mobility also in terms of actual status as it was not necessarily defined by and dependent upon the ritual status. Emulation of actual status required a change in the redistribution of society's resources. Also, the examples of tension between the ritual (Brahminic) and the actual (the Kshatriya) statuses have been brought to our notice by several scholars. However, it would not be correct to say that the two statuses were completely independent of one another. For example, caste system has performed innumerable functions including economic and political, and this is one strong reason for its continuity and change.

A study of social stratification based on evidence from Buddhist sources reveals two schemes of categorization of people: (i) *varna, jati and kula*; and (ii) a Brahminical division of society, namely, Brahmins, Kshatriyas, Vaisyas and Sudras on the one hand, and another based on non-Brahminical sources categorizing people into Kshatriyas, Brahmins and Grahapatis on the other. The Brahminical scheme uses *varna* and *jati*, and the non-Brahminical categorization is based on the term *kula*. The latter represents "a division of society into the domains of power, ritual and the economy."[23] In the Buddhist literature, the Kshatriyas are invariably enumerated above the Brahmins. Also tension is noticed between the Kshatriyas and the Brahmins. Buddha refuted the claim of Brahminical superiority. One finds a two-tier system of social ranking in the Buddhist literature. The system of social stratification is not as normative as portrayed in the Brahminical texts. Occupational divisions among the people were the basis of their identification. Thus, a system of stratification existed independent of the Brahminical scheme.[24]

According to Kosambi, the essential relationship in India is not based on kinship. Production and mutual exchange of commodities and bonds of production hold society together.[25] Caste was related to economic hierarchy and the two together paved way for feudalism. Feudalism was a form of social order. In the medieval period of Indian history, that is, from twelfth century till the advent of the British rule, basic structural changes occurred in the traditional Indian society. These changes comprised of the land tenure systems such as *iqta*, *mansabdari* and *jagirdari*, etc. which, in turn, brought about changes in the ruling class and the rural landed aristocracy. Below the rural aristocracy were big peasants. There was considerable stratification within the peasantry.

Nurul S. Hasan writes: "The Zamindar class played a vital role in the political, economic, and cultural life of medieval India."[26] However, Hasan makes this reference in the context of their role in extracting the agricultural surplus, appropriation and control of rural economy. "At the same time, the separatist, localist, and parochial trends received powerful patronage from the *zamindari* class."[27] The class of Zamindars was highly differentiated. Hasan classifies them into: (i) the autonomous chieftains, (ii) the intermediary Zamindars, and (iii) the primary Zamindars. The second and the third categories were found at the village level. Chaudhuris, Khots and Muqaddams were intermediaries, and the primary Zamindars included the holders of proprietary rights.[28]

Inequalities in the pre-British period existed in myriad ways. There were people who did not pay land revenue, and some paid only a nominal amount. There were others who paid the maximum. Such economic disparities were associated with caste hierarchy as well. The system of landgrants (*jagirs*) promoted creation of landed enclaves from among the ruler's caste and his kin groups. Some favourites, professionals, dancers and singers, and servants were also given *jagirs* in lieu of their services. The entire system became quite complex and inequalitarian. There were as many as 45 *jagirs* and 175 taxes in the erstwhile State of Jaipur. The *jagirs* were arranged in a rank-order based on their size and revenue, and the Jagirdars enjoyed power and privilege in accordance with the ranks of their *jagirs*. Taxes were also socially patterned as they were imposed differentially in terms of caste ranks and other positions.[29]

There were socially structured land control relationships in terms of the landlord and the tenant. But they were not monolithic as they were divided into innumerable strata. A social formation viewpoint explains that various landed strata were linked to definite socio-cultural and economic and political roles. Besides this, each caste group, for example, was differentially associated with other caste groups. A potter used to supply earthen pots to various families in the village community. He was treated as a *kamin* or servant by the Rajput landlords, but the 'untouchable' castes or even castes of 'equal status' could never treat him as a *kamin*, though like the Rajput landlords they were also his 'patrons'. Further, it would be wrong to assume that a potter was a *kamin* in all situations. He used to behave as a 'contra-priest'[30] on the occasions of marriage etc. in the families of castes higher than his own. A contra-priest is a person who is required to perform certain ritual functions on auspicious occasions at the families of castes higher than his own caste. Thus, inequality and equality coexisted, and no caste, class and power groups enjoyed absolute power. The very nature of interdependence upon each other provided certain rights and privileges to all social groups. But these were certainly of an uneven nature.

Frykenberg's suggestion for formulating new theoretical models seems worth mentioning here. His two ideas are: (i) ideas of movement, namely, about process and causation; and (ii) ideas of structural relativity, that is, of dynamic relationships of social entities moving within a defined structural whole.[31] Frykenberg considers ideas of structural relativity as intrinsic to the study of process and structure: "The dynamic relationships of all social entities moving within a defined structural whole can hardly be analyzed without the invention of working models, some simple and some extremely complex."[32] Land, labour and lord are appropriate elements according to Frykenberg. The British rule brought about drastic changes in the institutions of property, government and law, and these three significantly affected land, labour and lord, socially as well as economically.

Private ownership of land, land settlements, *zamindari* and *ryotwari* systems, centralization of governmental authority throughout the length and breadth of the country, bureaucracy, judiciary and new legislations changed the structural and normative patterns during the British period. Due to these changes, despite unwillingness of the British raj, the caste system became weak as a social hierarchy, and became stronger as a source of mobilization for social, economic and political gains. This process of caste mobilization for extra-ritual ends received further boost in the post-independence period d to adult franchise, elections, migration and education.

Both Cohn and Metcalf arrive at a similar conclusion in their studies of the eastern districts of Uttar Pradesh. Cohn writes: "Most of the Rajputs whose *zamindari* rights were sold continued to live as they lived before in their villages and *talukas*, dominating lower caste cultivators and offering sustained and at times effective opposition to auction purchases."[33] Thus, change in status from *zamindari* to ex-*zamindari* or what Metcalf calls "from *raja* to landlord"[34] could not substantially affect adversely their dominant position in Indian rural society. Change in legal status does not necessarily change the 'actual status' of the people.

This sort of hiatus between the ideal or expected change and the actual change and situation would not permit analysis of social change and mobility in terms of closed systems. Therefore, there is a need to go beyond the study of caste system and social mobility because social reality is much broader than what caste could encompass. Changes emanating from external sources, for example, during the British period, in terms of legislations, land tenure systems, technology, education and administration cannot be studied simply from a caste point of view. Unexpected or latent structural and cultural changes emerged during this period resulting into restructuring of hierarchical relations.

My own study of Rajasthan shows that the Jagirdars and Bhomias were allowed to retain best lands at the time of the resumption of jagirs. Some lands were not resumed at all. Jagirdars mobilized their caste association, namely, the Rajasthan Kshatriya Mahasabha, for allotment of *khudkasht* land, compensation and assessment of *jagirs* for land revenue. The government bowed to the pressure of the Jagirdars.[35] The substantial tenants were able to manage transfer of large landholdings in their names depriving the smaller tenants of their due share. This was a significant step in structuring social and economic inequalities. The legal status was withdrawn but there was no corresponding effect on the actual status. Downward mobility was not a significant result of this legislation in several cases. Upward mobility was, however, quite a noticeable phenomenon in the case of tenants.

Structuring of Social Inequality: An Analysis of a Few Selected Studies

We do not intend to discuss the patterns of social stratification in terms of caste, class and power as such in this essay. But a reference to Dumont's structuralist stance in regard to intercaste, intracaste and intrafamilial ranking is not completely out of context. The principle of hierarchy not only applies to caste, but also to principles of values, occupations, food and clothes and bride-givers and bride-takers. Dumont looks for cultural meaning of affinity and consanguinity.[36] In Dumont's *Homo Hierarchicus*,[37] Yogendra Singh discerns four notions of structuralism: (i) ideology, (ii) idealistic, (iii) transformational relationship, and (iv) comparison.[38] Hierarchy is an ideational notion; it pervades all aspects of Hindu society. Everything is seen in terms of 'pure' and 'impure', its binary tension and dialectics. Since pure and impure are parts of the same principle, they are complementary. But hierarchy is seen through the superiority of the pure over the impure. Dumont observes that there has been change in the society and not of the society, hence rules out a structural change in India's caste system.

Since we are interested in discerning change in the existing patterns of social inequality, we do not wish to go into the genesis of various approaches and methods of study of social stratification. It would be appropriate to lay hands on a few selected studies. Chakravarti discusses inequalities in rural India based on status, economic differences and power.[39] The analysis of social inequalities in terms of these three spheres is based on the assumption that a lower status in one sphere is not necessarily accompanied by the same in the other two spheres. Of these three domains, caste status is fixed by birth. But it is to be seen how ritual basis of caste continues to play a decisive role in determining social, economic and political status.

Structural incongruities have certainly emerged in the post-independence period. Caste has become segmental entity as it has lost its 'organic' character. The pure does not encompass today the less pure or impure. In fact, if the "less pure has acquired strength in economic and political spheres, it encompasses to a large extent the pure". The nature of intercaste relations is not so much valued today in terms of commensality as it is done in terms of wealth and power. Pollution-purity and untouchability have become more of casual rituals than a day-to-day reality. This is due to structural changes introduced in the countryside over a period of last four decades. Motivational factors or rational outlook have not brought structuring of social inequalities as much as the latter has changed values and aspirations of the rural people.

Two studies, one by Bailey[40] and second by Epstein[41] focus on structural change in the countryside. Bailey examines relationship between caste and new economy. As a result of the abolition of the traditional land tenure systems, new frontiers, namely, economic, political and administrative have taken land to market. Bailey analyzes new economy, land transactions, services and trade. The landlords have become ex-landlords, and the functionary and service castes have become landowners. The latter have taken their traditional produces to market and have earned profits which were not available to them in the traditional system.

Epstein's study reveals that structural innovation, namely, irrigation has brought about significant change in the village economy, but it has restricted social change by discouraging migration, education and employment outside the village. Lack of such an innovation has resulted into migration, education and employment in another village. Epstein analyzes structural change in two villages of Karnataka in terms of crops, houses, landholdings, livestock, family incomes and expenditures and market networks.

Social inequality is a structural and historical reality observable in diverse forms and in different contexts. Social inequality is, therefore, related to structure, ideology and behaviour of the people. Its consequences could be seen in terms of arrangement of the people and expressions of their life-styles and careers they pursue. Structure of inequality in a given society is generally found having dissonance between different dimensions. For example, the three dimensions of social inequality, namely, social, political and economic are not of the same magnitude in terms of producing inequalitarian relations, and therefore, these do not necessarily correspond with each other having one-to-one relationship. Thus, social inequality may be pronounced in one specific domain, whereas in others it may not be of the same magnitude. Such a state of inequality is normally a result of specific structural conditions and processes of change. Men are, therefore, not equally unequal. Impact of inequality is also uneven. Even ascriptive bases of inequality such as age, sex and kinship statuses do not have a uniform pattern of social effects.

Social inequality is a very sensitive aspect of social life. The notion that a person is higher than someone else or that one has a realization that his position is superior to some other member of his village community makes it sensitive and evaluative. It is not psychological evaluation that matters so much. Such evaluations are based on differential possession of resources including house, household goods, property, education, lucrative job and political power. Since role of these factors in determining social inequality has increased, the role of ascriptive factors such as birth, sex, age and fictive status has declined considerably.

Fallers states that social inequality has both normative and structural phenomena.[42] The normative aspect refers to evaluation, and the structural aspect refers to distribution of material resources and power. Berreman refers to a study of four dimensions of social inequality, namely, behavioural, interactional, material and existential.[43] Social inequality is a lived-in experience and a stark reality. It is a relative phenomenon.

Let us illustrate the structural basis of social inequality from our field studies in Rajasthan.[44] Brahmins are regarded high in ritual rank-order by other castes, but their influence and power in other domains depend mainly upon their economic and educational achievements. In one of the six villages we have studied Brahmins are dominant not because of their high ritual status, but because they enjoy dominant positions in economic and educational spheres. This is so to a large extent because being Brahmins they have more access to higher education and white-collar jobs than other caste groups. But it is not that all the families from among the Brahmins or even all the individual members from Brahmin families have such a privilege and opportunity. In another village, Brahmins have incongruity between their ritual status and economic and cultural (educational) achievements, and therefore, they do not enjoy power and dominance in the village community. Out of the remaining four villages, in one only Brahmins have considerable influence in the affairs of the village because of their better off economic and educational status. Thus, social inequality is a very complex phenomenon. It is not that high ritual status of Brahmins has become altogether redundant and insignificant. It is accorded importance on certain religious, ritual and ceremonial occasions, but it is ephemeral. A Brahmin priest becomes a commoner as soon as the particular episode is over. However, there are still some noticeable cultural and social distinctions between different caste groups particularly in regard to life-styles, performance of rituals and observance of some practices.

In regard to Rajputs, hierarchy based on the size of the *jagirs* is not closely associated with commensal and ritual bases of caste-based inequality. Norms in relation to pollution-purity and untouchability were never a significant element of the life-styles of Rajputs. They were always non-vegetarian and drinkers of alcohol, and their food habits made them to think that Brahmins and Banias particularly would observe norms related to pollution-purity and untouchability as they were vegetarian, teetotaler and performed rituals and worshipped gods and goddesses. Thus, theoretically, the Rajputs were number two in the caste hierarchy, but in practice they were number one in political sphere, and did not bother about their ritual rank as such. Generally, they were not engaged in gainful educational achievements. Because of the abolition of the *jagirdari* and *zamindari* systems, they have been affected severely. Now a good number of Rajputs are self-cultivators like their ex-tenants, and some of them today own much smaller landholdings than their own ex-tenants. A substantial number of Rajputs work as police constables and soldiers in Indian Army. Rajputs are one community which has witnessed a radical downgrading of their social status in the village community.

Conversely, the Jats who were tenants of the Rajput landlords, have improved their status considerably in economic and political spheres. In the economic sphere, the loss of Rajput landlords has been the gain of Jat tenants as they have acquired substantial landholdings. In the sphere of political power, they have taken maximum advantage of adult franchise and their preponderant numerical strength by arousing caste consciousness and mobilizing their members on the caste basis.

Thus, two obverse structural processes immediately after the first phase of land reforms created new cleavages within different caste groups and also brought about some 'levelling' effect on the structure of social inequality. Some of the Rajput families, though could not retain their traditional glory and power, tried to retain best lands, and diverted their savings and assets in economically gainful activities and enterprises. Similarly, the Jat cultivators who were substantially benefited by land reforms further consolidated their economic position by extracting maximum advantage of developmental schemes and facilities and by adopting new devices in the field of agriculture. Those groups and families which received a jolt could not recoup from that crisis, and have ended up with not only downward social mobility but also in some cases reached the level of pauperization.

A Comment on Caste as a Form of Social Inequality

Dumont's structuralism and its application by several others to the study of India's caste system have led us to think that there exists the dichotomy of hierarchy and equality, and holism and individualism. Srinivas seems to agree with Dumont's approach to the study of social inequality. He writes: "In short, there is, on the one hand, the syndrome of tradition, hierarchy and holism, while on the other hand, that of modernity, equality and individualism. There is no liberty in traditional societies for liberty can only be predicted of individuals and not of groups."[45] The obvious confession is that Hindu society is hierarchical and the modern western society is egalitarian.

If we look at the Indian scene today, it is quite evident that individuals migrate to towns and cities for higher education and better employment. Srinivas writes: "Caste society is holistic and hierarchical and is inimical to individualism but in spite of this individualism surfaces in the *sanyasi* or renouncer, who transcends society."[46] Srinivas and Dumont see individualism only in renouncing of the world and not in migration of a Marwari Bania from western Rajasthan to Assam, Bengal, Bihar, Tamil Nadu and Karnataka. A Rajasthani 'untouchable' labourer has been migrating to Delhi and Punjab for several decades for seeking employment particularly in the years of drought and famine. Always a selected few have gone out of their native places for higher education and white-collar jobs. These are vital sociological facts of India's rural life in the context of inequality.

According to Dumont, the basis of the caste system is the opposition between the pure and the impure, but with increased recession of pollution-purity syndrome, hierarchy does not continue to be an ideology. There is also no combination of 'two forces', that is, Brahmins and Kshatriyas (status and power). The intermediate castes have extracted maximum economic benefits from green revolution, and political gains from adult franchise and elections because of their numerical preponderance and improved economic standing. Dumont and Srinivas both do not see any exploitation in the *jajmani* system, because it is not recognized as such as per the norms of the system. Exploitation of the *kamin* (functionary) castes and untouchables was not only clearly perceptible, but it was also highly institutionalized. Today, we have new forms of exploitation which are not clearly visible under the new systems of relations of production in agriculture and politics and elections.

We have discussed elsewhere that occupation, education, power and styles of life are the main aspects of change in social stratification.[47] Distinctions based on these aspects are evaluated as the yardsticks of higher and lower status. There is no denying of the association of caste ranks with these aspects, but incongruities in them are indicative of weakening of the traditional social inequalities, and congruities speak of the continuity of caste groups or some families with fairly good economic position.

New forms of inequalities along with continuity of traditional inequalities in some measure in regard to various caste and class groups and families have emerged due to historical and cultural legacies and present-day distributive disparities. Class distinctions have even accentuated within the caste groups. Caste groups or some families have hindered not only emergence of class consciousness but have also created new enclaves of power and privilege. There is an undeniable element of casteness when only Harijan labourers are burnt alive, but at the same time this is also a case of class atrocity as the Harijans are generally poor, hence indulge in such inhuman acts.

Ownership, control and use of land in relation to caste partly become the basis of relations in rural India. Beteille identifies three forms of inequality: (i) between landlord and tenant; (ii) between landowner and wage labourer; and (iii) between large, medium and small proprietors.[48] Issues related to agrarian structure and change are sharply focused in a study of the district Basti in Uttar Pradesh. The two main issues are: (i) the 'land grab' movement in 1970 by the poor and helpless peasants; and (ii) the structural and emergent factors resulting in the termination and failure of this movement.[49] The questions raised by Rajendra Singh in this study are quite relevant for analyzing agrarian and social inequalities in the village community. These are: (1) How have various agrarian reforms affected caste, class and land relations? (2) Who have been the gainers and who the losers are of land as a result of these reforms? (3) What is their caste and class position today? (4) What is the impact of these reforms upon the emerging pattern of power structure in the district?[50]

Explorations, to find answers of these questions, show that there was an increase in the number of Zamindars and in the growth of class solidarity among them. There was pauperization both of Zamindars and *mahants*. And finally, a strong lower middle caste rich peasantry emerged.[51] We have discussed this process of change in terms of 'proletarianization' of the *jagirs* and Bhomias, and 'bourgeoisiefication' of the tenants in my study of six villages in Rajasthan. 'Downward' social mobility was quite perceptive in the case of a large number of landlord families.

Today, social inequalities in rural India cannot be diagnosed in terms of caste or class categories because of the very nature of social formation that has emerged in the post-independence period. Singh observes: "After examining the Basti situation, we find the inadequacy of class as well as caste. The agrarian society in Basti conforms neither to a class nor to a caste model."[52] Class dichotomies and conflicts can be seen in the context of caste which mould the subjective perceptions of the people in the countryside. Since mobility has been both upward and downward simultaneously, it is evident that various caste and class groups are highly differentiated. The hypothesis that the rich are getting richer and the poor poorer is not correct in all cases. Omvedt endorses Singh's view that caste is not necessarily equivalent to class, but it very clearly puts some limits.[53]

The idea of continuous hierarchies and discrete castes given by Dipankar Gupta refers to a commentary on Dumont's notion of caste as *Homo hierarchicus*. Gupta writes: "Any notion of hierarchy is arbitrary and is valid from the perspective of certain individual castes. To state that the pure hierarchy is one that is universally believed-in, or one which legitimizes the position of those who participate in the caste system, is misleading."[54] Besides pollution-purity, distinctions and 'diacritical notches' are observed strictly in the caste system. Castes equally pure refrain from merging their identities. Distinctions related to pollution and purity do not systematically affect caste status. In view of these formulations, Gupta examines the *jajmani* system, sanskritization, caste and politics and caste-class and social class. Inconsistencies and incongruities in behaviour of members of different caste groups in these spheres can be understood in terms of their discreteness.

The mode of production is a social formation in which we find interconnections of caste, kinship, family, marriage and even rituals with the forces of production and production relations.[55] Social inequalities are seen by Gough in terms of the emergence of a new bourgeoisie, the polarization of the peasantry, and the pauperization of the working class. Namboodiripad[56] and Ranadive[57] analyze class relationships as a domain assumption in the treatment of caste and kinship in India. Even *varna* and *jajmani* systems are explained in terms of class relations and are found embedded in the mode of production.[58] Caste is analyzed also in terms of physical force and economic power. Castes operate as enclaves functioning parallel to ecosystems. Marriages take place within these ecosystems, hence these become operative caste boundaries.

Conclusion

We have analyzed the nature and patterning of social inequality from the point of both structure and process. Structuring of social inequality refers to 'structure in time'. Our analysis shows that there are both internal or historical contradictions and external influences along with structural and normative sources influencing inequality. Placement of groups, families and individuals in high and low positions based on wealth, property, occupation and education refers to structural sources. Normative sources refer to evaluative standards. These are applied differentially to various spheres such as social and cultural (caste), power and economy. We have analyzed the question: Whether these spheres of social inequality are independent of each other or they are inseparable aspects of the same social formation.

Neither caste nor class alone can be a sufficient approach for studying social inequality. In fact, we have examined that social and economic dimensions of inequality coexist and are affected by each other. Upper castes have slided down in their status, and some of them have improved their position. Such a pattern is found almost among all caste groups. Thus, apparently equal groups are unequal in myriad ways and in their resourcefulness. Besides this, the social groups which occupied lower positions also enjoyed some rights and privileges.

Social inequality is structurally relational and relative phenomenon. Structural factors have brought about marked and manifest changes in the nature of social inequality. Ancient, medieval, British and contemporary periods in Indian history have shown role of these factors in terms of migration, invasions, warfare, land reforms, administration and education etc.

The caste system, which has been a pivotal infrastructure in shaping social relations, has not been 'static' and 'unchanging' as it is depicted in various writings. In fact, it has pervaded almost all aspects of social relations, and therefore, to see it as confined to ritual or religious phenomena would amount to undermining of its pan-Indian character. Both the contexts of caste, namely, historical and contextual, would permit us to know that the structural and the normative dimensions are inseparable, and therefore, a dichotomy of 'caste and class' or a trichotomy of 'caste, class and power'[59] as forms of social inequality or as systems of social stratification bring out only a fragmented picture of India's rural social formation. A social formation point of view for studying social inequality is based on the understanding specifically of structure, culture, history and dialectics of Indian society.

Notes

1. Dahrendorf, R., "On the origin of inequality among men," in Andre Beteille (ed.), *Social Inequality*, Penguin Books, 1969, p. 17.
2. Ibid., p. 19.
3. Sharma, K.L., "Caste and class in India: Some conceptual problems," *Sociological Bulletin*, Vol. 33, Nos. 1 & 2, 1984, p. 21.
4. Beteille, Andre, *Inequality among Men*, Delhi, Oxford University Press, 1977, p. 130.
5. Aron, Raymond, "Two definitions of class," in Andre Beteille (ed.), *Social Inequality*, Penguin books, 1969, pp. 75-77.
6. Beteille, Andre, *The Idea of Inequality and Other Essays*, Delhi, Oxford University Press, 1983, p. 34.
7. Marx, Karl and Frederick Engels, *The German Ideology*, Moscow, Progress Publishers, 1968, p. 187.
8. Ibid., p. 32.
9. Ibid., pp. 36-37.
10. Ibid., p. 37.
11. Ibid., p. 38.
12. Gerth, H.H. and Mills, C. Wright, *From Max Weber:Essays in Sociology*, London, Routledge and Kegan Paul, 1970, p. 12.
13. Ibid., p. 47.
14. Ibid., p. 59.
15. Nadel, S.F., *The Theory of Social Structure*, London, Cohen and West Ltd., 1969, p. 8.
16. Ibid., p. 126.
17. Bailey, F.G., *Tribe, Caste and Nation*, Manchester, Manchester University Press, 1960, pp. 6-10.
18. Ibid., p. 6.
19. Ruben, Walter, "Outline of the structure of ancient Indian society," in R.S., Sharma and Vivekanand Jha (eds.), *Indian Society:Historical Probings*, New Delhi, People's Publishing House, 1974, p. 92.
20. Ibid., p. 20.
21. Thapar, Romila, "Social mobility in ancient India with special reference to elite groups," in R.S. Sharma and Vivekanand Jha (eds.), op.cit., p. 95.
22. Ibid., p. 99.
23. Chakravarti, Uma, "Towards a historical sociology of stratification in ancient India: Evidence from Buddhist sources," *Economic and Political Weekly*, Vol. XX, No. 9, 1985, p. 357.
24. Ibid., pp. 356-60.

25. Kosambi, D.D., *An Introduction to the Study of Indian History*, Bombay, Popular Prakashan, 1975.
26. Hasan, S. Nurul, "Zamindars under the Mughal," in R.E. Frykenberg (ed.), *Land Control and Social Structure in Indian History* (Indian edition), New Delhi, Manohar Publications, 1979, p. 17.
27. Ibid., p. 17.
28. Ibid., pp. 17-31.
29. Sharma, K.L., "Land tenure systems, social structure and change: Some reflections on land reforms in Rajasthan," in Sheo Kumar Lal (ed.), *Sociological Perspective in Land Reforms*, New Delhi, Agricole Publishing Academy.
30. Gould, Harold A., "Priest and contrapriest: a structural analysis of jajmani relationships in the Hindu plains and the Nilgiri Hills," *Contributions to Indian Sociology*, New Series, No. 1, 1967, pp. 26-55.
31. Frykenberg, Robert Eric, "Introduction," in R.E. Frykenberg (ed.), op.cit., p. XX.
32. Ibid.
33. Cohn, Bernard S., "Structural change in Indian society," in R.E. Frykenberg (ed.), op. cit., p. 111.
34. Metcalf, Thomas R., "From Raja to Landlord: The Oudh Talukdars, 1850-1870," in R.E. Frykenberg (ed.), op.cit., p. 123.
35. Sharma, K.L., "Altering agrarian structure: Rajasthan land reforms," *State and Society*, Vol. 1, No. 3, pp. 64-78.
36. Sharma, Surendra, *Sociology in India: A Perspective from Sociology of Knowledge*, Jaipur, Rawat Publications, 1985, pp. 95-97.
37. Dumont, Louis, *Homo Hierarchicus*, London, Paladin Granada Publishing Ltd., 1970.
38. Singh, Yogendra, "Sociology of social stratification," Survey of Research in Sociology and Social Anthropology, 1969-1979 (ICSSR), Vol. II, New Delhi, Satvahan Publications, 1985, pp. 37-79.
39. Chakravarti, Anand, "Some aspects of inequality in rural India: A sociological perspective," in Andre Beteille (ed.), *Equally and Inequality:Theory and Practice*, Delhi, Oxford University Press, 1983, pp. 129-181.
40. Bailey, F.G., *Caste and Economic Frontier*, Manchester, Manchester University Press, 1957.
41. Epstein, T.S., *Economic Development and Social Change in South India*, Manchester: Manchester University Press, 1962.
42. Fallers, Llyod A., *Inequality:Social Stratification Reconsidered*, Chicago: The University of Chicago Press, 1973.

43. Berreman, G.D., *Caste and Other Inequalities: Essays on Inequality*, Meerut, Folklore Institute, 1979.
44. Sharma, K.L., *The Changing Rural Stratification System*, New Delhi, Orient Longman, 1974, Chapter 3.
45. Srinivas, M.N., "Some reflections on the nature of caste hierarchy," *Contributions to Indian Sociology*, Vol. 18, No. 2, 1984, p. 152.
46. Ibid., p. 153.
47. Sharma, K.L., *Essays on Social Stratification*, Jaipur, Rawat Publications, 1980, Chapter V.
48. Beteille, Andre, "Agrarian Relations in Tanjore District, South India," *Sociological Bulletin*, Vol. 21, No. 2, 1972, p. 135.
49. Singh, Rajendra, "Agrarian social structure and peasant unrest: A study of land-grab movement in District Basti, Eastern U.P.," *Sociological Bulletin*, Vol. 23, No. 1, 1974, p. 46.
50. Ibid., p.46.
51. Ibid., p.53.
52. Ibid., p.64.
53. Omvedt, Gail, "Caste, agrarian relations and agrarian conflicts," *Sociological Bulletin*, Vol. 29, No.2, 1980, p. 145, See also, *Land, Caste and Politics in Indian States* (ed.), Delhi, Authors Guild Publications, 1982.
54. Gupta, Dipankar, "Continuous hierarchies and discrete castes," *Economic and Political Weekly*, Vol. XIX, No. 48, 1984, p. 2049.
55. Gough, Kathleen E., "Modes of production in Southern India," *Economic and Political Weekly*, Vol. 15, Nos. 5, 6 and 7, 1980, pp. 337-64.
56. Namboodiripad, E.M.S., "Caste conflicts versus growing unity of popular democratic forces," *Economic and Political Weekly*, Vol. XiV, Nos-7 and 8, 1975, pp. 329-36.
57. Ranadive, B.T., "Caste, class and property relations," *Economic and Political Weekly*, No. XIV, Nos. 7 and 8, 1979, pp. 337-48.
58. Meillassoux, C., "Are there castes in India," *Economy and Society*, February, 1973.
59. Beteille, Andre, *Caste, Class and Power*, Bombay, Oxford University Press, 1966.

8

Social Stratification among Tribes in India

For a long time tribal people were seen as an undifferentiated lot. However, they have/had gradations based on age-sets, sex and kinship which did not form the basis of social stratification as found among the non-tribal people like property, wealth, power and authority. Several studies of social stratification, ranking systems and class formation among the tribes all over the world have reported absence of social differentiation in tribal societies. Social stratification, as an existential phenomenon among the tribes, is, however, different from that of the advanced agricultural and industrial societies. It is not unique as it is generally considered. The principles of social stratification such as ethnicity, class and power are the same everywhere. The difference lies in the operationalization and actual functioning of these principles due to structural differences in various tribal societies in regard to their history, level of economic development, nature of colonial impact and exposure to modern forces of social transformation. Thus to the extent the tribal people are different in terms of these criteria social stratification and class formation are also different among them in comparison to the non-tribal societies.

For a long time it has been debated by the academia and policy-makers whether tribals should be allowed to retain their cultural identity intact or they should be assimilated with the rest of Indian people. This culturological perspective is not specifically articulated for the study of social stratification as such among the tribal people, but rich data have been generated regarding intratribal and intertribal status distinctions (Vidyarthi, 1974). More specifically, the ethnic and class perspectives have been in currency for the study of tribal social stratification (see, for example, Sachchidananda, 1990; Badgaiyan, 1986; Doshi, 1990; Singh, 1985). Emphasis in the ethnic perspective is laid on inter-tribal distinctions in terms of historicity, land relations, colonial impact, contact with non-tribal people, economic development and socio-political awakening, etc. However, the class perspective emphasizes upon formation of class relations among tribes keeping in view their economy, patterns of exploitation, alienation, and backwardness. In a couple of studies convergence between the ethnic and the class perspectives has been greatly emphasized (see Badgaiyan, 1986; Doshi, 1990).

Finally, we may identify the major tribal ethnic structures in terms of their internal differentiations and interethnic differences and ties to ascertain ramifications of social stratification and class formation. Class formation, as a structural process, is based on increasing differentiation among the tribal people in terms of property, wealth, landownership, exploitation, pauperization, education, political power, social movements, migration and social mobility. We may relate these aspects of class formation with the ethnic structures to find out the nature of correspondence/non-congruence between ethnicity and class.

Defining Tribe

'Tribe' may be distinguished from 'caste', but it is not that 'tribe' is a homogeneous entity and 'caste' is characterized by complexity and heterogeneity. There are distinctions within a given tribe and between different tribes. Certainly, tribes are considerably distinct from the non-tribes. But then the question is: What is so distinctive about 'tribe' that makes it distinct from other entities such as caste, class, race, etc. Some tribes are quite large in size and are also spread over several states of India. Surely, tribes are not 'organically' related to each other as castes are under a common principle.

But tribes are also not exclusive systems as they are not small in size and bear a great deal of heterogeneity. Historically, a 'tribal society' has not been static, and yet it has retained its exclusivity from a 'caste society'. There are 427 tribes in India, and these can be classified on the basis of language, religion, degree of their isolation, and pattern of livelihood (Beteille, 1974). Some of these attributes of tribes often resemble with the non-tribal people in a given region than the tribal people of another region. The tribals are hunters, fishers, shifting cultivators, settled agriculturists, plantation workers and industrial wage earners, hence some of them resemble with the non-tribal people. The large tribes such the Bhils, Gonds, Santhals, Oraons and Mundas are not only settled agriculturists, some of them are found in modern occupations in like members of caste Hindus.

Tribal economy is also largely like the peasant economy. Division of labour based on gender, work specialization, tenurial differentiation and class distinctions are found among the tribal people like any non-tribal peasant community. Despite these similarities, tribes remain distinct from castes because of their geographical isolation, language or dialect and religion (Beteille, 1974). Even these criteria are not a rigid basis of distinguishing tribes from castes. For example, Meenas in Rajasthan are listed as a scheduled tribe, but they have always lived in multicaste villages as a part of the village system. Meenas were also one of the functionary castes under the *jajmani* system and, in fact, they are/were always referred as a caste. Certainly, tribes have been large and small both, but never without internal social differentiation. Beteille argues that a substantial number of tribal people are peasants today, hence tribes are in transition (Majumdar, 1937; Sinha, 1965; Oraon, 1969). There is class and social stratification (implying stratified peasantry) among tribes in India. In no way, tribes can today be treated as 'primitive'. Besides differentiation of peasantry, there is also a middle class among the tribal people. Migration, education, mobility, social and political awakening have contributed to the emergence of a small middle class. State-sponsored measures including the constitutional provisions and special programmes for their development have set in a new process of differentiation and stratification which would mean consideration of more or less same criteria of status determination which are normally applied to the non-tribal people.

There is more or less unanimity among the students of tribal social life in India regarding the presence of social stratification. However, Roy Burman (1984) cautions that social stratification by itself is not enough to mobilize the people to actively resist alienation of their land. More important is the nature of social stratification. Roy Burman cites a few examples in support of this observation. The Gonds were a highly stratified community, but no significant revolt took place amongst them till the forties of the present century. The presence of a state structure and the shifting nature of political contacts with the outside world led to both stratification and segmentation of Gond society. Like the non-tribal people, "the upper strata emerged as a multi-focal aristocracy." A new elite emerged among the Gonds, and the British rulers transformed them into new Zamindars. Thus, the Gonds synthesized the old and the new, the tribal and the peasant cultures. A tribal movement gets a start generally when it has support of a combination of factors including iniquitous relations, middle class interests, philanthropism and ethnic/community identity. But the point is that tribal people are like other people engaged in similar pursuits in the same area(s), and they are also different from them, and it is this difference/dissimilarity that makes social stratification in tribal society somewhat different from the non-tribal people.

Let us describe a 'functional' formulation of 'tribes' here. Tribes are not castes or caste-like entities though some of them have followed the path of sanskritization and conversion to Christianity and Islam. Tribes are a highly differentiated lot ethnically and culturally. Some adhere to 'tribalism', others have converted to Christianity by rejecting tribal pantheon, and some have taken up Hinduism by adopting vegetarianism, teetotalism and other Brahminic ideals and practices. Tribes are also differentiated based on landholdings, rural-urban background, education, occupation, income and political power. Tribes have been granted special treatment under the Constitution of India. They have also many attributes, practices and styles of life that distinguish them from the non-tribal people. It may be seen how their 'distinct' and 'general' characteristics get reconciled in their social life. What keeps them partly different from others, and what impinges upon their life to bring them closer to the non- tribal people? The tribal situation is complex in the sense that the tribals depend upon forest-based sources of livelihood, they are also engaged in settled agriculture, they are working in factories and industries, some of them are educated and are employed as professionals, civil servants and white-collar workers, and some are active politicians and social workers. Ethnic and cultural differentiation can be seen in terms of tribal identities and religious pursuits. Thus, the nature of social stratification is also quite complex corresponding with the heterogeneity of their socio-cultural and economic structure. Therefore, it would be unwise to consider tribes as the people dependent mainly upon forest produces, simple agriculture, living far off from modern civilization. They are a people who have a lot of attributes in common with the non-tribal population, and at the same time, have their own 'tribal identity'. Social stratification among the tribal people is, therefore, neither simply based on criteria like age and kinship nor it can be characterized by property, education, occupation, income and power. A semblance of the two sets of criteria may distinguish the tribal people from the non-tribal population.

Social Stratification Before Independence

Sachchidananda (1990) reports that social stratification in the states of West Bengal, Bihar, Madhya Pradesh and Orissa in the pre-colonial period could be observed through the ranks such as the *khutkattidars*, the village headmen and the masses. Later on some artisan castes such as blacksmiths, potters and weavers further differentiated the tribal society. From class point of view, the village society was divided into the *khutkattidars* and the *paria horoko* (masses). The later depended on the goodwill of the *khutkattidars* and were rated as second class citizens. The *khutkattidars* were the real owners of the village land. Sachchidananda writes: "The *khutkattidar* system was thus an arrangement for the management of land resources on a communal basis. The headman managed the affairs of the village with the help of some influential village leaders. He dispensed justice, fixed the dates of village deities and collected dues from landholders for payment as *chanda* (contribution) to the tribal chief". Under such a situation lineage or clan was the basis of socio-economic differentiation. The *khutkatti* system was mainly confined to the Munda tribe. Thapar and Siddiqui (1991) also find the *khutkatti* system as the basis of the Munda society. The *mundas, pahans* and *mahtos* were heads of their clans. Besides these heads of the clans/lineages, the *khutkattidars* were powerful as they collected a tribute from the *praja* living in the villages. Thapar and Siddiqui after tracing the history of social structure and its differentiation in ancient period write: "Thus, the tendency towards social stratification which had already begun with the *khutkatti* system was not only intensified and accelerated under the state, but was also made more complex with the interpolation of various levels of intermediaries". The tribal mode of production broke down and gave a way to the emergence of a new correlation of social status with landholding and power. The lineage rights over land became weak, and a feudal state on tribal society was superimposed. Tribal identity was also weakened by commodity production.

Individual ownership of land was found among other tribes. The headmanship was not confined to a member of a clan or lineage as it was in the case of the Munda tribe having the *khutkatti* system. But all the tribes had the institution of *headman* who acted as a patriarch. The *khutkattidars* were not completely autonomous as the king was the supreme authority in his state. Sachchidananda observes that such a system did not persist for long as feudal superstructure was set in place not only in Chhotanagpur but also among the Gonds in Madhya Pradesh. He writes: "Scions of the Raja's family carved out feudatory estates and principalities, the most famous of which was the kingdom of Chanda. The emergence of the feudal system marked the beginning of the breakdown of the tribal polity characterized by communal ownership of land" (Sachchidananda, 1990). At this stage, a clearly visible system of social stratification could be seen among the tribal people. A sort of economic explanation of this is provided by Sachchidananda though without using clearly relevant concepts and categories. He writes: "Social stratification based on differential command over economic resources began to emerge. The development of trade and commerce facilitated the growth of small urban centres. A variety of castes, ranging from *brahmans* and *rautias* to many artisan communities, flocked to these centres".

Sachchidananda mentions about the grant of *jagirs* by the Raja of Chhotanagpur in early seventeenth century. As a result of this a new class of merchants, money-lenders and Brahmin priests emerged. The emergence of this new class proved antithetical to the principle of communal and equalitarian character of the tribal society. Since the new grantees of lands in the tribal areas enjoyed more or less permanent and usufructuary rights, they soon began to exploit the tribal people uninhibitedly with the help of village officers such as the *munda* and the *pahan*. The *khutkatti* system also began to crumble down along with the *parha* system. Thus, a new basis of power and social status emerged and replaced the traditional arrangement. Land did not remain any more a communally owned and controlled phenomenon. However, the village officers like the *munda*, the *manki* and the *majhi* were given police powers by the British in their interests to establish their rule over the masses by granting a small minority such benefits which made them to fight for the *raj* and to suppress their own people.

It can safely be deduced from the available literature that isolation of the tribal people has been decreasing, and this has benefited some sections of the tribal society and, at the same time, new forms of social stratification among tribes in India has been variously characterized in terms of peasantization, detribalization, Hinduization, conversion to Christianity, etc. Some caste-Hindus because of pre-eminence of tribal society in a given region have adopted some tribal attributes, and such a process has been called as 'tribalization'. Despite these changes, tribal society can be distinguished from the Hindu, Muslim, Christian and other non-tribal communities. However, this does not imply that tribes in India have remained or continue to remain isolated, homogeneous, small in size and unique compared to the non-tribal people.

The British affected the tribal people in several ways. The intrusion of the British in the management of forests depossessed the tribals from their age-old control and use of forests. Besides the British officers, a lot of other sections like suppliers, traders, clerks and workers started living in the tribal areas. In course of time, some tribals were also benefited by the British encroachment, and they became a distinct class of the privileged few. Education was one way by which a select group of tribals became superior to the masses. Conversion to Christianity also helped the converts in education, employment, and in fact, in acclaiming a higher status for them.

Singh (1978) highlights some dysfunctional consequences of the British colonialism. The agency system established by the British was used for ruthless suppression of the tribal uprisings. The colonial system also strengthened the feudal elements in tribal society as it encouraged the chiefs and landlords to extract surplus from the tribals as much as possible for the well-being of the *raj* in India. The moneylenders had their heyday as no one was there to check the usurious activities perpetrated by them.

From various accounts, it is evident that during the British period class-based distinctions were replacing the traditional status system among the tribes of India. It could be seen in the alienation of land, control of forest economy by the state, emergence of moneylenders and traders, close but exploitative contacts by the non-tribals with the tribal people, etc. All these sections of society, including the British officers, Zamindars, moneylenders and traders and non-tribal agriculturists were superior in skills and resources even before they landed on the tribal soil. This implanted a hiatus between them and the tribals, and the policy of the government created status cleavages among the tribals. This is why some non-tribals are regarded as *diku* (exploiters). The tribals, in general, faced acute pauperization and were forced to migrate in search of employment to far off places in Bengal, Assam, Maharashtra, etc. The tribals are found divided even today due to the processes of acculturation started by the Christian missions and Hindu organizations. Conversion to Christianity and Hinduization brought about at least three orders, namely, Christian convert tribals, Hinduized tribals, and non-converts. All these tribals were also stratified internally based on their economic standing and ethnic status.

Interethnic relations between different groups with varying degrees of structural distance have been highlighted by Badgaiyan (1986). Ethnicity and class as the two main principles of social differentiation have provided multiple ways to the people for organizing their social relations. Within the same ethnic group there are wide-ranging class differences, and the hostile ethnic groups may be found in the same class. The searching questions posed by Badgaiyan are: (1) How people resolve the contradictory claims on their sentiments and impulses to act? (2) Do they allow their ethnic sentiments to ride over class interests or do they let class interests prevail over their ethnic obligations? (3) Is it the context that decides as to which affiliation will prevail over the other? (4) Do all ethnic groups behave the same way? (5) Are ethnic groups swayed more by primordial sentiments than by contextual logic? These questions are explicated in the context of the historical development of Munda society. The four phases noted by Badgaiyan are: (i) the traditional Munda society before the emergence of kingship among them; (ii) Munda society under kingship but before the imposition of British colonialism; (iii) Munda society under British colonialism; and (iv) Munda society in independent India. The account provided by Badgaiyan about the pre-British period resembles with those given by Sachchidananda and Thapar and Siddiqui.

The rent collectors in Chhotanagpur were recognized as Jagirdars (owners of land) after the British had taken over the Dewani of Bengal in 1765. The Jagirdars accelerated the process of expropriation of native owners of land. Ejection became an easy affair, and some proprietary cultivators were forced to become tenants and agricultural labourers. By the middle of the last century the number of Jagirdars had gone upto 600. In addition to rent, they imposed new taxes and levies. Badgaiyan writes: "Practorian obligations of service, gifts and presentation now became necessary for holding the land. Forced labour came to be extracted more and more. The Jagirdars introduced the *thekedars* to collect revenue. These *thekedars* used all their means and power to extract as much as they could from the tenants". Thus, three new classes, namely,

Jagirdars, *thekedars* and tenants emerged replacing the rent collectors and cultivators. With the intervention of the British, the moneylenders and the merchants also entered into socio-economic fabric of tribal life. Another dimension to social stratification among the tribes of middle India was added by the coming of Christianity as it brought about differentiation initially on religious basis and later on the basis of education, occupation and income. By the end of nineteenth century, the divide between the non-tribal elite and the tribal masses had become so wide that the Birsa movement emerged as a strong wave against the Hindus, Christians, Jagirdars, *thekedars* and colonialism.

Badgaiyan observes that by the end of the nineteenth century the tribal situation had become quite complex. For example, the Mundas had to deal with a number of other tribal groups like the Oraons, Hos and Cheros; they had also to deal with the non-tribal groups like the Hindus, Muslims, Sikhs and Christians and Birsaite sections from among themselves. These ethnic distinctions reflected to some extent status distinctions. The tribals who converted to Christianity were able to improve their socio-economic status by having modern education and white-collar employment, hence were generally considered superior than those who adhered to their traditional pattern of social life. All these developments accentuated the role of class in patterning of social relations. What Badgaiyan observes is that "the objective reality was thus characterized by a multiplicity of social groupings based on ethnicity and class, religion and language. But the Munda consciousness visualized this diversity falling into a trichotomy: tribals, *diku* and non-tribals but non-*dikus*".

Around this time, the word '*diku*' became quite expressive signifying non-tribal exploiters such as jagirdars, merchants and moneylenders. The character of the *dikus* has changed considerably after independence as the north Biharis employed in government departments are treated as *dikus* because they deprived the tribal people aspiring for white-collar jobs. In any case the word *diku* is used for the non-tribal exploiter of the tribal people. Thus, from the point of view of class, there are the classes of the exploiters and the exploited. However, both the classes are internally differentiated, hence no uniform pattern of exploitation. These outsiders also became local administrators and this too helped them in the oppression of the tribal people. But Singh (1978) takes a different view as he observes that the most of the tribal population in India was integrated within the administration of the provinces of British India or within that of the Indian states. He calls it the mode of protective administration. The administration established *chatties* along highways to supply the army which brought in merchants, traders and peddlers and set up cantonments and centres of administration and trade. The colonial system ended the relative isolation of the tribal society; brought it into the mainstream of the new administrative set-up, policies and programmes; but put an end to the political dominance of the tribes in the region; and roped the tribal communities which had been spared from the strain of the surplus generation by their states into a new system of production relations. Singh's observations thus do not synchronize with that of Sachchidananda and Badgaiyan. However, Singh makes a reference, though a passing one, about the dual policy followed by the *raj* as it strengthened the feudal crust on the one hand and the forces of market cutting the very roots of tribal economy and polity on the other. All these changes were reflected in social stratification. Let us now discuss the situation in the post-independence period.

Social Stratification Since Independence

K.S. Singh observes that the economic and political processes of tribal transformation get reflected in social stratification. Social stratification among tribes has always existed in various forms such as social and physical distance, notion of purity and pollution, prestige and status, habits and customs, and the like. The system of social stratification in the form of the feudatory chief Zamindars at the top, the well-to-do headmen in the middle and the general mass at the bottom has changed since independence. A class of insider *diku* and professional tribal moneylender as a result of the anti-land alienation laws has emerged in the post-independence period. A small section of the tribes has gone up in socio-economic hierarchy, and they are engaged in land transactions and moneylending.

In another context, Singh provides a four-fold classification of social movements with special reference to middle India. These movements are: (1) movements for political autonomy; (2) agrarian and forest-based movements; (3) sanskritization processes; and (4) cultural movements based on script and language. All these movements could be understood as efforts on the part of tribal society to find for itself a place of honour and status at least equal to other sections of Indian society. In other words, the tribal people expressed their anger against their political and economic suppression and also desired to move up in socio-cultural hierarchy as reflected in their efforts to convert and or adopt Christianity and Hindu way of life.

There are not many studies available on social stratification among the tribes in India. The Indian State has provisions in its constitution with regard to uplift of the tribal people living in different parts of India by reducing age-old socio-economic inequality. In the field of education, socio-economic and political awakening and employment part-successes have been achieved as a result of the policy of reservation of jobs, seats in educational institutions and earmarking of scheduled tribes' and scheduled castes' constituencies. The anticipated consequence of these provisions could be seen in new forms of socio-economic and political inequality between different tribal communities.

Sachchidananda seems to be (apparently though unintentionally) inclined towards an economic analysis of social stratification among the tribals of middle India. He writes: "Since the advent of colonial rule and the unrestricted movement of plainsmen into the tribal areas, the tribal population has been subjected to unemiting economic exploitation. Massive alienation of tribal lands to moneylenders and superior cultivating castes left the majority of agriculturists steeped in poverty and debt" (1990). Such a situation, characterized by isolation, economic backwardness, lack of education, social fragmentation, and distinctive ethnic, religious and linguistic affiliations, forced upon the state to declare the tribal people as a 'scheduled' category, providing them protective discriminatory treatment leading to their integration with the wider society in India. Sachchidananda's description of the tribal situation lacks requisite rigour as it neither makes use of the categories like class, class consciousness, class antagonism, change, relations of production and role of state, etc. nor it examines the role of ethnicity, isolation, assimilation, kinship, etc. as the main tools of his analysis. However, studies by Bose (1981), Pathy (1984) and Shah (1979, 1986) examine the tribal situation from the class perspective about which we would make a brief reference later on.

Sachchidananda (1990) reports that the weak impact of the measures taken by the Indian State for the welfare of the scheduled tribes has resulted into the continued dominance of the new outsiders as the colonial rulers have been replaced by the indigenous elites. The illegal transfer of land from tribals to non-tribals has become an established fact of life. Surplus land has not been distributed to the poor and deserving tribals. Even the land distributed is in fact so meagre and qualitatively so poor that it has not proved to be a viable source of livelihood. Industrialization has displaced the tribals as their lands have been taken over by the state. A large number of outsiders have again come to the tribal areas due to industrialization further widening the gap between the tribals and the non-tribals (*dikus*). Contractors, petty businessmen and government officials have taken strong roots in tribal society though still they look to be anachronisms and unwelcome elements. Even infrastructural facilities like roads, electricity and means of communication have been made available in the tribal areas keeping in view the needs of the outsiders rather than the tribal inhabitants. Education, employment and representation in legislative bodies from village panchayat to parliament through the policy of protective discrimination have created an elite section among the tribals rather than bringing about social mobility among the tribal masses.

Sachchidananda observes that "a significant impact of politico-economic change in independent India is the accentuation of social inequalities in tribal society." Sachchidananda's argument is that most tribal societies in middle India were egalitarian. Social stratification emerged among them in the pre-colonial and colonial periods in the form of semi-feudalism and exploitation by dividing the tribal society into the upper class and the commoners. The outside moneylenders were a third notable class which has been replaced by the inside *dikus* after independence. Social stratification is a relational and relative phenomenon, and therefore, it can be observed only in terms of relations between individuals, between individuals and groups and between groups over a period of time based on a certain value-frame. It has been reported earlier that social stratification has always existed among the tribes of India though its value-frame has changed from time to time. Social stratification existed not only between tribals and non-tribals, but it was also found among tribes, clans and lineages based on kinship—status, age, sex, hereditary—office, possessions, etc. After independence, education, employment and political power, though these are in a certain way interrelated phenomena, have become the main bases of social stratification among the tribal people. Since these did not exist earlier, their emergence after independence in a particular way cannot be taken as an accentuation of inequality. A small section of tribals has come directly close to the non-tribals through these new bases of social status, and some of the tribals have even gone higher than the non-tribal people based on these criteria. Other tribals have been beneficiaries at the seconendary and tertiary levels. A large number of tribals still remain unbenefited from these scarce resources like education, white-collar jobs and positions and offices of power. Class distinctions have crystallized among the tribals like the non-tribal people in terms of upper, middle and lower classes because all the people have not been benefited in equal measure, and it is hard to believe that a majority of the tribals have been harmed by the development process in the post-independence period. The high level of socio-political awakening among the Mundas, Oraons, Santhals, Hos, Bhils, Raj Gonds, Chaudharis, etc. is self-explanatory of their betterment compared to their own past during the British period.

The most important bases of social stratification among the tribes of middle India are ethnicity and class. Despite being interrelated aspects these are not found in the same proportions of interconnections and efficacy in all tribal societies. Tribal people who have been exposed more to the influences like Christianity, modern education, developmental programmes and industrialization would have more of *class* and *power* as the bases of status determination rather than ethnicity in the form of stratified lineages or clans. Let us have a look at these criteria in the context of the present-day tribal society.

Ethnicity

Ethnicity becomes distinctly observable if a community is viewed in terms of its independent existence rather than as an interdependent entity. The creation of scheduled areas, provisions for special measures for the development of tribal blocks, reservation for representation in parliament, state legislatures and local bodies and for admissions in schools and collages/universities and jobs have further strengthened the ethnic identities of the tribes of India.

Thus, in any given region, we may find ethnic differentiation within a given tribe in terms of the non-converts and the converts. The benefits accruing from adhering to one's own religion or from conversion to Hinduism, Christianity and Islam would determine to a large extent social status of the tribal people.

Fuchs (1977) is, however, right in his observation that most tribes are divided in two sections—a Hinduized upper section and a lower tribal section. He cites examples of the Gond (Raj Gond and Jungli Gond), Kokru (Muasi and Paharia), Bhilala (Bara Bhilala and Barela), Raj Banshi and others. Hinduized tribes have been relegated to the status of outcastes and untouchables. Only some tribes living in Chhotanagpur have developed some degree of consciousness and they also assert themselves almost equal to the non-tribal people. Fuchs shows his serious concern about adoption of the Hindu way of life by the tribes in central India, but his silence regarding conversion to Christianity speaks volumes of his approval. Fuchs also deplores the absence of a strong tribal solidarity among the aboriginals of central India. They do not have organizational support-base nor they are economically and socially well-placed.

Thapar and Siddiqui (1991) ask the question as to how tribal identity survived. Though they do not provide a complete answer but observe that the preservation of tribal identity was in part due to the nature of land relations. The expansion of tribal identity was to some extent watered down by the cultural legitimation of the tribal elite in terms of a wider Indian context (sanskritic courtly culture). With the emergence of a well established agricultural base and a network of trade connections not only further elaborated the system of social stratification but also weakened the exclusivity of tribal/ethnic identity. Thus, going by Thapar and Siddiqui's view, we may infer that the tribal identity was always coloured by economic differentiation and power hierarchy.

Class and ethnicity were inextricably intermixed in Chhotanagpur in the nineteenth century (Badgaiyan, 1986). In the context of the Mundas of Chhotanagpur, Badgaiyan mentions about *khutkatti* clan Mundas, non-*khutkatti* clan Mundas, non-Munda tribals and Hindu caste functionaries in the period before the emergence of kingship among them. The Munda and the Manki were not only heads of their clans and villages, respectively, but were also *khtkattidars*. Later on the *khutkatti* system was destroyed and replaced by Bhuinhari, Rajhas and Manjhihas tenures. There were non-tribal jagirdars in large number when the Munda society was under the system of kingship. Hinduism made inroads into the tribal heartland, and it was strengthened by the recruitment of Hindu militia and administrative staff. Brahmin priests and other functionaries found a convenient place for themselves with the patronage of the king as lower level feudatories, Hindu and Muslim merchants also found opportunities for trade and barter in the region.

In the first phase, new ethnic groups entered into the Munda society as a subordinate class, the producers of surplus; but in the second phase the class that entered was the subordinate class, the appropriators of surplus. Badgaiyan observes: "Entry of this new class radically changed the production relations. In order to justify and support the new production relations new concepts of ownership and authority as well as new ideology came to be imposed on the Munda society and polity". "The Munda themselves became greatly differentiated on class lines". Thus a new complexity arose between class and ethnicity. In fact, Badgaiyan also analyzes the patterns of dominance along with ethnicity and class. He refers to the subordination of all non-Munda ethnic groups in the early period followed by the subordination of the Mundas by a dominant section of the immigrant ethnic groups. The ethnic divide gets further blurred by sharing of class positions by the Mundas with the non-Mundas. There were Munda Zamindars and non-Munda Zamindars, and there were similarly Munda tenants and non-Munda tenants. Perhaps ethnicity has an edge over class because "relations between non-Munda Jagirdars and Munda tenants were reported to be far more strained and antagonistic than those obtaining between Munda jagirdars and Munda tenants". However, Badgaiyan infers a somewhat different conclusion from such a situation. He writes: "This leads one to hypothesize that agrarian relations are more strained when class stratification is compounded with ethnic differentiation." We may make two observations here: (i) the Munda Jagirdars had a legitimacy of their rule much before the non-Mundas encroached upon the tribal areas as jagirdars, hence they were not acceptable to the Mundas as their masters; and (ii) the strained relations between the Munda tenants and the non-Munda Jagirdars symbolized the non-acceptance of the alien rulers on the Munda land.

The ethnic structure of the Mundas became further weak due to two factors: (i) the British takeover of Bengal in 1765 (Bihar was part of Bengal); and (ii) Christianity. Rack-renting and ejection from Rajhas and Manjhihas land became frequent reducing the Mundas to the status of tenants and agricultural labourers. Forced labour was almost a routine activity. *Thekedars* as collectors of revenue were a new institution in the system of exploitation. Thus, with Jagirdars, *thekedars*, British administrators, money-lenders and merchants, the authority of Mundas and Mankis deteriorated further. Earlier Hinduism and later on Christianity proved to be an attack on the ethnically monolithic character of the Mundas as a community. The Birsa movement was a direct reaction to the onslaught committed on the Mundas by the British administration and Christianity.

Ethnic situation had become quite complex as the tribal groups came closer to each other and they also dealt with the non-tribal groups like the Hindus, Muslims, Sikhs, and Christians. Besides this, the Mundas had Hindu, Christian and Birsaite sections among themselves. Badgaiyan observed that it was not that everything was seen in terms of ethnicity alone. Social relations were defined by both ethnicity and class. Mundas and Hindus both had Jagirdars and tenants. Ethnicity was thus not coterminous with class. Objectively, there were several groupings based on ethnicity and class, religion and language. The Mundas perceived, according to Badgaiyan, three main groups, namely, tribals, *dikus* and non-tribals but non-*dikus*. Ethnicity and class coexist among the Mundas. Badgaiyan writes: "In the light of the behaviour of the Munda tenants and agricultural proletariats with regard to Munda and Hindu Jagirdars, it can be said that the ethnic solidarity is diluted by class differentiation and class hostility is heightened by ethnic differentiation." Class solidarity is eroded by ethnic differentiation. Identity of both class and ethnicity has resulted in greater solidarity among the Mundas. Today the question is: Whether ethnicity represents a bundle of primordial sentiments and ties or is it an identity which is contextually manipulated? Many a times ethnicity is articulated and twisted according to the compulsions of given situations. Badgaiyan writes: "Ethnicity is not just having a set of external attributes. It is essentially a question of subjective perception. It is this subjective perception that gives people a sense of belonging to an ethnic group." Members of one ethnic group could belong to more than one class, and members of one class could belong to more than one identity at a given point of time, and they may not be in mutual harmony.

Ethnicity in the context of wider socio-political and economic development has acquired a great deal of instrumental significance. Measures like the constitutional provisions and reservations and special schemes for development have strengthened rather than weakened the ethnic and primordial solidarities among the scheduled tribes. It is felt by the articulate section of the tribal people that they could persist with the existing benefits and also demand more and better amenities for their development by asserting their ethnic unity and solidarity as expressly as possible. In this way 'ethnicity' among tribes and 'caste' among Hindus have become a convenient means of political mobilization. Sachchidananda (1990) does not find any real contradiction between elaboration of stratification and hardening of ethnicity. Though apparently the two seem to be antithetical to each other, but in real life they are found in specific contexts without being antagonistic. Diversification and development impinge upon the monolithic character of the tribal society, hence weakening of ethnic solidarity becomes a logical and natural consequence, but 'ethnicization' is brought in by making best possible efforts to ensure availability of maximum benefits from the processes of development.

Expression of ethnic identity depends upon the contexts and the issues at a particular point of time. Lack of intertribal solidarity has always been one of the serious obstacles in achieving the most urgent common ends. Different tribes have not come together to share the same platform mainly because of the perception of exclusivity of one tribe and a sense of pride of being superior or at least not inferior compared to any other tribe. Mobilization even against the non-tribal people has suffered from such perceptions regarding intertribal and intratribal relations and notions of superiority and inferiority. However, ethnic identity has found its place in different spheres of life such as language, education, politics and culture. Students have formed from time to time associations and unions comprising *adivasis* alone.

A detailed treatment of the 'tribal question' in Chhotanagpur is provided by Weiner (1978) as a part of his study of *Sons of the Soil: Migration and Ethnic Conflict in India*. One gets the impression from Weiner's study that the main cause of the backwardness among the *adivasis* is economic as he emphasizes on the problems of land alienation, exploitation by *dikus* (earlier moneylenders and Zamindars and now white-collar workers, politicians and traders and businessmen), unemployment, etc. This explanation is based on the perceptions of the tribals themselves about their own problems. Their perceptions about the outsiders and their impact on politics in the region have been considered by Weiner as the basis of his argument in regard to what he calls 'tribal encounters' for analyzing relationship between tribals and migrants. The economic problem forced the tribals to emigrate in large numbers to work as plantation labourers in Assam and Bengal. Ethnicity is reflected in some of the statements made by the respondents. All *dikus* were Bihari Hindus and that they (tribals) were exploited by the Bihari landlords. The tribals lost their lands to non-tribals. Weiner observes that some well-to-do tribals who have acquired land, and some of them are themselves substantial money-lenders are not hated by the tribal folk. In fact, some tribals feel proud of their wealthy tribals, whereas they express antagonism against the wealthy non-tribals. Thus, Weiner clearly advocates an ethnicist perspective rather than a structural view for analyzing relations between tribals and nontribals. He writes: "given a choice, people prefer to hate others because of their religion, race, caste, or tribe, rather than because of their wealth. The wealthy in one's own community is a source of vicarious pride. The status (and accomplishment) of members of one's own community provides self-esteem to all members of the community. For this reason, it is not easy to create class cleavages and class parties in a multiethnic society except where class and ethnic cleavages coincide. Class antagonisms then become veiled expressions of ethnic hostility. This is probably why ideological parties of the left based upon class appeal have not done very well in India, and why peasant revolts against landlords are more likely to occur when the peasants and landlords belong to different religions or castes, or one is tribal and the other is not".

Migration of the tribals from their native places has certainly weakened ethnic bondage because class differentiation forces to treat themselves also as unskilled workers, mechanics, clerks, teachers, rural, semi-rural and urban inhabitants etc. Some tribals have become professionals like university teachers, doctors, engineers, lawyers, social workers and politicians. Professionals from among the tribals identify themselves more with the non-tribal middle class people rather than with the rest of the tribal people. Weiner overemphasizes the ethnic perspective undermining the role of class and power in weakening the ethnic character of the tribals on one hand and socio-political differentiation among the tribes on the other. All the queries made by Weiner refer to the ethnic question. Some of the questions are as follows:

(1) Why have the tribals remained 'backward'?

(2) Why are they looked down upon by non-tribals?

(3) Why have they not moved into skilled positions in industry, or into managerial posts?
(4) Why have they not successfully competed against the migrants who have moved into Chhotanagpur?
(5) What can be done to change the situation?.

Certainly, ethnicity holds its strong ground among the tribes of India, but it is also a fact that as a result of some reforms, administrative measures and implementation of given policies, ethnicity has become visibly weak and class differentiation has surfaced significantly. Therefore, a simple formulation referring to tribals versus non-tribals or local people versus outsiders in the context of jobs and opportunities forecloses the analysis of the role of class and power in the context of social changes since independence. Without any conscious effort, class differentiation itself brings about detribalization among the tribes of India. Conversions to Christianity and Islam and impact of Hinduism and other cultural forces have already shown a great deal of detribalization. The Christian tribals are superior to the non-converts in socio-structural terms. The Hinduized tribes consider themselves culturally superior to the non-converts as they have adopted vegetarianism and have discarded drinking of alcohol.

Despite conversion to Christianity, the ethnic dimension remains intact though in a somewhat new and changed form. Conversion to Christianity has brought about 'double allegiance' among the tribals as they are unable to forget their past and simultaneously they are made to be a part of a new world-view, namely, Christianity. This double identity, though broadens economic and socio-cultural base of the converts, but they are not able to get out of ethnic bondage in larger sense of the term. Most of the educated tribals converted to Christianity have/had their training in theology and have remained attached to one or other church. Missionary schools, colleges and other organizations have invited strong reactions in which some of these convert educated tribals are employed.

Class

Economic and political processes, accompanied by urbanization, industrialization and political awakening, have brought about visible differentiation among tribal people on class lines. Singh (1985) observes: "The major thrust of change has been from tribes into peasants. By the end of the eighteenth century communities of peasantized tribals had emerged in Assam, Rajasthan, middle India, etc." A hierarchy of land tenures in the form of tribal chiefs and occupancy tenants emerged with the coming of the British administration. Taking over of the forests from the control of the tribals made them to work as manual workers. With the emergence of industrialization in post-independence period tribal people have also become unskilled, semi-skilled and skilled workers in industries. A class of well-off non-tribal people coexisted with the tribals in the form of moneylenders, shopkeepers and white-collar workers. These non-tribals are now expressly considered as 'outside exploiters'. Class differentiation is a double-edged phenomenon because there has been a differential impact of the factors and forces of social change due to the uneven nature of intratribal and intertribal situations. As a result of this, we can find today hunting and food-gathering tribal people on the one end of the continuum and highly educated people engaged in government jobs and other lucrative persuits on the other. Thus, there is no uniform principle of hierarchization among the tribes of middle India. The differentiation between various tribes and between the families of a tribe in a given context indicate clearly that different segments of tribes and specific families have carved out particular 'social spaces' or placements for themselves. In many ways, they resemble with each other and also with the non-tribals though in varying degrees. Neither all tribal people have been equally involved in class and power struggles against their oppressors nor have they been benefited uniformly from the positive consequences of those collective or semi-collective mobilizations. But all tribals were not oppressed or deprived of in the same manner, hence their involvement in the emancipatory efforts has also varied. Some of these points have remained unattended in most of the studies of class and power among the tribes of middle India.

Observations made by Thapar and Siddiqui (1991) seem to be quite convincing about connection between socio-cultural and politico-economic dimensions among the Mundas in ancient period. They write: "The more fundamental changes however related to rights over land. The axis shifted from clan to territory: tenurial rights based on kinship were encroached upon by those based on professional services. The Raja granted lands and villages on perpetual tenures of military, administrative and personal services—the services required by the infrastructure of a state. The grantees were appointed to appropriate the maximum rights". Certainly, a distinction existed between the lineage lands or *bhuinhari* and the *rajhus* lands. Thapar and Siddiqui report presence of *manjhas* (grantee), *rajhus* (crown) and Kanwars, Thakurs and Lallas (who were given maintenance grants), and retainers. Thus, along with ethnic (clan, lineage) stratification, a quite elaborate class stratification existed. They write: "Thus, the tendency towards social stratification which had already begun with the *khutkatti* system was not only intensified and accelerated under the state, but was also made more complex with the interpolation of various levels of intermediaries". Now, from lineage, economic and political functions passed into the hands of professionals outside the lineage. A new nexus emerged between social status, landholding and power, though lineage still did not become defunct. It is evident from this account that feudalism had taken over the tribal society and the classes mentioned above also existed in the princely states till India achieved her independence.

The hypothesis put forward by Thapar and Siddiqui regarding decline of ethnicity and emergence of class relations also finds substantiation in Badgaiyan's systematic historical analysis of 'class and ethnicity' among the Mundas of Chhotanagpur. Badgaiyan provides a detailed account of the simultaneous emergence of feudalism and complex class structure among the Mundas, and observes that "social relations were defined not entirely by ethnic membership. They were influenced also by the class structure." However, the two were not coterminous nor were they reducible to each other. Another important point in Badgaiyan's analysis is regarding what he calls "objective reality and subjective dispositions" particularly in the context of *dikus* (exploiters) in Chhotanagpur. The Mundas consider all the non-tribal exploiters despite their ethnic and class differences as *dikus*. "The definition of an objective situation is subjective" (1986). The tribal exploiters today and earlier the tribal jagirdars have/had not been perceived as *dikus*. Thus, the objective reality and its subjective perception do not necessarily coincide, and therefore class and ethnicity coexist in certain respects and cut across each other in some contexts. When class and ethnicity are perceived in consonance, there is greater solidarity among the tribal people. Leaders of various tribal movements generally strive to emphasize on such an accord between ethnicity and class.

A large number of researchers observe that in the pre-British period with the encroachment of feudalism on tribal life, the process of emergence of a new class structure set in replacing the tribal patriarchal clannish system rooted into the *khutkatti* system of land tenure. Thus, feudal classes such as Raja, Jagirdars, grantees, *bhuinhars*, retainers, tenants on the one hand, and priests, merchants, moneylenders and masses emerged on the other. Such a change affected significantly the tribal polity too. Sachchidananda (1990) observes that the political authority of the head of the *parha* (confederation of villages) disappeared, and many Mundas migrated to other parts of tribal Bihar where they could retain their traditional institutions. In Madhya Pradesh and Orissa too, individual ownership of land had become a fact of life. The British used some traditional/hereditary village officers for collecting revenue by granting them powers of a police force. In Bihar, *munda, manki* and *majhi* thus became once again powerful under the British patronage. But the market forces further more rapidly accentuated in the British period along with new administrative system. Land alienation, moneylenders' usurious practices, heterogeneity brought in by the influx of non-tribal communities and new categories of people like traders, contractors and petite administrative officials not only proved a serious blow to the precolonial tribal system, but also accentuated two-pronged class-based stratification between the tribals and the non-tribals and among the tribals. Now one could easily find among the tribals proprietary tenants, tenants-at-will, sharecroppers and landless agricultural and manual workers. The classes other than these were formed by the non-tribals to a large extent. These included government employees and officers, professionals like doctors, lawyers and professors and merchants and traders. The post-independence period has witnessed strengthening of this class structure, and side by side some new communities and social categories too have acquired an access to some scarce and much desired positions and offices. The new political system has certainly created a class of tribal power elite. This new class is largely a transformation of the class of educated tribals of pre-independence period who were engaged in various reform and other movements and also employed as professionals and administrative workers.

Socially and culturally, the tribals have not assimilated to a considerable extent with the non-tribals. Conversions and adoptions of other religions and practices have created somewhat limited cleavages among the tribals rather than restructuring the tribal society. But this is not true in the same way about economic and political relations among the tribals and of the tribals with the non-tribals. Class structure and relations among the tribals resemble with the non-tribals, and so are power relations. The hiatus between the socio-cultural and politico-economic structures and relations could be attributed to the differential impact of macro-structural forces and factors which was perhaps intended by the colonial rulers and it is persisting even today because of the policies pursued by the Indian State since independence. Ethnicity has thus remained a force to reckon with for mobilizing the *adivasis* against the atrocious class structure which was superimposed upon them by the pre-colonial and the colonial rulers and continues to be there to a great extent even after independence.

Some recent studies of social stratification among tribal people highlight on class hierarchy and its socio-cultural consequences. A study of the Chaudhari tribe in Surat district of Gujarat by Shah (1979) shows the presence of four economic strata on the basis of occupation and ownership of land. These strata are: (i) agricultural labourers and poor cultivators; (ii) middle cultivators;

(iii) rich cultivators; and (iv) white-collar employees. The first three constitute more than 92 per cent of the total working population of the Chaudharis, while in the fourth category there are less than 3 per cent people. Shah (1991) writes: "Labourers and poor cultivators are at the bottom of the occupational hierarchy. It is the single largest stratum, constituting 61 per cent of cultivators, of which 24 per cent are almost landless and 37 per cent have land between one and five acres. Their main source of livelihood is manual labour." Shah provides other details about economic life of this largest segment of the Chaudharis of Gujarat. Of the middle cultivators 33 per cent own land between five and 15 acres. These are a better off section as 20 per cent of them have wells for irrigation and half of them have diesel or electric pumps. They use chemical fertilizers, and about 70 per cent of them have a pair of bullocks. Rich cultivators are about 5 per cent and own more than 16 acres of land. They are better off than the middle and poor cultivators. They have electric or diesel pumpsets, use chemical fertilizers, hire wage labourers, produce for market, and their womenfolk and children are educated and do not do manual work even on their own farms. All these three classes are related to agriculture though unevenly and enjoy different social statuses. The white-collar workers who are about 3 per cent of the population are engaged in non-agricultural white-collar jobs, particularly in lower level school teaching. Besides teachers, there are also clerks, postmen, *talatis*, *gram sevaks*, extension officers, etc. Some are employed in co-operative societies in various capacities. "Middle and rich cultivators dominate the stratum of educated white-collar employees."

In another study of stratification among the scheduled tribes in the Bharuch and Panch Mahals districts of Gujarat, Shah (1986) observes that status distinction based on achievement in such respects as wealth, property, income, occupation, education and power is emerging, and it is similar considerably with the pattern in the wider Indian society. Status determination based on ethnicity is being slowly replaced by the new criteria such as wealth, income, occupation, education and power. Economic and educational aspects and style of life are today the bases of newly emerging stratification. Differences in these aspects between the tribals and the non-tribals and within the tribals would provide an objective assessment of social stratification. The categories and groups in these two districts are more or less the same as Shah has found in Surat district. Different tribes are divided on the basis of interests. Besides land as the principal basis, there are differences of status based on education and life-style. Stratification is reflected in almost all aspects of social life of the tribal people. Contradictory changes have also been noted. Some have become quite rich and better-off, and others have slided down in class hierarchy. However, change in social stratification has not been uniform in Bharuch and Panch Mahals districts. Shah observes as follows: "There is sharper stratification in Bharuch than in Panch Mahals. The number of landless labourers is larger in the former area than in the latter district. The rich and the middle peasants of Bharuch purchased more land than their counterparts in Panch Mahals. So is the case with government benefits. The differences in life-style between the rich and the middle peasants on the one hand, and the poor peasants and the labourers on the other, are more widespread and sharper in Bharuch. These differences are perhaps because of uneven development in the two districts. Because the one which is more developed grows faster and develops sharper stratification, inequality increases and becomes sharp with development."

From both these studies of three districts of Gujarat, namely, Surat, Bharuch and Panch Mahals, Shah concludes that there is nothing like an all-India tribal culture and world-view. Tribals are also not isolated from the non-tribal people. It is a fact that they have become highly differentiated, socially and economically, and in certain respects the persisting socio-economic distinctions between them and the non-tribals have also accentuated mainly due to uneven consequences of lopsided development policies and their faulty execution. Despite this the tribal people are being 'integrated' with the wider society though not in a uniform manner. The better off tribals, namely, the middle class Chaudharis of Surat, have developed a certain commonness, cutting across tribal boundaries, with their counterparts of other tribes, in social and cultural matters and in life-styles. In fact, middle and rich cultivators as well as the middle class (white-collar workers) do not have a clash of interests, hence commonalty of attitudes and aspirations for further betterment of their status.

Bose (1981) also identifies four main classes among tribes in Gujarat, though mainly based on landholdings. These are: rich peasants, middle peasants, poor peasants, and agricultural labourers, and these have also been found by several researchers among the non-tribals as well. A given tribe is generally distributed among all the four classes. However, all the tribes are not the same as some are better off than others, and accordingly the proportions of different classes would also be different. Bose reports that the tribes in Gujarat today are equally affected by the processes of planned and unplanned change and by the continuous structural and institutional shifts in rural India. He writes: "They are stratified in terms of control over resources," hence the above mentioned four classes. This class hierarchy is reflected in all aspects of tribal life including education and political power. But Bose does not highlight the emerging patterns of social mobility among tribals brought about by developmental programmes and education as we find it in the two studies of three districts of Gujarat by Shah. Pathy's study (1984) of five tribal villages in Gujarat is similar in terms of its framework and methodology. The five economic categories in Pathy's study are: landlords, rich peasants, middle peasants, small peasants and farm workers. The distribution and characteristic features of these classes are the same as we find in the study conducted by Shah and Bose. It seems that in a broad sense, the studies of class stratification among the tribes of Gujarat reinforce each other. While referring to an earlier study by Pathy, *Political Economy of Kandhaland in Orissa*, Shah (1986) observes that "there is a case for closer examination in the tribal communities." Further, Shah finds that the rich have become richer, and the poor poorer, because of 'free competition' among the unequal competitors.

Roy Burman (1989) emphasizes on both class and ethnicity perspectives, but he does not spell out the nexus between class and ethnicity and status and class. The notion of status is inherently present in the ethnic identity and kinship system of the tribal society. In a recently published (edited) volume, Bhadra and Mondal

(1991) also emphasize the role of class and ethnicity as the main bases of social stratification in North-East India. There are tribes like Meenas of Rajasthan which have hardly any tribal features in terms of ethnicity and class, and yet they are scheduled as tribes. The Tharus of Bihar have all the prerequisites for being scheduled as a tribe, but they are not scheduled as such.

Singh though admits the emergence of social stratification as a historical reality created by the colonial administration and the processes of sanskritization and conversion to Christianity, but observes that "there are also contrary pulls in the opposition direction. The bonds of ethnicity and the appreciation of the political advantages of the tribe as an ethnic minority are still strong" (1985). This view is also shared by Sachchidananda. He writes while commenting on the class approach of Pathy: "These economic categories may be considered classes only in a limited sense; ethnic consciousness dominates over class consciousness. Similarly, production relations cannot be clearly characterized as feudal or capitalist. Primordial forms of slavery, revolving indebtedness of small peasants and agricultural labourers for consumption loans, the lack of a free labour market, forced labour, labour exchange, institutional credit and some commodity production confuse the total picture" (1990). But the question is: Do these four or five classes not exist among the tribes of Gujarat, Bihar or Rajasthan? Are they simply 'constructions' and not identifiable groups of people? Kulkarni (1979) observes that the question of class in the tribal society is more pervasive than the caste- tribal approach. Class interests do not obey caste or tribal boundaries (Sengupta, 1980). Land alienation is a class question. The demand for the formation of Jharkhand State is a class question. The 'tribal question', the 'forest-question' are all questions of 'class interests'. The forest policy in India in its present form serves the capitalists rather than the poor (Guha, 1983). 'Tribal unrest' is a class question. Both positive and negative consequences of the role performed by law and the state refer to the question of class in terms of gainers and loosers, more gainers and less gainers, more loosers and less loosers and so on. Thus, there are three viewpoints regarding ethnicity and class as the bases of social stratification: (i) mainly ethnicity, (ii) mainly class, and (iii) both class and ethnicity.

Concluding Remarks

Social stratification among the tribes of India is different compared to the non-tribes to the extent the tribal people are dissimilar in terms of their history, level of economic development and impact of modern forces of social change. Several studies of social stratification bring out the convergence of ethnicity and class as the main basis of status distinctions within and between different tribes. However, emphasis on ethnicity and class as exclusive bases of social stratification remains central to some scholars who look at the tribal social stratification either in terms of ethnic reality or as an economic phenomenon—a part of global class formation.

The *raj* created new structures and institutions and thereby provided a new system of social stratification. Landlords, contractors and money-lenders were alien to the tribal society before the advent of the British. Differentiation of the peasantry in terms of tenure-holders, tenants-at-will and jagirdars was also created by the British. A class of outside exploiters in terms of Zamindars and moneylenders was not known to the tribals till the British took over the forests.

Since Independence ethnicity is being viewed in a changed form as a means of mobilizing the tribal people with a view to have access to economic and political opportunities. Intertribal and tribal-non-tribal distinctions on the one hand and processes of conversion and initiation on the other are being highlighted by the tribals as the basis for demanding special treatment by the government. However, the tribals are not an exclusive component in India's fast changing social situation. A new middle class is emerging among them like the one we find among the non-tribals.

Ethnicity is on decline on the one hand, and it is being revived in myraid ways on the other. Detribalization and ethnicization coexist today both as a reality and as a strategy for change. Uniformity is not found in regard to convergence between ethnicity and class. Processes of socio-cultural and structural transformation are also not uniform in different parts of India. At the same time, now the 'forest question' and the 'tribal question' are being considered more as class questions. The phenomenon of power and dominance is increasingly dependent upon the questions of ethnicity and class.

References

Badgaiyan, S.D., 'Class and Ethnicity: Chhotanagpur in the 19th Century', in K.L. Sharma (ed.), *Social Stratification in India*, Delhi:Manohar Publications, 1986, pp. 293-308.

Beteille, Andre, *Six Essays in Comparative Sociology*, Delhi:Oxford University Press, 1974.

Bhadra, R.K. and Mondal, S.R. (eds.), *Stratification, Hierarchy and Ethnicity in North-East India*, Delhi: Daya Publishing House, 1991.

Bose, P.K., 'Stratification among Tribals in Gujarat', *EPW*, Vol. XVI, No. 6, February 7, 1981, pp. 191-196.

Doshi, S.L., 'Ethnicity and Class among the Bhils of Rajasthan', in K.L. Sharma (ed.), *Social Stratification in India*, Manohar Publications, Delhi, 1986, pp. 309-326.

Doshi, S.L., *Tribal Ethnicity, Class and Integration*, Jaipur: Rawat Publications, 1990.

Fuchs, Stephen, 'Central Indian Tribes' in Romesh Thapar (ed.), *Tribe, Caste and Religion*, Delhi: The Macmillan Co. of India, 1977, pp. 47-53.

Guha, Ramchandra, 'Forestry in British and Post-British India: A Historical Analysis', *EPW*, Vol. XVIII, Nos. 44, 45 & 46, 1983.

Kulkarni, S.D., 'Class and Caste in Tribal Movement', *EPW*, Vol. XIV, Nos. 7 & 8, Annual No., February 1979, pp. 465-68.

———, 'Adivasis, Law and Social Justice', *EPW*, Vol. XX, No. 28, 1985, pp. 1171-1174.

Majumdar, D.N., *A Tribe in Transition:A Study in Culture Pattern*, Longmans, 1937, quoted from Andre Beteille (1974).

Oraons, Martin, 'A Tribal People in an Industrial Setting', in A.R. Desai (ed.), *Rural Sociology in India*, Bombay: Popular Prakashan, 1969, pp. 232-241.

Pathy, Jagnath, *Tribal Peasantry:Dynamics of Development*, New Delhi:Inter-India Publications, 1984.

Roy Burman, B.K., 'Challenges and Responses in Tribal India', in M.S.A. Rao (ed.), *Social Movements in India*, Delhi:Manohar Publications, 1984, pp. 319-340.

———, 'Problems and Prospects of Tribal Development in North-East India', *EPW*, Vol. XXIV, No. 13, April 1, 1989, pp. 693-697.

Sachchidananda, *Profiles of Tribal Culture in Bihar*, Calcutta:K.L. Mukhopadhyay, 1965.

———, 'Patterns of Politico-Economic Change among Tribals in Middle India' in Francine R. Frankel and M.S.A. Rao (ed.), *Dominance and State Power in Modern India: Decline of a Social Order*, Delhi:Oxford University Press, 1990, pp. 278- 320.

Sengupta, Nirmal, 'Class and Tribe in Jharkhand', *EPW*, Vol. XV, No. 4, 1980, pp. 664-671.

Sengupta, Nirmal (ed.), *Fourth World Dynamics:Jharkhand*, Delhi: Authors Guild Publications, 1982.

Shah, Ghanshyam, 'Tribal Identity and Class Differentiations:A Case Study of the Chaudhari Tribe', *EPW*, Annual Number, Vol. XIV, Nos. 7 & 8, February, 1979, pp. 459-69.

———, 'Stratification among the Scheduled Tribes in the Bharuch and Panch Mahals Districts of Gujarat', in S.C. Malik (ed.), *Determinants of Social Status in India*, Delhi: Moti Lal Banarsidas, 1986, pp. 149-183.

———, Social Movements in India: A Review of the Literature, New Delhi: Sage Publications, 1990.

Singh, K.S., 'Colonial Transformation of Tribal Society in Middle India', *EPW*, Vol. XIII, No. 30, 1978, pp. 1221-32.

———, *Tribal Society in India:An Anthropo-Historical Perspective*, Delhi: Manohar Publications, 1985.

Sinha, Surajit, 'Tribe-Caste and Tribe-Peasant Continua in Central India,' *Man in India*, Vol. 45, No. 1, 1965.

Thapar, Romila and Siddiqui, Majid Hayat, 'Tribals in History: The Case of Chhotanagpur', in Dipankar Gupta (ed.), *Social Stratification*, Delhi: Oxford University Press, 1991, pp. 419-430.

Vidyarthi, L.P., 'Tribal Ethnography in India', *A Survey of Research in Sociology and Social Anthropology*, Vol. III, ICSSR, Popular Prakashan, Bombay, 1974, pp. 31-133.

Weiner, Myron, *Sons of the Soil, Migration and Ethnic Conflict in India*, Princeton:Princeton University Press, 1978.

9

Levels of Mobility in Caste Structure

Four viewpoints about mobility in caste structure could be ascertained. Firstly, Srinivas (1966) has emphasized the need for sanskritization and westernization as conceptual tools for understanding mobility in caste system. He holds that 'corporate mobility' still remains basic at the caste or *jati* level, as familial mobility does not obtain public recognition. Secondly, on the contrary, Stein (1968) points out that the mobility of families and individuals was pronounced in medieval South India, and this should help to analyze and understand the present-day mobility in caste structure. Thirdly, Marriott (1968) thinks that caste could be understood within the frames of reference, such as the rural versus metropolitan and traditional *varna* versus modern national frames of reference for ranking. And fourthly, Lynch (1968) and Damle (1968) apply *reference group* theory to understand caste and individual mobilities in India.

These approaches to caste mobility are singularistic and do not encompass the totality of mobility taking place today in caste system. One would agree with Lynch's observation that there was no agreement about the conception of caste and the units that structure it. If such an ambiguity persists, then the units which move, remain unclear. I would further agree with Lynch that mobility within the caste system is not really distinguished from change of the system. Change within or between castes does not necessarily constitute mobility within the caste system, unless one accepts mobility as the only significant kind of change in Indian society. A more meaningful form of mobility should entail changes in ritual hierarchy than the enhanced power position of a particular caste.

The above approaches to caste mobility are inadequate as none of them is singularly adequate enough to explain the entire gamut of mobility in the caste system. Sanskritization covers only socio-cultural aspects of change and confines to 'group mobility' of a caste. It does not take a note of individual frontiers of mobility and the motives and factors that underlie such mobility. Stein's analysis of mobility in medieval India is no doubt quite meaningful and adds a new dimension to the understanding of caste system, but it has undermined the strength of caste ethnocentrism or group solidarity based on caste allegiance. Marriott's approach is, in fact, 'confusing', and its application remains ununderstandable in terms of rural versus metropolitan caste categories. The analyses of Lynch and Damle are undoubtedly an addition to the analysis of caste mobility, but how to transform a 'culture bound', ad hoc concept of sanskritization into a structural one, and how to explain structural changes and their implicit and explicit repercussions on caste mobility through the reference group theory, remain unclear.

Here it could be proposed that mobility in caste structure could be understood better if we analyze it at different levels namely, family, group and individual. This would also remove the ambiguity about the units which move or do not move. This further helps in delineating the extent of mobility and also the quality and quantum of mobility. A distinction between caste and non-caste structures (Heibert, 1969) also becomes relevant in this context, and their interrelationship becomes understandable. These three levels of mobility encompass the entirety of mobility in the caste system. Mobility at the familial level could be better explained in terms of repercussions of structural reforms. Reference group theory helps in the analysis of mobility at the level of individual, and corporate mobility is better understandable by the concept of sanskritization and other related concepts.

Levels of Mobility

There are three important levels at which mobility takes place in caste structure: (1) mobility of one or a minority of families within a caste to a higher/lower position; (2) mobility of a group or majority of families within a caste to a higher or lower position; and (3) mobility of individual members within a family belonging to certain caste(s). These levels of mobility in the caste structure indicate that mobility takes place at individual, family and group levels. Mobility in caste structure at these levels takes place simultaneously. Mobility at one level is not in contrast with the same process at other levels. The same family may bear mobility at all the three levels. This is also true for other two levels. Thus, mobility in caste structure is both interrelated and discrete.

Mobility of a Minority of Families within a Caste

Mobility at the level of family is inspired by differential privileges and positions that families and individuals enjoy in the village community. Families of the same caste, of other castes in the same village and of other villages and towns may operate as reference points for mobility at the family level. Mobility at the family level depends basically upon the attributes of the family concerned without necessarily being determined by the rank of a caste. All the families belonging to a caste do not possess a common set of attributes which may enable them equally to have mobility. Thus, the families within the same caste witness differential patterns of mobility without any change in caste structure. Such a mobility accentuates 'class-like' differentiation (Leach, 1960) within the hitherto same social group (caste). These increased distinctions of status and prestige may be termed as 'positional' changes (Srinivas, 1966) within the segments of the village community. These changes in the direction of upward status mobility are basically achievement-oriented, however, role of ascriptive determinants, such as, caste rank, family background, landed property, etc. cannot be overlooked and undermined.

Improvement of economic and social position through more agricultural production, business, prestigious occupations and education contribute to enhancement of status of certain families. In our study of six villages in Rajasthan, we have noted that some families of the Brahmins have taken up higher income providing and lucrative jobs by achieving higher education. In Bawari village, a science graduate is an agriculture extension officer. Three families from Bhutera village have established business at Delhi. In Harmara, three families have got educated all the adult male members and secured white-collar jobs for them. This is true for some families of Roopgarh and Murwara as well.

Similarly, some families of Rajputs, Charans and Banias in Roopgarh, Sabalpura and Harmara have elevated their positions in terms of both improvement in economic position and higher education. In Roopgarh, for example, leaving aside the families which have graduates and matriculates, there are families which having engineers, university teachers and persons in all-India services. In Harmara, a Bania is a medical doctor, and a Charan is an engineer. Such a mobility based on higher education and consequent higher occupation and income is mainly confined to the upper castes and class people.

Mobility at the level of family among the intermediate castes, however, is of a slightly different nature. It is not higher education and corresponding higher occupation, income and prestige that determine mobility in the case of the families of the Jats, Gujars, Malis, Khatis, Ahirs and Gadarias. Enhancement of economic position in the case of these castes is through more land and more income providing occupations. For example, fifteen families of the Jats have manoeuvred more than 100 acres of land at the time of the abolition. These families have built up *pucca* houses and spent conspicuously on marriages and other occasions during the last fifteen years. Some families of these castes run petty shops in towns and this has enhanced their economic status. There are, however, some families which have a few members as school teachers, police constables, and the like.

Such a mobility is, however, relatively absent among the lower and 'untouchable' castes. This is mainly due to their poor family background and low caste ranks. The exceptions are of a Nai telephone operator and a school teacher in Roopgarh and a Gadaria railway inspector in Murwara. Mobility at group level is more pervasive and pronounced among these castes.

As a result of mobility in caste structure at the level of family, horizontal status distinctions have increased and some significant patterns in regard to dress, use of utensils, house type, hospitality, expenditure on marriages and food, etc. have emerged. Use of costly clothes, *saris* (in place of traditional dress), stainless steel utensils, furniture have become a status symbol for these families.

Mobility at this level does not bear a corporate basis. In fact, some families have mobilized their respective resources individually to improve their status. They might have felt frustrated regarding their status comparing it with their own status in the past or to the status of other communities and families in the other villages and towns. The families which did not have resources to enhance their status enjoyed lower status within the same caste. Such status polarizations refer to a class-like horizontal distinctions (Majumdar, 1958). Status mobility of such a character cannot be termed as 'vertical mobility', because vertical mobility implies lessening of status distinctions. Vertical mobility brings about perceptible reduction in hierarchical distance as the lower takes the place of its immediate higher castes. Such a process of mobility in course of time generates hopes for an equalitarian character of society. But this is not happening in India. Caste structure remains more or less the same in spite of structural changes induced through structural innovations.

Mobility at the family level, which is of horizontal (class-like) nature, cannot be explained with the concepts of sanskritization and westernization or secularization. Because these concepts do not take a cognizance of motivations and aspirations of these few families. Sanskritization is essentially an analytical tool in the context of group mobility and particularly with reference to 'dominant caste' (Srinivas, 1959). As we have made clear that at this level mobility is not of a 'group' and 'even' character, and as such sanskritization does not help in understanding mobility at the level of family. Westernization too does not provide a basis for taking a note of resources, capabilities and aspirations of these families. Westernization implies only 'references' for mobility, but it lacks a provision for understanding the motivations and aspirations of the 'climbing' families. As such varied forms of reference group, for example, membership (own caste families) and non-membership groups and both 'negative' and 'positive' (Merton, 1962) help analysis of such a mobility.

Mobility of a Group or a Majority of Families of a Group

Mobility of a group or a majority of families of a caste is not essentially in contrast with mobility at the level of family. The same family may have mobility simultaneously at both the levels. The major distinction between the two levels is that the 'corporate' (group) interests are given priority at the caste level, whereas at the family level the interests of family concerned predominate. In the former, collective striving is involved, while in the latter individualistic-achievement is stressed for status upgrading. Another distinction is that mobility at the caste level generally operates with regard to socio-cultural customs or matters regarding pollution-purity while mobility at the family level takes place in the socio-economic and political domains, and it is concerned with real power and influence in the village community.

In the six villages studied by the author, Khatis, Nais, Meenas, Chamars, Naiks and Brahmins have tried to improve their caste positions by discarding certain practices and occupations attached to their respective castes which they considered impure and degrading. For example, the Khatis (carpenters) in Roopgarh, Sabalpura and Harmara used to accept *kucha* food and water from most of the clean peasant castes, such as Jats, Malis, Gujars, Kumhars and Ahirs about fifteen years ago. But now they refuse to take *kucha* food from these agricultural castes and claim a higher caste rank equivalent to the Brahmins, and label themselves as the 'Jangir' Brahmins—the direct descendants of the Lord Viswakarma (the creator of the world) and have started putting on the sacred thread.

The Nais (barbers), with the exception of two families, have discarded cleaning of defiled (*jutha*) plates for the last ten years considering that this lowered down their caste rank. The Jats (peasants) of Roopgarh, Sabalpura and Bhutera have started naming themselves 'Singh' (a Rajput style of nomenclature) since the abolition of the *zamindari* and *jagirdari* systems. Likewise, the Meenas (watchmen) have left chowkidari and committing thievery up with a view to upgrade their caste rank. The Chamars ('untouchable' leather-workers) have discarded their traditional occupations such as disposal of carcass, skinning the dead animals, mending old shoes and other menial and 'forced' labour with the exception of three families, one each in Roopgarh, Sabalpura and Bawari. Chamars in two villages of Bharatpur now name themselves as 'Jatav'—a name resembling with 'Jat'—a landowning caste in the area.

Among the Naiks (another 'untouchable' caste) women performed as midwives about fifteen years ago in Roopgarh and Sabalpura. As midwives they had to attend the mothers of the newly-born children and clean the dirt including excreta and urine of both child and mother. Considering these services polluting and status degrading, the Naiks decided collectively to discard midwifery.

The above illustrations are of the castes which have tried to sanskritize their behaviour patterns by discarding polluting and degrading callings and practices and by adopting occupations of the superior castes which guaranteed higher social status. Here we can say that mobility in caste structure is generally of a corporate nature. Efforts are collectively made to upgrade caste position, however, individuals also try to upgrade their socio-cultural position within the caste by discarding eating meat and drinking wine or by having regular bath, worship and the sacred thread.

We would like to make here a reference about the concepts of sanskritization and dominant caste as they are helpful in understanding of corporate mobility in caste structure in spite of their ad hoc character. It has been pointed out that sanskritization is a group process and it helps in understanding of group mobility. Sanskritization does not reduce 'economic inequalities' nor it challenges the dominant caste(s). Bailey (1960) points out that sanskritization is a corporate activity and it is an attack on hierarchy, and therefore, it is a process towards 'general levelling of culture.' But the dominant castes are not so ignorant and unaware about the movements of the sanskritizing castes. They take defensive mechanisms and maintain/create rather more status distinctions than what existed before through articulation of new status bases which are generally beyond the reach of the lower caste and class people. As such sanskritized castes hardly get higher recognition by the privileged caste groups. The non-privileged sanskritizing castes do not possess material means and mechanisms to compete with the dominant caste groups. As such sanskritization increases generally ineffective status distinctions within the same caste without attacking the caste structure as such. For example, the Nais who do not clean *jutha* plates consider themselves superior to those who continue to adhere to the traditional occupation. Such intracaste distinctions are found in all the sanskritized castes. The privileged sections do not constitute a homogeneous status group, but they are generally superior to those who have not been privileged, and the former continue to be influential because of their bigger landholdings, higher education, and prestigious jobs, which are beyond the reach of the non-privileged sections of rural society. Therefore, we can firmly say that sanskritization does not reduce economic inequalities, but it may enhance cultural levelling.

In political sphere, sanskritization is not by rule a corporate activity. Status conflicts within the same castes are found between the dominant families. As such sanskritization is a misfit for political analysis in the village community.

Thus, it is not correct to say that sanskritization does not apply where caste hierarchy is disputed and hazy, and where dominant caste does not exist or does not inspire the members of other castes to sanskritize their behaviour patterns (Srivastava, 1969). Srivastava suggests that the 'progressive family' is a more viable reference group for understanding mobility. He refers to the Koiris of Barigaon who did not imitate the behaviour patterns of the dominant caste of the Chhatris and imitated behaviour patterns of their own caste from a nearby village. About another village Asalpur he mentions that there is no dominant caste in the village and the Raigars imitated the Raigars who lived in Ahmedabad.

Our view is that sanskritization helps in the understanding of group mobility. But group mobility does not encompass totality of mobility in caste structure. There is group mobility, and this is mainly in socio-cultural aspects. The prevalence of hierarchy supports the existence of dominant groups, castes or sub-castes, however, there may be decisively one or more dominant castes/sub castes. The sanskritizing castes generally cannot imitate the ways of twice-born dominant castes or other higher castes, as this is influenced by the rank of the dominant caste. The lower castes imitate the life-ways of the immediate higher castes and this pattern applies to all the sanskritizing castes. Sanskritization is thus a contextual phenomenon (Singh, 1968).

In the context of group mobility, sanskritization is not a futile concept. Srivastava's argument that the 'progressive families' of the Koiris and the Raigars were *reference groups* for their respective castes. But from where and how these reference group families borrowed superior status indices. Srivastava probably means that 'complex culture' of towns and cities provided superior contexts to these reference families. This is not a correct view, as the reference to a Koiri family was in a nearby village, and if this family was affected by industrial-urban complex culture, other families of the Koiris could have also been affected by this 'external culture'. The Raigars of Asalpur have taken up mythical king Raghu as their ancestral figure.

These examples prove imitation of the Kshatriya and the Brahmanic cultures. Besides this, imitation of the higher castes is not a difficult adventure in the cities. The impact of complex culture could be observed more in terms of higher education, removal of untouchability, migration, etc. instead of religious adaptations. What Srivastava analyzes is very much sanskritization in reality. His reference is for socio-cultural adaptations and corporate activities which are essence of sanskritization.

Thus, sanskritization is applicable to the understanding of group mobility vis-a-vis caste structure particularly with reference to socio-cultural behaviour patterns. Sanskritization is to be used as a tool of analysis regarding dominant castes or groups and caste ranking and ranks of the sanskritizing castes. Sanskritization does not necessarily reduce 'economic inequalities' nor does it challenge caste hierarchy, however, it symbolizes an increased sense of awareness among the non-privileged sections.

Mobility of an Individual Within a Family

The mobility of an individual within family implies enhancement or degradation of status of an individual without necessarily affecting the social position of his family and caste to which he belongs. Caste (group) mobility and family mobility are, however, interrelated, and therefore, this distinction between family mobility and individual mobility within the context of caste is devised mainly for analytical purposes.

Mobility at the level of individual is more concerned with psychological processes, such as aspirations, ambitions, frustrations, etc. and therefore, it can be better explained by the *theory of reference group behaviour*. Individual mobility is observable when we find that some individuals are esteemed high irrespective of their caste, class and family statues. It is a mobility in personal status of an individual which is a combination of his caste status and non-caste status. A particular member in a family is highly respected, whereas his real elder brother and cousins are not, sometimes including his own sons. The aspirations of individual members thus differ even when they belong to the same joint family. Such examples of mobility at the individual level are a few only, that, however, indicate a class-like pattern of mobility within an organically closed stratification system. These individuals are invariably social workers, men of integrity and character and generally educated. While observing these individuals, we may find individuals to whom we could label as 'negative' reference individuals in Mertonian sense.

Education and sanskritization are two main factors responsible for mobility at the individual level. We find that in all the six villages of Rajasthan studied by us, the graduates and matriculates are respected more than other members of their families and their age-groups irrespective of their caste and economic status. Similarly, vegetarian, teetotaler, regular worshiper and bathtaker are esteemed more than the non-vegetarian and non-believer in God and non- worshiper. Thus, sanskritized individuals are rated higher than the non-sanskritized ones.

The mode of orientation in the mobility at the individual level is essentially achievement-oriented, and therefore, such a mobility is least corporate in character and action. Individualism prevails over collectivism within the family, however, the latter is generally benefited by the achievements of its individual members.

Patterns of Mobility in Caste Structure

Structural enforcements that were brought to mitigate the caste distinctions have been proved ineffective so far. The legal enactments have strengthened caste sentiments and loyalties. Some changes, particularly land reforms, have, however, brought significant class-like changes within the caste structure. Horizontal status distinctions within the caste have considerably increased. The processes, though not considerably effective to change the caste structure, are of 'proletarianization' and 'bourgeoisiefication' (Sharma, 1969). Some former Zamindars have become petty peasants and the former tenants have become big peasants. Economic inequalities are thus reduced in some cases. But to achieve an egalitarian pattern of society such more effective radical changes are needed. As such decentralization of power, abolition of untouchability and caste system and adult suffrage have almost been infructuous.

The following patterns of mobility may, however, be discerned in caste structure on the basis of foregoing analysis:

(a) Marginally going up

Some families and groups of families have raised their status marginally within their own castes. This change is reflected through changes in their customs, practices, occupations, education and income. These changes essentially imply a social climbing.

(b) Marginally going down

The reverse of the pattern of marginally going up is the pattern of marginally going down. Adherence to the so-called defiling and degrading callings and practices lowers down status compared to those who have discarded the degrading occupations and taken up the clean and prestigious occupations and practices. This applies to some families of several lower and upper castes.

(c) Maintaining status quo

There are families and castes which have faced a number of attacks on their caste ranks. The landowning and priestly castes, such as the Rajputs, Brahmins and Jats have been facing new challenges and situations since Independence, but they have been adjusting themselves in such a way that no significant shifts have taken place in their caste ranks. The loss they had suffered has been compensated with regard to high education, lucrative jobs, cash income and political power.

Conclusion

Reference group theory is certainly a better conceptual frame than the concepts of sanskritization and westernization. The latter concepts are of an ad hoc nature. They lack refinement at conceptual level. Mobility at individual level in terms of aspirations, frustration, morale and commitment can be better understood with the theory of reference group behaviour. Mobility in caste structure at different levels could be explained through the application of a set of perspectives.

The applicability of the reference group theory, however, still remains to be tested to understand structural (induced) changes emanating from legislation, land reforms, and democratic decentralization etc. which do not involve groups and individuals as such but the systems in existence. Structural changes do not take a cognizance of aspirations and frustrations of the individuals and groups *per se*. The objective is an overhauling of the existing systems with a view to reduce or remove structural inconsistencies, inequalities and contradictions and to ensure an egalitarian system of social relationships.

Sanskritization and westernization can be defined only in cultural terms. But Lynch (1968) maintains that sanskritization can be defined structurally too. The major difficulty of sanskritization is of being 'culture-bound', which could, however, be overcome by an application of a frame of analysis that uses generalized types of reference groups (identification, imitation, negation) and generalized types of status (dominant and salient). With such a frame of analysis sanskritization could be compared with movements of mobility in other societies and their similarities and dissimilarities could be compared and analyzed. But these arguments of Lynch do not stand the test of validity. Sanskritization as a concept is applicable basically within the frame of caste structure. Again, mobility at all the levels as referred above cannot be understood with the concept of sanskritization because there is a gross negligence of realization of the role of initiative and incentive, individual aspirations and resourcefulness. Thus, the structural changes which are induced through extra-caste mechanisms but have definite repercussions on caste structure are not understandable either with reference group theory or sanskritization. However, the analysis of mobility in caste structure could be better understood at different levels of mobility as analyzed above.

Finally, it could be pointed out that if the concept of sanskritization is used in the wider sense as referred to by Lunch, it does not remain sanskritization as defined by either Srinivas or Bailey. It becomes altogether a new concept perhaps unacceptable to Srinivas. Structural changes are understandable through reference group theory or not remains still an unsolved question. Merton has used reference group theory for socio-psychological analysis at intermediate level (middle range). Whether it could also be extended to an analysis of a macro social and psychological phenomena remains an unsolved puzzle.

References

Bailey, F.G., *Tribe, Caste and Nation*, Bombay: Oxford University Press, 1969.

Damle, Y.B., 'Reference Group Theory with regard to Mobility in Caste,' in James Silverberg (ed.), *Social Mobility in the Caste System in India*, The Hague: Mouton and Co., 1968.

Heibert, Paul G., 'Caste and Personal rank in an Indian Village,' *American Anthropologist*, Vol. 71, No. 3, June 1969, pp. 434-454.

Leach, E.R. (ed.), *Aspects of Caste in South India, Ceylon and North-West Pakistan*, London: Cambridge University Press, 1960, pp. 1-10.

Lynch, Owen M., 'The Politics of Untouchability: A Case from Agra, India,' in Milton Singer and Bernard C. Cohn (eds.), *Structure and Change in Indian Society*, Chicago: Aldine Publishing Company, 1968, pp. 209-240.

Majumdar, D.N., *Caste and Communication in an Indian Village*, Bombay: Asia Publishing House, 1958.

Marriott, McKim, 'Multiple Reference in Indian Caste Systems,' in James Silverberg (ed.) *op.cit.*

Merton, R.K., *Social Theory and Social Structure*, Glencoe: The Free Press of Glencoe, 1962.

Sharma, K.L., 'Stresses in Caste Stratification: A Study of Six Villages in Rajasthan,' *Economic and Political Weekly*, Vol. 4, No. 3, January 18, 1969, pp. 217-222.

Singh, Yogendra, 'Caste and Class: Some Aspects of Continuity and Change,' *Sociological Bulletin*, Vol XVII, No. 2, September 1968, pp. 165-186.

Srinivas, M.N., 'The Dominant Caste in Rampura,' *American Anthropologist*, Vol. 61, No. 1, 1959, pp. 1-16.

———, *Social Change in Modern India*, Berkeley: University of California Press, 1966.

Srivastava, Sahab Lal, 'The Concept of Sanskritization: A Re-evaluation,' *Economic and Political Weekly*, Vol 4, No. 16, April 19, 1969, pp. 695-698.

Stein, Berton, 'Social Mobility and Medieval South Indian Hindu Sects', in James Silverberg (ed.), Op. cit., pp. 189-200.

10

Downward Social Mobility: Some Observations

Downward social mobility has not yet been analyzed adequately by sociologists. Our objective is to highlight some of the dimensions and contexts, forms and factors, of downward social mobility in Indian society. Why has downward social mobility not engaged the attention of social scientists? The belief that downward mobility is involitional and not desired at the levels of group, individual and family and, therefore, it does not occur, appears to have been responsible for its neglect. Such a view is unwarranted and unfounded. Downward social mobility does occur and is a complex process involving social and economic, cultural and motivational, factors.

Furthermore, we need to distinguish between *specific* and *generalized* downward status mobility, for in India a lag has been observed between upward socio-religious mobility and economic or political mobility. Several sanskritizing castes have moved up in the caste hierarchy by discarding their 'polluting' callings without, however, a corresponding change in their economic and political position (Harper, 1968; Sharma, 1970a). Indeed, when the lower castes imitate the cultural traits of upper castes, their economic position often declines owing to the abandonment of lucrative economic activities. When this lack of fit between a rising social (caste) position and a declining economic position persists for a period of years, their generalized status may decline below what it was when they started to emulate the upper castes. Downward economic mobility here is an unplanned consequence of planned upward social mobility. Efforts to change the agrarian social structure, such as land reforms, would also force lower status upon the landlords. This 'withdrawal of status respect' (Hagen, 1962) has varied motivational and other repercussions on the privileged sections of the society. Downward social mobility is, thus, a structural and historical reality observable in diverse forms and in different contexts.

Social decline may affect a lone individual or a social group as a whole (Sorokin, 1964). Mobility is not a symmetrical phenomenon (Miller, 1969). The patterns of mobility do not bear a definitive character. A nation can be high in one measure of mobility and low in another. The same may be found with an individual and/or a group. Therefore, sometimes it is difficult to connect the mobility of one kind with another. A nation may have most downward movement and may also have most upward mobility at the same time. It may be difficult to relate the aspects of downward movement with that of upward mobility at the national level. Similarly, an individual may have upward economic movement and downward social movement simultaneously and *vice versa*.

As a result of industrialization (Miller, 1969), the agricultural and manual workers become non-manual and skilled workers, but the sons of elite fathers are not always entitled to or able to enter their fathers' social positions. Thus, downward mobility is more indicative of social fluidity than upward mobility. Whatever combination of upward and downward mobility may prevail in a society, it is clear that when a society drops the sons of the privileged strata out of their original positions or blocks their entry into these positions, it is more open and mobile than a society which has only progressive upward mobility but no mechanism for downgrading the elites. Thus, there are societies having more upward mobility without having more fluidity in social structure and *vice versa*. On the basis of Miller's data, two essential points emerge: that downward and upward mobility indicate greater fluidity than upward mobility alone and the two can appear in four combinations which are as follows:

(a) high downward and high upward mobility (+ +);
(b) high downward and low upward mobility (+ –);
(c) low downward and high upward mobility (– +); and
(d) low downward and low upward mobility (– –).

Our purpose is to locate the processes of downward social mobility in Indian society rather than to examine the applicability of Miller's model. We submit that downward social mobility has not been very much pronounced in India partly because of the organically closed character of its social system and partly because of the political structures and conditions that existed in the past. In our view, upward mobility has also been quite slow in India for the same reasons.

Downward social mobility is generally unplanned, non-deliberate and involitional (Saberwal, 1972). Saberwal distinguishes between: (a) a change in the society's *organizational* principles, and (b) a *positional* change for the individuals concerned. For the first case, he cites the abolition of princely privileges and the leather-workers' decline due to a growing preference for factory-made shoes in the town he studied. With regard to positional changes, Saberwal cites an example of a candidate who repeatedly contests and loses expensive elections and consequently his position declines compared to what it had been earlier. Saberwal's remarks on downward mobility are, however, casual and incidental, and his main concern was with upward status mobility. A satisfactory framework for analyzing social mobility, we submit, must allow adequately for motivation or consciousness. Downward mobility due to organizational change should be related to structure, ideology and behaviour of the people and its consequences should also be taken into consideration. Thus, there is a need to investigate social decline in the context of both organizational or structural change and positional change. In other words, downward social mobility resulting from social and economic innovations and transformations on the one hand, and the failure of the groups and individuals to maintain the status of the ascending generation on the other hand, has not been seriously investigated.

II

The possibility of social mobility in the nineteenth century and earlier in the caste system is now generally accepted. Stein (1968) has noted the case of a group of Sudra Srivaishnavas who achieved upward mobility through religious roles at the Tiruvengadam temple at Tirupati in the fifteenth century. Elsewhere some castes have been able to upgrade their caste rank by getting political power and royal degrees. In course of time, these upwardly mobile castes received priestly recognition and also underwent changes in nomenclature, traditional occupation and ritual idioms. A number of lower castes in course of time achieved Kshatriya status by migrating to other places and establishing dominion over the native people (Panikkar, 1955).

While the fact of upward caste mobility has been noted by many analysts, its consequences for those whose position has remained unchanged has not been adequately explored. Our point is that upward mobility, if restricted to some caste groups only, accentuates structural cleavages and imbalances. Some castes move up, and others remain where they have been. This differential movement adversely affects those castes which remain static. Some castes which were inferior in past may now move up to a higher position in the caste hierarchy. This is true not only of castes; but within the caste, different families and within the families different individuals are also differentially affected by such a group-specific upward mobility. Thus, without moving down or even without being affected by generalized decline, the relative position of groups, families and individuals might decline as a result of the upward mobility of other units of society. Such a consequential decline has been conspicuously neglected in sociological analysis and only upward mobility has engaged the attention of sociologists so far.

Ahmad (1971) reports that low or 'backward' castes advancing higher status claims went on increasing at different censuses in different states from 1901 to 1931. In 1901, the number of castes claiming high status was only 21. The number increased to 148 in 1931. In many cases a single caste made more than one claim and these claims changed in the successive censuses. A number of castes claimed Kshatriya status in 1921 census and the same castes claimed the Brahmin status in 1931. Similarly, many castes claimed Vaishya status in 1921 and Kshatriya status in 1931. It would be necessary to know about the castes which superseded and the castes which were superseded and the factors which contributed to this discriminating mobility.

Since the field of downward mobility is still largely unexplored, we are more interested here in analyzing its manifestations than its structural constraints. This would enable us to postulate some hypotheses for empirical investigation. Thus, we propose to analyze the processes underlying downward mobility. However, it will not be possible for us to analyze interactional relations between those who slide down and those who go up in social hierarchy. Again, our analysis is limited to the phenomenon of sliding down in economic hierarchy mainly in village societies, but we would also relate it to caste segments and to other aspects of social life. We present first a formalized view of the forms and contexts of downward mobility and in the last section of the paper we refer to concrete cases of downward mobility.

The term 'mobility' means upward mobility and the term 'decline' refers to downward mobility. Decline can be categorized into: (a) generalized decline, and (b) domain-specific decline. Generalized decline refers to total decline of a unit of society, i.e., individual, family, group and nation. Domain-specific decline would mean downward mobility of these units in a particular domain or aspect. Domain-specific decline may also result from mobility of a particular type, or as an unplanned or unforeseen consequence of a particular type of mobility. Generalized decline can be categorized into structural decline and positional decline on the basis of the nature of the decline itself. Structural decline follows changes in the organizational principles of the society, whereas positional decline, in contrast, implies only a movement of persons within a continuing structure of society. Structural decline can, on the basis of the nature of its effectivity for the units, be further classified into primary structural decline and secondary structural decline. Primary structural decline refers to radical changes which may be due to pressure from above; for example, from the threat of war by a big power and/or from elitist reformative policies, or from pressure from below, e.g., from a Maoist revolution. In either case, the decline would reflect certain normative pressures. However, the nature of the normative pressure would be different in these two situations of primary structural decline. Secondary structural decline refers to indirect and immediately less effective changes to which individuals and groups are exposed. Primary structural decline is brought about by the direct impact of these forces of change on the affected groups whereas the decline of these groups may set off, though indirectly, the decline of other groups as well. Secondary structural decline may be an intended or unintended consequence of the structural changes. The analytical diagram of downward social mobility and its various forms have been presented in Chart 1.

Primary Structural Decline

Primary decline may follow the creation of new structural principles, organizations and units which replace the old ones. Such a change may restructure the existing status system, including property relations, denying the erstwhile privileged groups and individuals their traditional prerogatives and conferring these upon the underdogs of the old order. The abolition of the *jagirdari* and *zamindari* systems, for example, expropriated the rights of the old landowning classes and conferred peasant proprietary rights on the ex-tenants. This is the formal situation; we shall consider the realities shortly. Changes in organizational principles and structural innovations, such as non-recognition of the traditional village and caste councils and installation of statutory panchayati raj agencies, have also led to downward mobility. The effects of these measures could be seen on the office-bearers and landowners in terms of their statutory non-recognition and sliding down socially, politically and economically in the village community.

Primary decline takes place when highly placed sections or groups are forced by the militant pressure groups to come down to a lower level at par with the commoners. It is symbolic of structural

CHART 1

UPWARD AND DOWNWARD SOCIAL MOBILITY

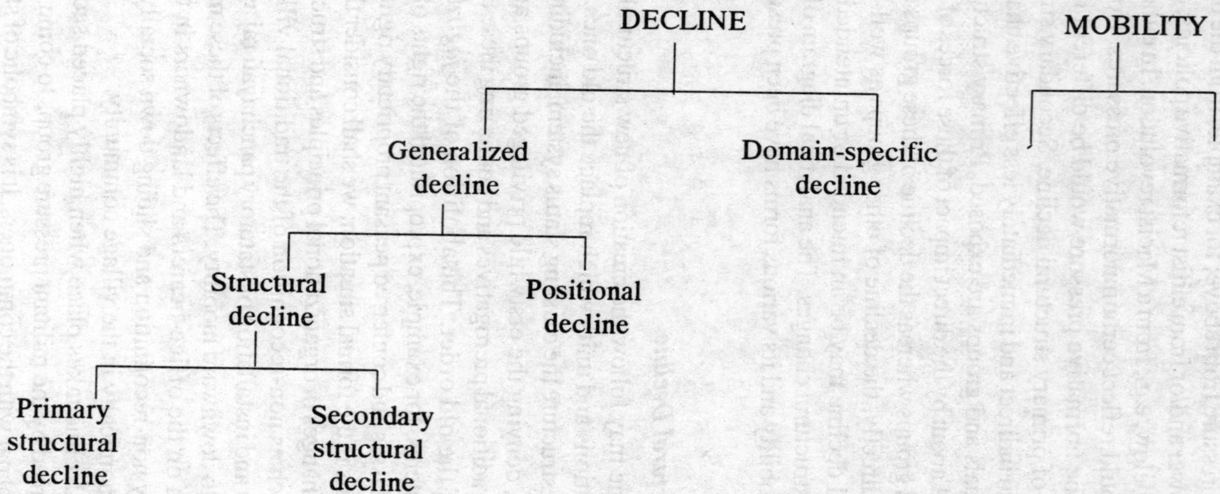

(This diagrammatic presentation has been suggested by Dr. Satish Saberwal.)

upheavals and revolutions. The privileged have no choice but to accept the dictates of such an organized force. Such a pattern of decline of old established groups requires a high degree of mobilization accompanied by intense polarization of interests and sharpening of ideological conflict. Naxalite movement in West Bengal, Kerala and in some other parts could be said to have caused the decline of *jotdars*, absentee landowners and rich peasant proprietors at least to some extent and for some time. However, this enforced downward mobility was foiled through a counter-offensive launched by the youth wing of another political party after some time. Our point is that ideological and class polarization is always found operating in the background of primary structural decline as a result of pressures from below. These form part of a strategy of structural change and the emergence of a new social order. Primary decline can also occur as a result of 'elitist' intervention from above.

Secondary Structural Decline

Changes in organizational principles may affect some people directly and immediately as we have noted above; they may affect some others indirectly, as for instance, the dependents of the landed gentry consequent upon *zamindari* abolition. Land reforms have also led to secondary structural decline of working peasants and marginal tenants. Since land reforms gave tenurial stability, it motivated the big tenants for agricultural innovations and mechanization of farming. "With agriculture developing along capitalist lines the process of ruination and proletarianization of the bulk of the peasantry is growing more intensely all the time" (Kotovsky, 1964). The emergence of rich capitalist peasantry on the one hand and pauperization of the working peasant households and their reduction to the status of proletarian households on the other has also been identified (Saith and Tankha, 1972) as an indirect result of the 'green revolution'. The process of impoverishment of most small peasant households has increased recently. Saith and Tankha observed that rapid expansion of the forces of production has intensified the process of differentiation and, consequently, of polarization of the peasantry. This process transforms the rich surplus-making peasants into machine-using capitalist farmers. "The same process, however, spells the ruination of small working-peasant classes. An inescapable conclusion must be that the 'diffusion of prosperity' hypothesis (we referred to in an earlier section)... does not stand up to scrutiny" (Saith and Tankha, 1972). The accentuation of economic inequalities denoted by the emergence of capitalist farmers on the one end and pauperized peasant-workers on the other was perhaps an unintended and indirect consequence of land reforms and later of the green revolution. Thus, secondary structural decline results both from intended and unintended consequences of innovations and it takes place both at the level of individuals and of groups. It forms part of the generalized decline.

Positional Decline

Positional decline can be defined as decline of an individual or a group from one social position to another. A number of factors or a combination of factors may be responsible for this decline. Demotion of individuals due to changes in occupations, or due to transfer of persons from one place to another and such other setbacks could be identified as positional decline. These downward movements do not involve a change in the principles of the structure. Positional decline, however, affects the dominant status of persons and groups and, therefore, it would affect other domains of social life of those groups and individuals.

Positional mobility and positional decline are characteristic features of a relatively stable society. Srinivas (1966) observes that as a result of the process of sanskritization only positional changes in the system have taken place. He writes: "...a caste moves up, above its neighbours, and another comes down, but all this takes place in an essentially stable hierarchical order. The system itself does not change" (1966). Saberwal (1972) also states: "In contrast, there may only be positional change for the individuals concerned, resulting from an imprudent use of scarce resources as, for example, in repeatedly contesting and losing expensive elections, or in failing to maintain relationships important for generating resources which sustain one's status." Positional decline is thus a part of generalized decline, and as such it is related to policies and programmes and their implementation. But it does not result from structural changes as such. Positional decline does not pose a threat to the existing structures.

Bailey (1957), Lynch (1968) and Rowe (1968) have also brought to our notice certain processes of social mobility. Though some of these processes represent 'unsuccessful' attempts (Rowe, 1968), others were related to the 'decline' of the landowning castes (Bailey, 1957). The unsuccessful attempts refer to positional decline of the lower castes who aspired for higher status. The decline of the landowning castes refers to structural decline. However, both unsuccessful attempts and sliding down of landowners are a part of generalized decline.

Domain-Specific Decline

Domain-specific decline stands in contrast to generalized decline. In fact, it is to some extent unplanned and unexpected because it results from upward mobility, and the actor's motivation is directed towards going up in the hierarchy. As such domain-specific decline takes place as an unforeseen consequence. However, it is not coercive as the affected persons can also neutralize the negative consequences by retreating to the position they had before they moved upward. Hypothetically, we could say that if the actors apprehended the specific dysfunctional consequences, perhaps these could have been avoided either by non-activity or by deploying some mechanisms to avert the negative repercussions.

We do not mean that these changes are irreversible. There could be counter-mechanisms and instrumentalities by which some people might undo the positive consequences of mobility. But our point is that in the case of domain-specific decline, choice to avert it is considerably greater than in the case of the two other forms of structural decline, i.e., primary structural decline and secondary structural decline. Since domain-specific decline is generally a result of volitional mobility, its avoidance is also possible when its cost becomes much more than the gains of mobility.

A certain amount of simultaneous rejection and acceptance of caste ethic is also clearly observable. In seeking ritual identity with the higher castes, the lower castes seem partly to reject the ideology of the caste system; but by imitating the behaviour pattern and cultural idioms of the upper castes, with a view to upgrade their rank, these castes also accept very much the caste ideology. The lower castes, on the other hand, have united against the upper castes through political participation in order to have adequate representation in different agencies and institutions. All these accounts of mobility, both upward and downward, reveal that these mobility movements have not secured the claimed higher status for the lower castes because status acquisition is now more a matter of command over resources (Sharma, 1970). Therefore, imitating discarded life-ways of the upper castes, or adopting new caste names would be unhelpful for upward status aspirants. In these accounts domain-specific decline is implicit and this has not been analyzed. We shall discuss this point in detail in the next section.

A number of sanskritizing castes have adopted upper caste names, such as Singh, Rawat, Verma, Sharma, Berua and Bariba. They have adopted the sects or cults, such as Kabir, Raidas and Ramdeo Panth, Vaishnava Sampradaya and Bhagat Sampradaya (Sanyal and Roy Burman, 1970). In March 1973 in Delhi, thousands of Harijans embraced Buddhism. The manifestoes of these castes are related to socio-cultural reforms including rejection of the 'polluting' callings. These castes have mobilized their members through traditional caste panchayats. However, some formal associations have also been active in the mobility endeavours (Sanyal and Roy Burman, 1970). The analyses of these mobility movements have not taken cognizance of 'substantial' mobility, that is, the status accorded to the aspiring low castes by the upper castes and the gains they have received actually in terms of higher education, standard of living and active participation in decision-making in different spheres at various levels.

The problem of decline is not as simple as it appears to be. The dilemma arises from the gap that exists between our legal-political structure and the existential conditions. Ours is a system which is perhaps most open in theory (i.e., in terms of the principles of the

Constitution) but at the practical level chances of upward mobility are limited to only certain sections of the society. This is obviously because of historical and institutional reasons. Therefore, upward mobility and primary structural decline have not been simultaneous and movements seeking upward mobility have generally been 'unsuccessful'. The movement of workers from manual to non-manual positions and *vice versa* has not been crucially significant because of the conspicuously low rate of industrialization. Structurally speaking, the most significant are the changes resulting in the decline of a section of the erstwhile landed aristocracy. At the same time, the same institutional changes have also resulted in the upgrading of peasant proprietors and big tenants on the one hand and the pauperization of the poor peasants and village functionaries on the other (Kotovsky, 1964; Joshi, 1971; Saith and Tankha, 1972). Thus, these changes do not necessarily ensure a reduction in inequalities. This is what we call unintended secondary decline.

Domain-specific decline could also be related to differential resource ownership. Socio-cultural upward mobility demands a different set of means and resources than what upward occupational or economic mobility would require. The effectiveness of these institutional changes is minimized when there is no substantial difference between the magnitude of downward decline and that of mobility taking place at a given time and when the operational norms too at the upper level continue to be the same. Thus, because of differential prerequisites for mobility in different spheres, it is quite possible to find a group which is not capable of moving up in one sphere but is capable of upward movement in another domain. We have also evidence to prove that the affluent peasants are those who were big tenants and who enjoyed security of land in the past. Thus, a complex of factors in diverse forms constitutes the existential background of downward mobility.

Jagirdari and *zamindari* were two systems of land tenure the abolition of which affected differentially the people under these systems. *Jagirs* constituted bigger estates than the *zamindaris*. *Jagirs* were granted to certain military commanders, ministers and courtiers by the state chiefs or princes. The grantees appropriated the revenue for their own support or that of a military force which they were bound to maintain. Thus, the Jagirdar was an intermediary between the tiller and the state, but for all practical purposes he acted as the master of his *jagir* not only in relation to the tenants but also in relation to the entire people under his command.

'Charge' lands were *zamindari* lands. A person appointed to manage the tract under his influence was designated as the landholder or the Zamindar of his territory. The duty of such a Zamindar was strictly to collect revenue and retain only his sanctioned share of the total revenue. The Jagirdar was the sole owner of his estate, and generally the jurisdiction of a *jagir* spread over several villages. There were a number of Zamindars (particularly in 'severality villages') in the same village who shared the benefits accruing to them from the *zamindari* system. On the other hand, a Jagirdar used to manage his land through Zamindars and a 'formal bureaucratic' organization, i.e., the Jagirdar had several Zamindars as his grantees. The Jagirdar had to pay only a fixed amount as tribute to the king, and he was free to manage his *jagir* in his own way. Thus, the systems of *jagirdari* and *zamindari* were different on the basis of their size, resources, rights and privileges. The diverse nature of the *jagirdari* and *zamindari* systems affected differentially the rural class structure in the two types of villages as a result of the abolition of these systems.

Several Zamindars shared land on the basis of their 'charge' right or kinship status. Therefore, size of their landholdings was quite small even before the abolition. The small size of the landholding made it possible for them to retain the major portions in their own accounts by claiming for themselves a self-cultivating status at the time of the abolition.

The situation in the case of the Jagirdar was different. He was the sole owner of his estate and, therefore, only he was affected by the abolition (though several retainers were also affected and perhaps much more than the Jagirdar). The number of substantial beneficiaries in the *zamindari* villages (in many 'severality villages') was quite insignificant. But the number of substantial beneficiaries in the *jagirdari* villages was quite significant. The Jagirdar, being the sole owner of the land, could retain only a small fraction of it at the time of the abolition. Consequently, a number of tenants received land rights due to the abolition. However, the big tenants were benefited more than the small and marginal ones.*

It was found in the study of six villages in Rajasthan (Sharma, 1968) that in some villages, Rajputs, Brahmins and Jats who were Zamindars before the abolition, cannot now support themselves on the meagre or uneconomic landholdings they have retained after the abolition and, consequently, they have to work as manual and agricultural labourers. The retainers and the Zamindars under the Jagirdars were left with uneconomic holdings. They could not seriously anticipate the gravity of the abolition and, therefore, did not eject their tenants. Secondly, their dependence upon the Jagirdars was so much that they could not think of their independent existence without that of the Jagirdar. The number of such sufferers is, however, quite small.

Some of the Rajputs who are impoverished today work as manual and agricultural labourers either on the construction sites or on the farms of the rich peasants who are lower to them in caste hierarchy. The author found in one of the six villages that a Rajput who enjoyed social prestige was working as a labourer on the famine relief work site along with the ex-untouchable labourers. Some other Rajputs have been working as labourers for a decade or so. Some Brahmins, Gujars and other clean caste persons were also working as labourers. In 1965-66, about fifteen families of ex-Zamindars were engaged in manual activities in these six villages. We may add here that none of these poor ex-Zamindar families worked as wage labourers before the abolition of *zamindari* system. However, some of them were partly absentee landlords and partly self-cultivators and worked casually on their farms in the capacity of owner-cultivators.

---

* Simiar observation has been made by P.C. Joshi (1971) in terms of differential transfer of landholdings as a result of land reforms in the *zamindari* and *ryotwari* areas. The latter had peasant proprietors and the former consisted of absentee landowners. Therefore, the distribution of land as a result of the abolition among the tenants has been much more in *zamindari* areas than the *ryotwari* areas. We would say that in *jagirdari* areas the impact of the abolition has been still greater due to the reasons discussed above.

Similarly, the positions of Jagirdars and some big Zamindars have declined considerably. The Jagirdars of the two of the six villages owned lakhs of bighas of land before the abolition, and had jurisdiction over a number of villages. After the abolition, they have not only slided down socially, politically and juridically but their economic position too has declined enormously as they do not own land now even half a per cent of what they owned in the past. But they are still better off than even the richest peasants in these villages.

The processes of mobility affect differentially the various sections of the rural society. Those who have moved up affect negatively those who could not do so. Earlier the landowners were at the top of class hierarchy; now the ex-landowner-cum-cultivators and ex-tenant-cum-proprietors are at the top of it. The studies by Saith and Tankha, Kotovsky and Joshi reveal that the agrarian system has changed from the feudalistic to the commercial and the capitalist type. This change has led to the ruination of the working peasants further.

It has been noted (Singh, 1969) that as a result of the *zamindari* abolition, the Zamindars initially stayed away from statutory village panchayats. But, later on, they found that the statutory panchayat could be a forum through which they could exert some influence and exercise their power. So this led to heightened tensions and conflicts between the Zamindars and the climbers. Since the Zamindars still owned major resources they were able to get control over statutory panchayats. But the shock of the 'withdrawal of status respect' produced, especially among the Jagirdars, apathy and withdrawal from village polity, decision-making and welfare activities (Sharma, 1974).

In one village, to a Jagirdar who had ruled over a dozen revenue villages, the rough and tumble of village politics seemed to be too degrading for involvement. The Jagirdar's tendency to withdraw, thus, allowed the rich peasants to rise without a confrontation. In another village, the Jagirdar was unanimously elected Sarpanch for two consecutive terms, but he did not take any interest in the village affairs, and stayed away at Jaipur. People started criticizing him for his lack of interest in village activities. When he came to know about this criticism, he withdrew from panchayat elections for the third term, but asked one of his subordinates to contest. The nominee of the Jagirdar was defeated with a big margin by a Jat candidate. Thereafter, the Jagirdar completely withdrew from village politics.

It may be noted that, as compared to the Jagirdar, the Zamindar was closer, in terms of social status, to the peasant proprietors; and the abolition of intermediary tenures reduced the gap still further. Consequently, the political arena has now numerous contestants, ex-Zamindars as well as new peasant proprietors.

We have already made it clear that domain-specific decline has been pronounced in the case of the depressed and lower castes. These castes aspired for higher status generally within the caste hierarchy. The upper castes frustrated their efforts and they also lost their traditional occupations and found themselves in a state of underemployment and hardships. The other effect is the bifurcation of these castes into 'deviants' and 'conformists'. Those who conformed to the new norms were deviants but since they constituted the majority, they claimed higher status; those on the other end who conformed to the traditional norms were a minority and were labelled as conservative and given a lower status as they were still associated with degrading styles of life and occupation.

The barbers decided to discard cleaning of defiled plates which was a part of their traditional obligations. They, however, retained other activities including hair-cutting. All the barbers did not abide by this decision. This created another sub-caste of barbers. Those barbers who conformed to the traditional norms received more patronage now than before. On the other hand, those barbers who conformed to the new norms had to face economic hardships due to the displeasure of the patrons as a result of this change. Some of the families, however, silently carried on the traditional activities though overtly they claimed that they had left these polluting activities (Sharma, 1974).

Similarly, the Balais (leather workers) tried in vain to elevate their status by imitating Brahminical customs and practices. They gave up leather work, disposal of carcass and colouring of rawhides, etc. As in the case of the barbers, this led to a division among the Balais. They also had to face acute difficulties like the barbers and perhaps much more because of their greater dependence upon the upper castes. Their meagre lands were not adequate for their livelihood. Underemployment resulting from their move compelled them to migrate to the cities in search of employment as construction labourers.

The Regars (leather workers) took to leather work fifteen years ago when the Balais left their callings. Recently, however, they have discarded working with leather. The Regars protested against the atrocities of the patrons (particularly Jats) saying that they exploited them even more than was done by the ex-Zamindars. The movement to discard these obligations spread during 1971-72 from Rajasthan to Delhi, Haryana and parts of western Uttar Pradesh. They were harassed by the *jajmans* and even beaten up at many places during the period. For about six months they stuck to their own decision. Within this small period they had to face difficulties of employment and alienation. After about six months they returned to their original position. Unlike the Balais, none of the Regars came to Delhi before this incident. Drought has further accentuated the consequences of discarding traditional occupational obligations.

This is a very short period to establish the existence of downward mobility. This shows that the system does not allow upward mobility to certain sections of society in a given context. It also becomes clear that the Regars were successful in discarding their occupations but could not stick to their decision. The pains of coming down economically could not be borne by them and, therefore, they retreated to their original position. The other castes who left their traditional obligations and had to lose some economic support include Brahmins, Naiks (ex-untouchables) and Meenas (watchmen).

Domain-specific decline has really been demoralizing for the affected groups and individuals, particularly when they had to revert to their original positions. Firstly, they were harassed when they left the traditional and *jajmani* obligations and, secondly, their persecution increased when they, accepting the supremacy of the *jajmans* or patrons, retreated to their original position. Such a mobility has also resulted in a heightened sense of insecurity. Migration became inevitable in many cases when the sanskritized groups and individuals did not revert to their traditional position.

Concluding Remarks

Downward social mobility is a complex process involving social, economic, cultural and motivational factors, and occurs in different contexts and forms. We have made a distinction between domain-specific decline and generalized decline. Generalized decline could be further categorized into structural decline and positional decline. Structural decline consists of primary structural decline and secondary structural decline. Our scheme takes note of direct as well as indirect consequences of the structural changes on the affected persons, families and groups. Positional decline can be defined as decline of an individual or a group from one social position to another. Such a decline does not involve a change of principles of the structure. All generalized mobility is related to normative pressure. Domain-specific decline is not a part of generalized decline. It takes place often as a negative consequence of mobility, but is not coercive because retreat to the original position is possible. Downward mobility lends greater fluidity to the social structure than upward mobility.

We have noted that different land tenure systems and their abolition have affected differentially the people under these systems. In the case of the Zamindars downward mobility has been less compared to the Jagirdars. But the ex-Jagirdars still occupy dominant economic position. The abolition, that is, the withdrawal of status respect, has led to their detachment from village politics. The Zamindars have, however, emerged as potential rivals to the emerging peasant proprietors. Again, as a result of the abolition, some sections of the people have gone up and others have come down in social hierarchy. Both unequally and equally placed people have been affected differentially by the same measure. Domain-specific decline is generally a consequence of upward mobility. It is a characteristic feature of the depressed and lower castes who try to go up by discarding certain traditional occupations and obligations.

References

Ahmad, Imtiaz, 1971, "Caste Mobility Movements in North India", *The Indian Economic and Social History Review*, Vol. 8, No. 2.

Bailey, F.G., 1957, *Caste and the Economic Frontier*, Manchester: Manchester University Press.

Feldman, Arnold S., 1960, "Economic Development and Social Mobility", *Economic Development and Cultural Change*, Vol. 8, No. 3.

Hagen, Everett E., 1962, *On the Theory of Social Change* (An adaptation), Bombay: Vakils, Feffer and Simons (Pvt.) Ltd.

Harper, Edward B., 1968, "Social Consequences of an 'Unsuccessful' Low Caste Movement", in James Silverberg (ed.), *Social Mobility in the Caste System in India*, The Hague:Mouton.

Joshi, P.C., 1971, "Agrarian Social Structure and Social Change", Delhi:Institute of Economic Growth (mimeographed; this is a revised version of the paper which was originally published in *Sankhya*, Series B, Vol. 31, parts 3 and 4, 1969).

Kotovsky, Grigory, 1964, *Agrarian Reforms in India*, New Delhi: People's Publishing House.

Lipset, S.M. and Zetterberg, Hans L., 1970, "A Theory of Social Mobility", in R. Bendix and S.M. Lipset (eds.), *Class, Status and Power*, London:Routledge and Kegan Paul.

Lynch, O.M., 1968, "The Politics of Untouchability: A Case from Agra, India", Milton Singer and Bernard Cohn (eds.), *Structure and Change in Indian Society*, Chicago: Aldine Publishing Co.

Miller, S.M., 1969, "Comparative Social Mobility", in Celia, Heller H. (ed.), *Structured Social Inequality*, New York: The Macmillan Company.

Panikkar, K.M., 1955, *Hindu Society at Cross Roads*, Bombay: Asia Publishing House.

Rowe, William, 1968, "The New Chauhans: A Caste Mobility Movement in North India", in James Silverberg (ed.), *Social Mobility in the Caste System in India*, The Hague: Mouton.

Saberwal, Satish, 1972, "Status, Mobility and Network in a Panjabi Industrial Town", in Satish Saberwal (ed.), *Beyond The Village*, Simla:Indian Institute of Advanced Study.

Saith, Ashwani and Tankha, Ajay, 1972, "Agrarian Transition and the Differentiation of the Peasantry: A Study of a West U.P. Village", *Economic and Political Weekly*, Vol. VII, No. 14.

Sanyal, S. and Roy Burman, B.K., 1970, *Social Mobility Movements Among Scheduled Castes and Scheduled Tribes of India*, New Delhi:

Government of India Publications.

Sharma, K.L., 1974, *The Changing Rural Stratification System (A Comparative Study of Six Villages in Rajasthan)*, New Delhi: Orient Longmans.

———, 1970a, "Modernization and Rural Stratification: An Application at the Micro-Level", *Economic and Political Weekly*, Vol. V, No. 37.

———, 1970b, "Changing Class Stratification in Rural Rajasthan", *Man in India*, Vol 50, No. 3.

Singh, Yogendra, 1969, "Social Structure and Panchayats", in M.V. Mathur and Iqbal Narain (eds.), *Panchayati Raj, Planning and Democracy*, Bombay: Asia Publishing House.

Sorokin, P.A., 1964, *Social And Cultural Mobility*, London: The Free Press of Glencoe.

Srinivas, M.N., 1966, *Social Change in Modern India*, Bombay: Allied Publishers.

Stein, Burton, 1968, "Social Mobility and Medieval South Indian Hindu Sects", in James Silverberg (ed.), *Social Mobility in the Caste System in India*, The Hague:Mouton.

11

Caste, Class and Social Mobility among the Scheduled Castes

A nation-wide study of the educational problems of the scheduled castes and the scheduled tribes was undertaken a couple of years ago.[1] A lot of data about students at various levels of education in regard to their enrolment, drop-out, hostel accommodation, scholarship, performance, attitudes, aspirations, etc. were gathered through the 'conventional' techniques of *schedule* and *interview*. However, data were also collected from secondary sources, namely, census reports, reports of Scheduled Castes and Scheduled Tribes Commission and governmental reports. One of the serious limitations from which these studies suffer is that neither they have been rooted into the analysis of social structure nor they have any bearing on caste and class structure of Indian society. At the outset it may be stated that a proper study of social mobility among the scheduled castes must have its bearing upon social structure of 'caste society', that is, division of Indian society into caste and class groupings. Changes in the non-scheduled castes' society would also have its repercussions on the structure of the scheduled castes. Therefore, a meaningful discussion would be possible if caste/class relations *vis-a-vis* scheduled castes are properly analyzed and all the 'ideological' points in the definitional and relational aspects of these two 'concepts', that is, caste and class, are discussed. What have been those conditions as a result of which several anti-Brahmin, anti-twice-born movements and other emulative movements by the scheduled castes have emerged? Self-consciousness among these sections could be a result of the inhuman and exploitative conditions in which the scheduled castes were forced to live for centuries. It is quite possible that factors external to the caste system were strong enough to loosen its rigid strings tied to the scheduled castes and other lower sections. In such a situation, it was perhaps wise for the upper castes to grant certain concessions to the lower castes, and make search for new avenues of status, honour and power. Social mobility among the scheduled castes should, therefore, be examined in view of their structural position in the caste system. Before we discuss the various viewpoints regarding caste and class, it is necessary to refer some points about social mobility. Regarding the social position of the scheduled castes in a village of Coimbatore district, Den Ouden[2] points out the following questions:

Do the scheduled castes comprise a recognizable category within the domain of regional norms and actual behaviour? To what extent do they constitute part of a more inclusive grouping in the eyes of the higher castes?

Do the middle and high castes distinguish levels among the low castes?

Do the low castes make similar distinctions?

Is there a 'barrier of pollution' hindering or preventing the vertical mobility of the low caste?

What sets the untouchable (and possibly sections within this category) apart from other castes?

Ouden rightly observes: "My principal concern was to identify and to interpret changes in the stratification system, to locate the causes of these changes and to evaluate their consequences for the low castes and their membership."[3] Changes in caste rules structuring intercaste relations may be of the following nature as observed by Ouden:[4]

(a) Rules continue to exist but occur in the castes to which the rules refer.
(b) Rules continue to exist but situations formerly governed by these rules have declined in importance, some such situations are even disappearing.

(c) Rules lose stringency, weakened by new situations arising to which the rules hardly, if at all, apply.
(d) Rules become undermined by conflicting rules; more and more individuals conform to a new ideology and convert to new values and norms.

Ouden meticulously takes into account the role of caste hierarchy *vis-a-vis* 'caste relevant' and 'caste-irrelevant' roles. He also takes into account the role played by an individual in improving his position within the caste system. However, the question regarding caste and class, both conceptually and operationally, remains unanalyzed in Ouden's work. Therefore, first we will deal with the viewpoints and approaches concerning caste and class, and then our emphasis will be on the nature of social mobility among the scheduled castes *vis-a-vis* caste and class as systems of social stratification affecting it.

I

Despite various difficulties in defining the caste system, a large number of sociologists, anthropologists, social historians and indologists have engaged themselves in the study of caste system at the neglect of the studies of class, political power, etc. Studies of caste have been innumerable. The main features of the caste system, according to these studies, are: a common name, common decent, hereditary calling, and homogeneity of caste members. Risely, Senart and Ketkar were among the early writers who studied caste exclusively as an Indian system.[5] Later on, Furnivall, Hutton and Sherring in particular pleaded that caste system was 'functional' for the whole of the Hindu society.[6] Even Marx's notion of the Asiatic mode of production and Maine's idea of caste as a case of non-contractual 'status-society' contributed to the stability and continuity of the caste system. Indologists such as Ghurye, Kapadia, Karve and recently Dumont have given caste system a renewed ideological strength rooted into India's specificity and cultural distinctiveness.

Singh observes that the abstracted and ahistorical detachment of caste from tribe, attribution of exaggerated autonomy to systems of religion and village community and the omission of the exploitative and alienative role of colonialism in India on its society and economy from most sociological analyses of its institutions, prove adequately the ideological foundation of such theorizing.[7] Dube and Singh both realized that the demand for indigenization of social science paradigms now so widely voiced by social scientists in India is a product of such historical conditioning of concepts and theories.[8] However, such a demand for indigenization of social science paradigms and schema is not a recent one only. Marxist scholars like Thorner[9] pleaded for it in 1950s for a better understanding of agrarian relations. Even some non-Marxist scholars and indologists such as Karve and Saran made similar demands.[10] However, reasons for them were different from that of Thorner. Mukerji[11] made a vehement plea for making Indian tradition as the sole basis of analyzing social change. Desai[12] realized the role of colonialism in Indian society, polity and economy, and felt that the Marxist concepts and paradigms could provide a fuller understanding of the Indian society. One of the criticisms against the lack of proper paradigms is the western education and academic socialization of Indian sociologists and social anthropologists. Srinivas has been accused of a wrong application of the British functionalism by Mencher, Leach and Saberwal.[13]

Ideological contents have been predominant in the various approaches to the study of caste system. These elements were reflected even in the methodology and data which were used for substantiating the numerous explanations about the origin and functioning of the caste system. However, caste was never treated as a 'social formation', which also included components other than traditionally known as 'caste' components of Indian society. Some scholars for certain ideological reasons again equated caste with entirety of Indian social system. Whatever may be the reasons for stability and continuity of the caste system, the following formulation seems appropriate:

"My basic assumption is that the continuity of the caste system is a solid proof of its adaptive capacities. It has adapted to innumerable varied situations, forces, and constraints. Because of its adaptability, caste has evolved simultaneously in several directions and adjusted with ideologically antagonistic systems, adjusting its principles whenever necessary. It has never paved the way to the emergence of an alternate system of stratification and social relations, though the contents of its functions and other paraphernalia changed from time to time".[14]

Sinha[15] observes certain trends in regard to the studies of caste in India. These trends which refer to stability and change of the caste system could be taken for studying caste system as a part of a 'social formation' which certainly comprised of class, ethnicity, power, religion and economy along with caste. How all these aspects were webbed into each other should provide a proper understanding of the historicity of social formation of Indian society. Caste and class were parts of this formation in various ways. Such a perspective has not been formulated, nor a realization about indigenization of concepts and theories could provide the necessary understanding of Indian social structure as a social formation. As Singh has rightly hinted that historical and fragmented nature of understanding has been at the core of the studies of social stratification.

One of the serious limitations of the studies of social stratification is that caste has been considered as a logical opposite of the 'class' system. The class system has been thought of a basic feature of the western world. Beteille[16] has outlined the basic features of the 'caste' model of Indian society while examining its usefulness as a scheme of analysis. Beteille's trio of 'caste, class and power' is an imitation of Weber's theory of social stratification, namely, 'class, statute and party.'[17] The other Weberian adaptations are 'caste, class and politics'[18] and 'caste, religion and power'[19]. These adaptations have undermined the role of historicity of Indian society while accepting Weber's notions of rationality and historical specificity. Secondly, Weber's macro-analysis implied a certain method of study and research which has been neglected by Beteille, Bhatt and Aggarwal in their empirical studies of social stratification.

Caste and class are not polar opposites. Changes in caste and class have not occurred as 'replacements.'[20] The view that "caste is changing into class", or change is "from hierarchy to stratification" or "from closed to open system" (the first implying caste and the latter referring to class) are not, therefore, true. At no point of time caste system was a 'closed' system, and class was not so 'open' system even in the western world. Therefore, the notions that class inheres mobility, openness and freedom to individuals are implanted in the minds of Indian intellectuals through western text-books and funding of researches. Caste was named by the western academics as a feature of an archaic society and characterized it by all those features which were just opposite to that of the 'class' system. Class has existed along with caste as an inseparable phenomenon. It is a different thing that caste has been a more 'elaborate' system of ranking in some regions than others, and similarly class-like relations have been more pronounced and visible among certain groups and in certain contexts than others. It is admitted by several scholars that caste incorporates the elements of class, and class has a cultural style of functioning in Indian society. Historians of both Marxist and non-Marxist dispositions have pointed out the coexistence of class relations with caste stratification. Therefore, the ideas that 'caste alone' could explain Indian social reality or that 'class alone' could explain Indian problems or both 'caste and class' should be taken as the basis of understanding of Indian society are not very relevant. Alternative to all these views should be the notion of 'social formation' which explains the totality of social relations from various viewpoints and at various levels in terms of historicity of the Indian society.

Borrowed approaches such as functional, dialectical, psychological and structuralism are inadequate to explain the totality of social formation and its dynamics. As we have pointed out earlier that the impact of western scholarship has been immense on Indian sociology. The two most popular views about caste are: (i) it is a cultural phenomenon; and (ii) it is a structural form of social stratification. Caste as a cultural phenomenon is mainly upheld by Dumont and Leach,[21] and as a structural form it is upheld by Barth and Berreman.[22] Caste as a cultural phenomenon is particularistic and Indian in substance, and according to the 'structural' view it is a form of general theory of social stratification.

It is true that systems analogous to caste are found elsewhere also, and it is also true that caste system is one of several stratifications found in other societies. Singh[23] taking a clue from these two views formulates a paradigm of social stratification in view of cultural versus structural, and particular versus universal characteristics of social system. He suggests four types: (1) cultural-universalistic; (2) cultural-particularistic; (3) structural-universalistic; and (4) structural-particularistic. Singh does not indicate his preference for one of these types that resembles with the Indian situation; however, it seems that his view is nearer to the structural-particularistic category.

In a recent study, Singh[24] categorizes the theoretic concerns in the seventies in the studies of social stratification as: (1) structural-functional, (2) structuralist, (3) structural-historical, and (4) historical-materialist or Marxist. These approaches are not discussed here in detail. However, some of the basic points in regard to caste-class debate could be mentioned. Class relations are subsumed by caste and any departure from caste in terms of incongruence between caste, status, wealth and power is considered as emergence of class relationships by the structural-functionalists. Structural-functional studies are characterized by mobility within the caste (sanskritization), and norms relating to mobility are of a consensual sort. These studies lack historicity. However, in some studies, structural mobility (downward social mobility, namely, proletarianization and bourgeoisiefication, namely, upward social mobility) have been reported. Resilience is the main feature of caste, according to the structural-functionalists. Future of caste is seen quite safe as it is a localized system of social relations.[25] Kolenda and others do not agree with the view that 'organic solidarity' existed in a congruent fashion at any time in the caste system. Bailey and Beteille assumed 'organic solidarity' in the traditional caste system.[26] Not only Kolenda does refer to a point which goes 'beyond organic solidarity', several historians such as Panikkar, Stein and Thapar have pleaded that there was never perfect congruence between caste, class and power; and mobility and migration were quite normal activities in ancient and medieval India.[27]

Another serious limitation of structural-functional approach is its reliance on analytical abstraction in the form of statistical-mathematical indicators or analytical typologies.[28] D'Souza treats class as a category conceptually abstracted, hence class does not exist as a community unlike caste.[29] Class is defined operationally in terms of certain indices. Marxists would accept this as a non-humanistic view of a system of social relations. It is considered as a 'Brahminical' or 'hierarchical' model of caste society. Leach[30] has labelled Srinivas as the father of 'Brahminocentric' sociology. The 'dalitcentric' sociology or 'upside down' view has been advocated by Mencher, Parvathamma and several others in some recent writings.[31]

Dumont's *Homo Hierarchicus*[32] is the most significant representative of the structuralist approach to the study of caste system in India. Singh[33] points out that pivotal notions of structuralism such as ideology, dialectics, transformational relationship and comparison have been brought in the analysis of caste stratification in India by Dumont. For Dumont, 'hierarchy' is 'ideology' and hierarchy implies 'pure' and 'impure' in regard to all sorts of social relations, hence binary tension or dialectics. 'Pure' and 'impure' are separate in all aspects as well together as parts of the theory of caste hierarchy. 'Hierarchy' also implies the relationship of 'encompassing' and the 'encompassed'. The 'pure' encompasses the 'less pure' or 'impure'. This applies to all the sections and aspects of society. Thus, according to Dumont, change is *in the society* and not *of the society*.

Dumont's view falls in the category of 'cultural-universalistic' type of social stratification. According to Singh, Dumont's structuralism suffers both theoretically and substantively. Pure and impure are fused together instead of being disjunct. The notion of 'contra-priest'[34] by Gould also negates such a separation between the two at a substantive level. Dumont wrongly understands that tradition displies representation of structural relations irrespective of time, place and situation, and which might have changed disproportionately to the changes in the tradition. It is not at all a new idea that caste and class have been treated as binary notions by Dumont. All along the western scholars have done it for the reasons best known to them[35]. Singh observes: "The structuralist's treatment of dialectics is dissociated from history. History, indeed, links essence to existence, form to content, superstructure and theory to practice. Devoid of such a sense of historical conjecture structuralism amounts to a set of conceptual schema, devoid of a basis in evolutionary changes in society. Its transformational relationships being ahistorical abound in tautologies."[36] Dumont's structuralism is no exception to these criticisms.

Structural-historical approach has been applied by both Marxists and non-Marxists scholars. The main emphasis is on structural orientation, historical evolutionary typologies and processual analysis of structures as social movements.[37] The question of origin of caste has recently been resurfaced by Klass.[38] Marxists[39] such as Namboodiripad and Ranadive have made propositions about the nature of caste. The scholars of both the dispositions have not been able to prove their common thesis that social stratification in India has emerged from its ancient egalitarian character. Secondly, the view that from clan-like organization caste has emerged, is not factually tenable. On the contrary, class has emerged from inequalitarian system like caste due to recent change in it. To us, structural-historical approach does not refer to origin of caste or clan or class. It offers a new theoretic interest implying Indian society as a social formation with its different aspects having interlinkages and interrelationships which have evolved over the years due to their constraints and contradictions. This approach has not been applied earnestly by historians, sociologists and anthropologists. Singh[40] is inclined to have a preference for this approach, but he has not analyzed the phenomenon of social stratification with such clear theoretic and methodological preparedness. Some studies of the social origin of equality/inequality have been undertaken but mainly as parts of the studies of social movements without having a direct bearing upon the structural-historical approach.

Marxist categories and concepts have been used in the understanding of national movement in India. The basic tenets of the Marxist approach refer to locating the historical forces in the mode of production and the contradictions of classes. It is essentially evolutionary and developmental and has a dialectical quality of self-transformation. Gough[41] combines Marxist approach with the anthropological tradition of field-work. She considers mode of production as a social formation in which she finds interconnections of caste, kinship, family, marriage and even rituals with forces of production and production relations. Her study of colonial rule in Thanjavur explains the emergence of new bourgeoisie, polarization of peasantry, and the pauperization of the working class due to historical transformations in the modes of production. Totality of contradictions in social stratification could be seen through the contradictions in the mode of production. Thus, Marxists like Gough and even ideologies like Namboodiripad and Ranadive consider class relationships as the domain assumption in the understanding of caste and kinship in India. Even *varna* and *jajmani* systems could be explained in terms of class relations as embeded in the mode of production.[42] The mode of production framework[43] has been put to test at the village level by Djurfeldt Goran and Lindberg, Heera Singh, Thorner, Saith and Tanakha, Bhardwaj and Das.

Caste-class congruence and/or incongruence has been examined in several studies of social movements. 'Caste feudalism' refers to class relations, or caste relations encapsulate class relations, or that caste relations are another name for class relations—are some of the recent expressions based on several studies conducted by social scientists in India.

There are four basic features for understanding caste and class relations and their transformations in regard to Indian society. These are: (1) dialectics, (2) history, (3) culture, and (4) structure. Dialectics does not simply refer to binary fission in the cognitive structure of the society. It refers to the effective notions which bring about contradictions and highlights relations between unequal segments and men and women. History is not again a conjectural construction based on mythology, scriptures and idealistic formulation, but it provides a substantial account of existent conditions of work and relationship; culture does not include just cultural practices, rituals, *rites de passage*, etc., it defines the rules of the game, the nature of relations between the haves and the have-nots and so on. Structure is no doubt a product of dialectical contradictions, historical forces, and certain rules of the game, but it becomes a 'formation' once it has emerged, and in return, becomes a sort of 'force' to determine in some way the course of history, nature of contradictions and the evaluational standards. Thus, structure refers to relations between social segments at a given point of time, but as a historical product and reality. Having these elements as the kernel of structural-historical approach, changes in caste and class structures could be considered as 'transformational' rather than replacements. All the debates regarding caste and class such as caste is closed and class is open, caste is 'organic' in its structure rather than 'segmentary', there is either caste or class, both caste and class are there, class is replacing caste, caste is weakening, class is emerging, etc. may be taken up with this perspective for a better understanding of social stratification.

Jajmani was never an 'organic' system in reality, though apparently it provided such an impression. The idea of 'contra-priest' even cannot undermine the hierarchy which is built into the *jajmani* system. It is necessary to understand the following patterns of change with a historical perspective:

(1) Downward mobility and proletarianization.
(2) Upward mobility and embourgeoisiement.
(3) Urban income for rural people and mobility in the village.
(4) Rural non-agricultural income and mobility.

II

Bougle[44] writes: "To sum up on these points: hereditary specialization, hierarchical organization, reciprocal repulsion, as far as any social form can realize itself in its purity, the caste system is realized in India. At the very least it penetrates Hindu society to a level unknown elsewhere. It plays some part in other civilizations but in India it has invaded the whole. It is in this sense that we may speak of the caste system as a phenomenon peculiar to India." Srinivas,[45] following Bougle, observes pre- eminence of religious values in the caste system, and these values centre around the ideas of pollution and purity. However, Hocart[46] finds that religion encompasses power, hence priesthood is not 'absolute' in nature. Relations between Brahmin and Kshatriya are defined in terms of certain reciprocity, namely, the former represents the 'religious' authority, and the latter enjoys 'political' power.

Srinivas refers to various types of purity and impurity in regard to the Coorgs of South India. He writes: "Normal ritual status is the status which a person enjoys most of the times."[47] Further, he observes: "Ritual impurity, normal ritual status, and ritual purity form a hierarchy. If a person in an impure condition touches another in a condition of either purity or normal ritual status, the latter becomes impure. If a person in a condition of normal ritual status touches another in a pure condition, the latter losses his purity and is reduced to normal ritual status. That is, normal ritual status is a mild form of impurity."[48] Dumont and Pocock, however, observe: "We must discard the reassuring but unjustified expression of 'normal' ritual status."[49] Normal ritual status, which is mildly impure is really outside the realm of the hierarchy of pure and impure in the context of the caste system in India. Ritual bath could eliminate such impurity and after the occasion is over, it could recur. Relations between castes in the caste system are not based on this sort of ephemeral purity or reimpurity after the purification.

Srinivas adds to the confusion that is also realized by Dumont and Pocock[50] when he writes: "The concept of pollution governs relations between different castes. This concept is absolutely fundamental to the caste system."[51] Srinivas further writes: "Some occupations are considered defiling because of the contact with some defiling object or other necessary to their practice. Swine-herding is defiling because swine defiles. Leather defiles, and consequently the making and repairing of shoes is an occupation of the untouchables... Finally, any occupation, however, remotely implying the destruction of sentient life in any form would be prohibited to the high castes."[52] According to Srinivas, sanskritization is the only way to remove impurity or minimize it. We may quote two points made by Dumont and Pocock about Srinivas' notion of pollution and purity among the Coorgs. One is that an object or a person is purer, or less pure (or of course more or less impure) than another. Secondly, a person or an object is impure in relation to one another, for example, when there is avoidable relationship between the two.[53]

Srinivasian sociology is commented upon by Parvathamma:

"In all the writings of Srinivas, the Brahmin-non-Brahmin values are juxtaposed."[54] Hierarchy remains basic to Srinivas' thinking in regard to all aspects of human life even if it is not so pronounced or less existent. Srinivas does not try to analyze the tensions and contradictions which could be caused by what he calls 'sanskritization'. His main emphasis still remains on concepts of dominance and solidarity.[55]

It is not only Srinivas, Dumont, Marriott, Mandelbaum, etc. also have overworked on the themes of caste hierarchy, pollution-purity, religion, rituals and other allied aspects. Their impact on the younger scholars relating to the study of caste has resulted into the neglect of the study of social structure in totality as a social formation. The notions of pollution-purity, hierarchy and dominance have made a strong impact on the minds of scholars, reformers and political leaders as they do not see the social structure beyond these parameters. It is, therefore, necessary first to look into the measures taken for the welfare of the scheduled castes, and then to relate them to the reality of relations between the scheduled castes and caste-Hindus.

III

We are not comparing India's Harijans with Muslims or Blacks for the simple reason that they are a part and parcel of India's social formation at all the levels of its evolution and development. The Blacks have had never been part of the Whites and the same is true about India's Muslims and the tribes. We do not have to go into the genesis of the names 'untouchables', 'ex-untouchables', 'Harijans' or 'scheduled castes,' *dalits* which have been used for the lowest sections of Hindu society. Issacs[56] makes a detailed reference to the beginnings and uses of these names for the scheduled castes of today.

To us, there are two patterns of social mobility among the scheduled castes:[57] (i) the welfare measures have brought about mobility among some selected sections of the scheduled castes, adversely affecting hegemony of the dominant castes in the fields of education and employment; and (ii) social mobility among the scheduled castes is also directly a result of certain socio-cultural movements which in turn has created anti-upper caste attitudes and awareness about their own low position. It is not that these two patterns are quite independent of each other. Since the scheduled castes were also a highly differentiated lot before Independence, that differentiation could be reflected in these broad patterns of social mobility among them. Certain sections of the scheduled castes have taken more advantages of the constitutional safeguards and welfare measures, hence they have more migration to urban centres, education and white-collar employment. The others who perhaps due to their earlier weak position among the scheduled castes had to choose the path of 'sanskritization' for social mobility, and this created tensions without much benefits in concrete terms. Though latently 'sanskritization' might have brought some benefits to the scheduled castes.

We have observed in an earlier article[58] that the scheduled castes suffer today not only because of the imposed social and cultural disabilities but perhaps much more because of the imbalances created by the emergence of structural differentiation within them due to the policies and plans undertaken ostensibly for their uplift and welfare. The differential benefits received by the scheduled castes is a major reason for these continuing inequalities. The two patterns of social mobility on the one hand accentuate class-like distinctions among the scheduled castes, and on the other the demands of equality in relation to the mobile sections of the caste Hindus are not met. Data about Rajasthan in regard to enrolment, hostels and scholarships relating to SCs have amply revealed inter-district, intradistrict, intercaste and disparities.

The atrocities on Harijans and their exploitation by the dominant Hindu castes may be analyzed in view of the distinctions which we find among the scheduled castes *vis-a-vis* their relations with caste Hindus. All types of Harijans have not been equally victims of atrocities of the landlords, rich peasants and upper castes.[59] To say that it is a situation of total class war between caste Hindus and Harijans is not a correct observation. The relations between caste landlords and Harijan labourers are quite intriguing.[60]

The institution of untouchability is not functioning in a wholesome way. Its pollutional aspect has receded, but its reflections are seen quite effectively in economic and social relations. Untouchables have changed along with the changes in structural and cultural aspects of Indian society. The areas of untouchability and non-untouchability have become crystal clear in recent years. Like caste resilience, untouchability has more or less disappeared. It is not that caste has withered away with all its class-like character, and untouchability has been continuing and *vice-versa*. Since caste in the garb of class remains a pivotal force to a large extent, untouchability refers to a situation of exploitation, suppression and powerlessness of the wretched of the earth. Naturally, the exploiters are the well-off caste Hindu landlords and big peasants. Harijans or untouchables may not be doing today what they were forced to do a couple of decades ago, but the Harijans remain under the economic and social hegemony of the landed interests.

IV

Article 46 of the Constitution of India provides: "The state shall promote with special care the educational and economic interests of the weaker sections of the people and, in particular, of the scheduled castes and scheduled tribes, and shall protect them from social injustice and all forms of exploitation."[61] In view of this clause several provisions have been made for the reservation of seats for the scheduled castes in the states of union and in the parliament and reservation for jobs and services at various levels.

Further, Article 17 declares: "Untouchability is abolished and its practice in any form is forbidden. The enforcement of any disability arising out of untouchability shall be an offence punishable in accordance with law."[62] In pursuance of these constitutional provisions, several programmes have been undertaken for the uplift of the scheduled castes.[63]

The question is: "How close to equality are scheduled castes?"[64] Chandi Das reviews the achievements of social welfare programmes for scheduled castes for two decades and finds that their position compared to that of the non-scheduled castes is still very inferior as regards titles to land as well as size of landholdings.

He further writes: "Their depressed position is reflected again in their economic and social mobility. Their rates of urbanization and education, compared to those of non-scheduled castes, are low. And their economic poverty is poignantly underscored in the fact that, as between districts which are at the same level of development, the average per capita income of those with a higher proportion of scheduled castes is much lower."[65] A similar observation is made by Ramaswamy.[66] The policy of preferential treatment of scheduled castes has been in practice for over two decades, but has barely scraped the surface of the problem. Even in the urban areas only a fraction of the posts in the administration which are reserved for them is actually filled. The same is the case in regard to completion of formal education even upto secondary level.

In regard to educational opportunities for the scheduled castes, Premi[67] observes that new inequalities are creeping up among the scheduled castes themselves. She writes: "Mere existence of facilities does not ensure their optimum use. Awareness and acceptance are essential for utilization. To maximize the use it is necessary to generate better awareness. More publicity is needed to ensure the wider use of the facilities and to find out the reasons for the poor use".[68] Premi arrives at the following conclusion:[69]

(i) Education among the scheduled castes may not filter down as expected.

(ii) Equal access for unequal groups is not true equality.

Chauhan[70] observes that the spread of education among the scheduled castes has created social classes among them on lines parallel to those existing in higher society. Chitnis[71] concludes that the scheme of post-matric scholarship is neither equitably distributed not optimally used. Caste patterns within the scheduled castes determine differential distribution and utilization of scholarship and other amenities. Ramaswamy,[72] in another article, reconfirms unevenness among the scheduled castes independent of the imbalances created by education and other measures for their welfare. She writes: "In terms of social and economic status, there are clear differences among the scheduled castes. There is a well recognized hierarchy among them. Not all of them are untouchables, even among those that are, there are degrees of pollution. There are also religious cleavages among the scheduled castes."[73] Each one of the scheduled castes is aware about its identity among themselves, and at the same time is conscious of their shared status as scheduled caste.

The realization that unevenness exists among the scheduled castes has led to the exploration of what is popularly known as 'scheduled caste elites'. Harold's *India's Ex-Untouchables*, Saberwal's *Scheduled Caste Elites of Punjab*, Sachchidananda's *The Harijan Elite* and Deshpande's *Scheduled Caste Elites and Social Change* are some of the most well known titles on this theme. Issacs interviewed 50 educated persons from the scheduled castes; Saberwal added eight more, that is, he interviewed 58; Sachchidananda interviewed 200; and Deshpande slided down much below Issacs, and interviewed only 29 Harijan elites.

Two points of methodological and substantive nature emerge from these studies of scheduled castes and their elites: (i) The reliance is on the information which the researchers could gather from their respondents (elites in this case); and (ii) it is by and large realized that 'unevenness' among the scheduled castes inherently prevalent as well as created by the implementation of policies and programmes for their welfare is mainly responsible for their backwardness. Awareness about this unevenness could have a levelling effect on the weaker sections. However, it would not be correct that nature of elites could be understood by interviewing them. The number of respondents studied is not significant. The nature of investigation is important. Secondly, that diffusion of ideas about the welfare programmes and awareness about their status in the post-independence period could minimize the gap between the caste Hindus and the scheduled castes is also based on erroneous premises. It is quite likely that we get neither proper understanding of the structure of the scheduled castes *vis-a-vis* caste Hindus nor of the substantial reduction of the hiatus between the scheduled castes and caste Hindus as the problems of the scheduled castes are dealt at the surface level only.

Patwardhan observes: "The overall perspective is that there is an increasing possibility for upward mobility for all the Harijans."[74] She further states that there are two processes of mobility:

(i) through corporate efforts; and (ii) by competing between castes and within a caste.[75] Patwardhan also notices intercaste variability in regard to social mobility, and "sacred and secular models in different contexts." Migration, education and white-collar jobs, particularly outside the village, have been the main source of social mobility among the scheduled castes. The gist of Partwardhan's analysis is that social mobility among the scheduled castes has been immense and a multiplicity of factors have contributed to this particularly since independence. However, Patwardhan's view that 'ascription' does not play such a role in social mobility looks only superficial. Ascription- achievement dichotomy is not viable for understanding mobility at the empirical level. Ascription promotes achievement, and in turn such an achievement adds to ascription, and in this way, in real life, it is found as a complicating process, and if it continues for decades and centuries no significant change may be brought by Constitution or Untouchability Offenses Act of 1955 or other measures. In a recent study, Malik[76] observes that as a consequence of social mobility among scheduled castes, their social status, pattern of interaction, levels of aspirations, family pattern, employment of wives and awareness of government policies have also changed. However, these aspects have been studied without knowing the basic structural questions and the complexity of ascription and achievement. Duskin and Lynch refer to unity among the scheduled castes beyond the village particularly for political action in towns and cities.[77] Menchar and Mahar also find the similar political mobilization among the scheduled castes.[78] Mobilization of such a sort may be counterproductive, and consequently the non-scheduled castes also mobilize themselves perhaps with greater resources and vigour than the scheduled castes.

V

All Harijans are not equally victims of atrocities committed by the landlords, the rich peasants and the upper castes.[79] Why is it so? Is it perhaps due to the fact that the Harijans who are not victims belong to a higher 'class' than other Harijans who fall a prey to the rich landlords? The following questions are quite revelant:

Why some of the families of Harijans are tortured and exploited?

Why the Harijans of a particular village who have generally a low and poor status among the Harijans are victimized?

Why only certain sections of Harijans have extracted most of the benefits extended to them by the central and state governments and voluntary agencies?

Why some castes and groups have advanced in the field of education, and others have migrated to towns from their native places just for bare survival?

Why atrocities are committed only on Harijans and not on their non-untouchable counterparts (in the sense of class) from among the caste Hindus?

Massacre, loot and rape of the scheduled castes in Belchi, Agra, Pant Nagar, Marathwada, Bajitpur and other places are known to all of us.[80] In an attempt to understand the role of caste system *vis-a-vis* class struggle and class organization, the Atyachar Virodhi Samiti in Maharashtra was constituted.[81] It observes: "The caste system functions both as a relation of production and as an ideology."[82] The Samiti further observes: "The caste system functions as an extremely effective method of economic exploitation. The class which has economic power also acquires political power and social prestige which helps it to perpetuate, consolidate and justify its position in the hierarchy. Caste hierarchies also effect ownership of land. Economic hierarchy is closely linked with social hierarchy. The caste system is not merely division of labour. It is also a division of labourers. Capitalist relations make agricultural and industrial labourers into a distinct *class in itself*, but the caste system prevents them from being a *class for itself*."[83] Caste and religion are used to perpetuate a particular class structure. Caste persists as a part of feudal ideology. The Samiti observes that caste system has prevented formation of consciousness and struggle on class lines with any commonalty of interest or unity of function. This function is one of the main resources for its persistence. The Samiti agrees with Mencher's observation that "conflicts between social classes stem ultimately from the social relations of production." The new functions of the caste resemble with the old class-like functions of the caste system, hence discouragement to the emergence of class consciousness. Such a situation is not peculiar to Maharashtra only. Singh[84] has reported about a similar situation in Punjab. One could find 'class character' in the 'spectre of caste war' in Gujarat in regard to reservation of seats for scheduled castes in state's medical colleges.[85]

The above point is very well brought out by Bose[86] in a study of the riots in Gujarat. He observes that literacy, education and employment are the most important indicators of social mobility among the scheduled castes, and geographical spread of the violence is closely related to social mobility of the scheduled castes affected by violence.[87] Those sections of the scheduled castes who are relatively better educated, more mobile and have some access to jobs have been most seriously affected by the present caste riots. The areas, thus affected, have also a relative concentration of the scheduled castes. Bose also admits that there may be deep-rooted caste prejudices among the upper castes against the Harijans, but at the same time it is also a fact that the rivalry is now between the well-off scheduled castes and the caste Hindus who are entrenched into lucrative jobs, positions of power and high status. In effect, it is a 'class war' between the apparent caste riots, between the scheduled castes and *savarnas*. I.P. Desai, who has earlier written a book on *Untouchability in Rural Gujarat*, also looks at the relations between the scheduled castes and the caste Hindus from a class point of view. Ingle[88] finds that Untouchability Offences Act, 1955 has been flouted by caste Hindus in Maharashtra quite frequently, and without much corresponding corrective steps. Desai observes: "The system of reservations, even though introduced by the state, has now become a weapon in the hands of the various deprived groups in their struggle against socially entrenched upper caste and upper class interests."[89] The upper castes and classes want to maintain the social and economic *status quo* under the cover of seemingly progressive ideology and demand that 'merit' and not 'caste' should be the determining factor in higher education, jobs, promotions, etc. The scheduled castes and the scheduled tribes and other socially disadvantaged groups through their agitation have tried to attack on this status quo by insisting upon reservations which apparently might appear as a particularistic ideology.

Some empirical studies at the village level reveal a high concentration of socially backward castes among the tenant cultivators.[90] Reddy and Murthy find that as many as 73 per cent of the pure tenant cultivators belong to the backward castes, and of the owner-cum-tenant cultivators 70 per cent belong to these backward castes. The backward caste tenant cultivators are predominant in the small and medium size groups. The socially backward castes in Andhra consists of Settibaliji and Harijan, and the socially advanced castes consist of Brahmin, Kapu, Devanga and others. Thus, most of the tenants of small and medium size belong to economically and socially depressed castes and pure rent receivers except 12 per cent who belong to the dominant castes. The latter are getting more benefits from technological changes than the small size cultivators.

While discussing realities of agrarian relations in India, Mukherjee[91] discusses caste/class dichotomy and observes that at the root of different forms of social organization, namely, caste and class are the common causal factors which have brought caste, religion and class on the same political and economic dimensions. He cites the example of caste riots and observes: "Caste riots are frequent in those areas where the castewise 'social' deprivations are manifestly correlated with the classwise economic deprivations, such as in Bihar, Maharashtra, Tamil nadu, etc."[92] According to Mukherjee, these caste contradictions are due to inherent class contradictions in the caste system.

Vagiswari[93] compares the income and occupation of Harijans and non-Harijans. He finds that the position of the Harijans has worsened over the past ten to twenty years. He estimated that the per capita annual income of the Harijans in 1970 was Rs. 227 as against Rs. 406 for the non-Harijans. He finds that in terms of all economic indicators—size of landholding, employment, occupation, savings—the position of Harijans had progressively worsened between 1950 and 1970; also it had deteriorated compared to the non-Harijans during the same period.

Consequently, the *dalits* or Harijans are attacked, murdered, their womenfolk raped, and other cruel and inhuman treatment is meted out to them. The accounts of such atrocities are innumerable.[94] In case the scheduled castes react even mildly against the atrocities, they are forced to pay a very high price including social boycott, denial of public facilities and employment on farms by the landlords. Such incidents have taken place quite frequently in Bihar, Uttar Pradesh, Gujarat, Maharashtra, Tamil Nadu, Rajasthan, etc. In the Belchi killings on May 27, 1977, nine Harijans and two others—all agricultural labourers were tortured and then burnt alive by dominant caste Hindus.[95] Singh provides a vivid account of atrocities and oppression of the scheduled castes in Madhya Pradesh.[96]

In a forthright despatch, Sinha[97] comments on Bihar situation and observes that it is class war against Harijans, and not atrocities. In 1977, Bihar, among all states, accounted for the largest number of cases of atrocities against Harijans. The outrages occurred in Kargdhar, Belchi, Pathadda, Chhaundano, Gopalpur and Dharampur. People were killed or persecuted not because they were Harijans, but also because they were agricultural labourers and sharecroppers working with the rich and dominant landlords, hence cruelties against them were of the nature of a class war as the interests of the two did not coincide and class contradictions had become more than manifest. The issues behind these happenings were struggles for minimum wages, the occupancy rights of the sharecroppers, and a challenge to the absolute feudal power of the landlords. Therefore, such atrocities (class war) could be against the non-Harijan proletariat, the backward castes, and even against the poor intermediate and upper castes proletariat. Logically this view could be accepted on the basis of class war thesis. But it is only partially true. There is an element of Harijanness in the atrocities committed by the caste Hindus on the Harijans.[98] There is a difference between a situation of atrocity and that of oppression and exploitation. There is a difference between a Brahmin proletariat and a Harijan proletariat, hence the differential treatment meted to the two by a Brahmin or Rajput landlord for the same reason. What is known as "the rise of the Kulak power at the centre and in the states", can be held responsible for the oppression of the scheduled castes. The attitude of patronhood or patronage has slowly been disappearing away particularly since independence.

Mukherjee,[99] while writing about the peasant revolt in Bhojpur district of Bihar, observes that *izzat* (dignity) and *uncheneeche jaat ka sanghrush* (upper-lower caste conflict) are the two main causes of bitterness between the upper and lower castes and class people. He writes: "The dehumanization of the lower castes is violent and physical: rampant sexual tyranny perpetuated by the upper castes on lower caste women; the pride of Bhumihars, whose unwritten law prohibits lower classes to remain seated in their presence even at their doorstep; its viewing even the wearing of a clean *dhoti* or receiving education as intolerable ignorance; the 'hakim' suffix after every sentence; at places, the taking of *dole*, i.e., the Bhumihar or Rajput landlord's privilege to sleep with the new bride of a lower caste labourer on the wedding night."[100] Movement for creation of Jharkhand State for the *adivasis* and slogans like "Harijanisthan lar ke leinge" (we will fight for a state for Harijans) are expressions of the oppression and sufferings of the Harijans and tribals at the hands of the dominant castes/classes in Bihar.

In Marathwada, the riots began due to renaming of Marathwada University as Dr. Babasaheb Ambedkar University in July 1978. The Students Action Committee, which naturally consisted of non-*dalit* student activists, launched an agitation against the *dalits* which continued for 67 days. The Protection of Civil Rights Act did not help the victims in getting out of the inhuman situation prevailing in the region. The movement provoked violence including killing of people, molestation and rape of Harijan women, burning of Harijan houses and huts, pillaging their *basties*, evicting them from their houses and villages, killing of their cattle, denying them drinking water and refusing them work, etc.[101] This act of the caste Hindu capitalists, landlords with the help of the state power was planned to give a serious setback to the *dalit* movement and its vocal leadership. Thus, an explanation for understanding the pitiable position of Harijans should be searched in the character of social structure of Indian society. The causes of their exploitation, oppression and intimidation are not casual, short lived, and contingent in nature. Dignity and upper-lower caste/class have been the two focal points of discord and contradictions throughout the history of the Hindu society.

A study was conducted by the Harijan Sevak Sangh in 1976 in 179 villages of nine districts of Madhya Pradesh. It is reported that important programmes like land distribution, irrigation, distribution of homestead plots, debt redemption, freeing of bonded labour and financial help schemes were only marginally implemented. Most of the 54 lakh Harijans in the state are agricultural labourers or landless peasants and their future is in the hands of a few big farmers. They were paid as low as Rs. 1.50 for a day's labour. They were put to all sorts of inhuman treatment and indignity. Uttar Pradesh tops the list of atrocities, and Madhya Pradesh comes next to Uttar Pradesh. In the first half of 1973-74, 254 cases were reported, and 18 of these were murder, 37 rape, 38 arson, 81 grievously hurt cases, and 80 offences under Untouchability Offences Act. During 1974-75, 11812 cases were registered.

In 1977, there were 8,905 cases of alleged atrocities on the scheduled castes, and that highest number of atrocities were reported from Uttar Pradesh (4,974), but according to another source the number was 5,739, and in 1976 it was 3,428 and in 1975 it was 6,760— higher than those of both 1976 and 1977. As many as 2,133 incidents of atrocities were reported from Madhya Pradesh. Other states had: Andhra Pradesh (70), Bihar (421), Gujarat (331), Kerala (136), Maharashtra (367), Rajasthan (179), and Punjab (81). The report refers to land disputes, payment of wages at lower rates, indebtedness and forced labour, forcing the Harijans to perform manual jobs and creating obstruction in the use of public places, particularly drinking water wells.

In 1975-76 and 1876-77, the scheduled castes and Scheduled Tribes Commission received, 2,295 and 1,761 complaints, respectively, regarding harassment and untouchability, land and agriculture, housing and education from the scheduled castes and the scheduled tribes. The Commission reports that all the cases are not reported, and out of the reported cases, only some are found punishable because of legalities and other factors such as lack of evidence, etc.[102]

Conclusion

There was a time when studies on caste by ethnographers, anthropologists, sociologists and lately by political scientists, economists and historians became quite popular. Every aspect of the society was viewed in the idiom of caste. To the students who studied caste, class remained almost invisible as a social reality. But others who studied class quite consciously thought that 'caste divisions' persisted along with 'real class divisions' in Indian society. Scholars of either hue and orientation did not see the existence of the social formation of Indian society which absorbed caste, class, race, ethnicity, minorities, religions and regions. The change in the emphasis on the studies from caste to class, or from hierarchy to stratification, or from closed to open stratification or change in the application of the methods of study from 'indological' to 'empirical' and now 'experimental' are no doubt indicators of the realization of the need for studying what is more relevant than what was in the past. However, even these shifts in the foci of studies and research are not properly perceived. To think of Indian society simply in terms of 'caste' as the social formation implying harmony, hegemony, reciprocity, hierarchy, division of labour and stability of the society and vice versa from a class point of view would create confusions and misconceptions.

A scholar of the eminence of Srinivas[103] does not take cognizance, perhaps inadvertently, of the continuity of 'social formation' of Indian society, and prefers to adhere to "caste model" of Indian society. He refers to 'rural caste' and 'urban caste' like some American scholars such as Rosen and Marriott.[104] Caste and class, theoretically speaking, are principles of status determination, hence not concerned with 'rural' or 'urban' people as such. Rural and urban are patterns of living and not principles of ranking. Srinivas observes that "even today agricultural production requires the co-operation of several castes, and even traditionally competition between different castes did occur though it was not very common."[105] He further notes that "caste idiom is widespread", but does not realize that it could also be called as 'class idiom', or idiom of Indian society itself. Srinivas states that there are caste continuities, discontinuities, and fuzzy/areas without clear-cut boundaries with multiple and contrary forces at work. Thus, Srinivas refuses to admit existence of 'class relations'.

We have pointed out that mode of production and differentiation of peasantry are dynamic in nature. Transformation in these could be understood by a framework which includes dialectics, history, culture, and structure. Structural-historical perspective is found quite useful. The rules and regulations to bring about social mobility among the scheduled castes have become quite ineffective. The frame of pure and impure and sanskritization has been unable to account for structural changes among the scheduled castes. Differentiation among the scheduled castes has accentuated unevenness of a new sort among them. Atrocities and violence against the scheduled castes are a clear indicator of a 'class war' between the well-off caste Hindus and the well-off scheduled castes. Oppression and exploitation are not new to the scheduled castes. The only difference is that now there is more possibility of making a hue and cry than before whenever violence takes place. A class view of the status of the scheduled castes in the caste system could reveal the dynamics of social mobility. Srinivas is perhaps not prepared to accept clearly that caste has also been a system of class relations as well. He says: "there is fuzziness," this is just to avoid the issue and clinch to his well known position of 'caste sociologist'. Leach[106] feels that the tradition of British empiricism has been used the way it suits for the purposes of analyses—it has become a matter of convenience rather than a matter of scientific investigation. Leach's fear is that such an attitude in use of empiricism brings in the subjectivity and cultural idiosyncracies of the researcher. We are very often accused of doing Brahmin or Rajput or Raiyot sociology. We have to guard ourselves from such accusations by bringing refinement in our methodology and understanding.

Notes

1. Chitnis, S., "Education for Equality: Case of Scheduled Castes", *Economic and Political Weekly*, Vol. VII, Nos. 31, 32 and 33, August, 1972; and Chitnis. S., *A Long Way to Go*, Surat: Centre for Social Studies (mimeographed).
2. Den, Ouden, J.H.B., De Onnanraakbaran Von Konkunad, Wageningen: H.Veenman and Zonen B.V., Wageningen, 1975, p. 227.
3. Ibid.
4. Ibid., pp. 227-30.
5. Risley, H.H., *The People of India*, Delhi: Orient Books, 1960, p. 47; Senart, E., *Caste in India: The Facts and the System*, London: Metheun & Co. 1930, p. 35; and Ketkar, S.V., *History of Caste in India*, Jaipur: Rawat Publications, 1990, p. 15.
6. Furnivall, J.S., *Netherlands, India: A Study of Plural Economy*, Cambridge: Cambridge University Press, 1939; Hutton, J.H., *Caste in India*, London: Oxford University Press, 1963; and Sherring, M.A., *Hindu Castes and Tribes*, Delhi: Cosmo Publications, 1974.
7. Singh, Y., "The role of Social Sciences in India: A Sociology of Knowledge," *Sociological Bulletin*, Vol. 22, No. 1, March, 1973, pp. 14-28.
8. Dube, S.C. (ed.), *Social Sciences and Social Realities: Role of the Social Sciences in Contemporary India*, Simla: Indian Institute of Advanced Study, 1976; Singh, Y., "Constraints, Contradictions and Interdisciplinary Orientation: The Indian Context", *International Social Science Journal*, Vol. 31, No. 1, 1979.
9. Thorner, D., *Land and Labour in India*, Bombay: Asia Publishing House, 1974.
10. Karve, I., *Kinship Organisation in India*, Bombay: Asia Publishing House, 1953; and Saran, A.K., "A Review of Contributions to Indian Sociology", *Eastern Anthropologist*, Vol. 15, 1962, pp. 53-68.
11. Mukerji, D.P., *Diversities*, Delhi: Peoples Publishing House. 1958, pp. 228-241.
12. Desai, A.R., *Social Background of Indian Nationalism*, Bombay: Popular Prakashan, 1948.
13. Mencher, J.P., "The Caste System Upside Down, or The Not-So-Mysterious East", *Current Anthropology*, Vol. 15, No. 4, December, 1974; Leach, E.R., "Introduction: What Should We Mean By Caste?" in E.R. Leach (ed.), *Aspects of Caste in South India, Ceylon and North-West Pakistan*, Cambridge: Cambridge University Press, 1960, pp. 113-46; and Saberwal, S., "Sociologists and Inequality in

India: The Historical Context", *Economic and Political Weekly*, Vol. XIV, Nos. 7 and 8, February, 1979.

14. Sharma, K.L., "New Introduction", in J. Murdoch, *Review of Caste in India*, Jaipur: Rawat Publications, 1977, p. VII.
15. Sinha, S., "Caste in India", A Survey of Research in Sociology and Social Anthropology, Vol. I, ICSSR, Bombay: Popular Prakashan, pp. 248-49.
16. Beteille, A., "The Politics of Non-antagonistic Strata", *Contributions to Indian Sociology* (New Series), 1969, pp. 17-31.
17. Beteille, A., *Caste, Class and Power*, California: California University Press, 1965.
18. Bhatt, A., *Caste, Class and Politics*, Delhi: Manohar Book Service, 1975.
19. Aggarwal, P.C., *Caste, Religion and Power*, New Delhi: Shri Ram Centre for Industrial Relations, 1971.
20. Sharma, K.L., *Essays on Social Stratification*, Jaipur: Rawat Publications, 1980.
21. Dumont, L., *Homo Hierarchicus*, London: Paladin, 1970; Leach, E.R. (ed.), op.cit., 1960, pp. 1-10.
22. Barth, F., "The System of Social Stratification in Swat, North Pakistan", in E.R. Leach (ed.), op.cit., 1960, pp. 113-46; Berreman, G.D., "Stratification, Pluralism and Interaction: A Comparative Analysis of Caste", in Anthony De Reuck and Julie Knight (eds.), *Caste and Race*, London: J&A Churchil Ltd., 1967, pp. 45-73.
23. Singh, Y., "Sociology of Social Stratification in India", A Survey of Research in Sociology and Social Anthropology, Vol. 1, Bombay: Popular Prakashan, 1974, pp. 311- 82.
24. Singh, Y., "Sociology of Social Stratification in India-II" (Draft) Prepared for Second Survey of Research in Sociology and Social Anthropology, New Delhi: ICSSR, 1981, p. 10.
25. Kolenda, P., *Caste in Contemporary India: Beyond Organic Solidarity*, California: Benjamin Dimmings Publishing Co. 1978.
26. Bailey, F.G., "Closed Social Stratification in India", *European Journal of Sociology*, Vol. IV, No. 1, 1963, pp. 107- 24; and Beteille, A., op.cit., 1965, pp. 224-46.
27. Panikkar, K.M., *Hindu Society at the Crossroads*, Bombay: Asia Publishing House, 1955; Stein, B., "Social Mobility and Medieval South Indian Hindu Sects," in James, Silverberg (ed.), *Social Mobility in the Caste System in India*, The Hague: Mouton, 1968, pp. 78-94; and Thaper, R., "Social Mobility in Ancient Indian Society", in

R.S. Sharma (ed.), *Indian Society: Historical Probings*, New Delhi: People's Publishing House, 1974, pp. 95-123.
28. Singh, Y., op.cit., 1981, p. 12.
29. D'Souza, V.S., "Social Inequalities and Development in India", *Economic and Political Weekly*, Vol. X, No. 19, May 10, 1975, pp. 770-73.
30. Leach, E.R., "Social Anthropology: A Natural Science of Society?" *Radcliffe-Brown Lecture Proceedings of the British Academy*, Vol. LXII, London, 1976.
31. Mencher, J.P., op. cit., 1974, pp. 469-93; and Parvathamma, C., "The Remembering Village: A Brahminical Odyssey", *Contributions to Indian Sociology* (New Series), Vol. 12, No. 1, January-June, 1978, pp. 91-96.
32. Dumont, L., op.cit., 1974.
33. Singh, Y., op.cit., 1981, p. 15.
34. Gould, A.H., "Priest and Contrapriest: A Structural Analysis of Jajmani Relationships in the Hindu Plains and the Nilgiri Hills", *Contributions to Indian Sociology* (New Series), No. 1, 1967, pp. 26-55.
35. Sharma, K.L., op.cit., 1980, pp. 1-25.
36. Singh, Y., op.cit., 1981, p. 20.
37. Ibid.
38. Klass, M., *Caste: The Emergence of the System in South Asia*, Philadelphia: Institute for the Study of Human Issues, 1978.
39. Namboodiripad, E.M.S., "Caste Conflicts Vs. Growing Unity of Popular Democratic Forces", *Economic and Political Weekly*, Vol. XIV, Nos. 7 and 8, February, 1979, pp. 319-26; and Ranadive, B.T., "Caste, Class and Poverty Relations", *Economic and Political Weekly*, Vol. XIV, Nos. 7 and 8, February, 1979, pp. 337-48.
40. Singh, Y., op.cit, 1979, p. 303.
41. Gough, K.E., "Modes of Production in Southern India", *Economic and Political Weekly*, Vol., XV, Nos., 5,6 and 7, February, 1980, pp. 337-64.
42. Meillassoux, C., "Are there Castes in India?", *Economy and Society*, February, 1973, pp. 89-111.
43. Goran, D. and Lindberg, J., *Behind Poverty: The Social Formation of a Tamil Village*, The Scandinavian Institute of Asian Studies (Monograph Series), London: Curzon Press, 1975; Singh, H., "Kin, Caste and Kisan Movement: Some Questions to the Conventional Sociology of Kin and Caste", *The Journal of Peasant Studies*, Vol., 7, No. 1, October, 1979; Thorner, D., "Capitalist Farming in India,"

Economic and Political Weekly, Vol. IV, No. 52, December 27, 1969; Saith, A., and Tanakha, A., "Agrarian Transition and the Differentiation of Peasantry: A Study of West UP Village", *Economic and Political Weekly*, Vol. VII, No. 14, April, 1972, pp. 712-23; and Bhardwaj, K., and Das, P.K., "Tenurial Conditions and Mode of Exploitation: A Study of Some Villages in Orissa", *Economic and Political Weekly*, Vol. X, Nos. 5, 6 and 7, February, 1975, pp. 222-23.

44. Bougle, C., "The Essence and Reality of the Caste System", Contributions to Indian Sociology, No. II, 1958, p. 29.
45. Srinivas, M.N., *Religion and Society among the Coorgs of South India*, Bombay: Oxford University Press, 1952, pp. 26-28.
46. Hocart, A.M., *Caste*, London: Methew & Co., 1950, p. 56.
47. Srinivas, M.N., op.cit., 1952, p. 106.
48. Ibid, pp. 106-107.
49. Dumont, L., and Pocock, D.F., "Pure and Impure:M.N. Srinivas' Religion and Society among the Coorgs", *Contributions to Indian Sociology*, No. III, July, 1959, p. 17.
50. Ibid., pp. 17-18.
51. Srinivas, M.N., op.cit., 1952, p. 26.
52. Ibid., p. 28.
53. Dumont, L., Pocock, D.F., op.cit, 1959, pp. 23-24.
54. Parvathamma, C., op.cit., 1978, p. 91.
55. Ibid., p. 95.
56. Issacs, H.R., *India's Ex-untouchables*, Bombay: Asia Publishing House, 1965.
57. Sharma, K.L., op.cit, 1980, p. 183.
58. Sharma, K.L., "Class Stratification and Atrocities", *Seminar*, Vol. 243, November, 1979.
59. Sharma, K.L., op.cit., 1980, pp. 169-170.
60. Ibid., p. 170.
61. Constitution of India, Government of India, Article 46.
62. Ibid., Article 17.
63. Dube, S.N. and Mathur, U., "Welfare Programmes for Scheduled Castes: Content and Administration", *Economic and Political Weekly*, Vol. VII, No. 4, January, 1972, pp. 165-175.
64. Chandi, D.R., "How Close to Equality are Scheduled Castes?", *Economic and Political Weekly*, Vol. IV, No. 24, June 14, 1969, pp. 975-79.
65. Ibid., p. 975.

66. Ramaswamy, U., "Scheduled Castes in Andhra: Some Aspects of Social Change", *Economic and Political Weekly*, Vol. IX, No. 29, July 20, 1974: and Ramaswamy, U., "Self-Identity among Scheduled Castes: A Study of Andhra", *Economic and Political Weekly*, Vol. IX, No. 47, November, 1974, pp. 1153-58.
67. Premi, K., "Educational Opportunities for the Scheduled Castes: Role of Protective Discrimination in Equalization", *Economic and Political Weekly*, Vol. IX, Nos. 45 and 46, November 9, 1974, pp. 1902-1910.
68. Ibid.
69. Ibid., p. 1909.
70. Chauhan, B.R., "Social Problems regarding the Education among the Scheduled Castes", in M.S. Gore, I.P. Desai and Suma Chitnis (eds.), *Papers in Sociology of Education in India*, New Delhi: NCERT, 1967, p. 246.
71. Chitnis, S., op.cit., 1972, pp. 1675-81.
72. Ramaswamy, U., op.cit., 1974, pp. 1159-64.
73. Ibid., p. 1959.
74. Patwardhan, S., *Change among India's Harijans*, Delhi:Orient Longmans, 1973, p. 186.
75. Ibid., pp. 188-89.
76. Malik, S., *Social Integration of Scheduled Castes*, New Delhi:Abhinav Publications, 1979.
77. Duskin, L., "Caste Associations in Bangalore", *Economic and Political Weekly*, Vol. XV, No. 37, September 13, 1980, pp. 155-57; and Lynch, O.M., *The Politics of Untouchability*, Delhi: National Publishing House, 1974, pp. 20- 31.
78. Mencher, J.P., "Community and Change in an ex-Untouchable Community of South India," in J. Michael Mahar (ed.), *The Untouchables in Contemporary India*, Arizona: The University of Arizona Press, 1968, pp. 37-56; and Mahar, M.J., "Agents of Dharma in a North Indian Village", in J. Michael Mahar (ed.), op.cit., 1968, pp. 17-36.
79. Sharma, K.L., op.cit., 1979, pp. 22-25.
80. Reports on Khanjawala near Delhi and Belchi in Bihar may be found in *Economic and Political Weekly*, Vol. XIV, Nos. 5 and 6, February, 1979.
81. Atyachar Virodhi Samiti was formed by a group of activists in Maharashtra who gave report on Maharashtra riots. Atyachar Virodhi Samiti, "Marathwada Riots: A Report", *Economic and Political Weekly*, Vol. XIV, No. 19, May 12, 1979.

82. Ibid., p. 851.
83. Ibid.
84. Singh, A.P., "Farm Workers Vs. Rich Peasants: Caste and Class in Panjab Villages", *Economic and Political Weekly*, Vol. XIV, Nos. 42 and 43, October 27, 1979, pp. 1751-52.
85. Yagnik, A., "Gujarat Spectre of Caste War", *Economic and Political Weekly*, Vol. XVI, No. 13, March, 1981, pp. 553-55.
86. Bose, P.K., "Social Mobility and Caste Violence: A Study of Gujarat Riots", *Economic and Political Weekly*, Vol. XVI, No. 16, April 18, 1981, pp. 713-16.
87. Ibid.
88. Ingle, M.D., *Untouchability and Role of Legislation: A Sociological Analysis* (M.Phil. Dissertation), New Delhi: Centre for the Study of Social Systems, Jawaharlal Nehru University, 1979.
89. Desai, I.P., "Anti-Reservation Agitation and Structure of Gujarat Society", *Economic and Political Weekly*, Vol. XVI, No. 8, May 2, 1981, p. 819.
90. Reddy, V.N. and Murthy, C.S., "Backward Castes and Tenancy: A Village Study", *Economic and Political Weekly*, Vol. XIII, No. 26, July 1, 1978, pp. 1061-76.
91. Mukherjee, R., "Realities of Agrarian Relations in India", *Economic and Political Weekly*, Vol. XVI, No. 4, January 24, 1981, pp. 109-116.
92. Ibid., p. 112.
93. Vagiswari, A., *Income Earning Trends and Social Status of Harijan Community in Tamil Nadu*, Madras: Institute of Development Studies, 1972.
94. Bombay attack on Dalit Panthers may be found under the title "Bombay: Attack on Dalit Panthers", *Economic and Political Weekly*, Vol. IX, No. 3, January 19, 1974, pp. 51-52.
95. Bhushan, S., "Bihar: The Belchi Killings", *Economic and Political Weekly*, Vol. XII, No. 25, June 18, 1977, p. 1974.
96. Singh, N.K., "Madhya Pradesh: After the Massacrs", *Economic and Political Weekly*, Vol. XII, No. 25, June 18, 1977, pp. 1800-02.
97. Sinha, A., "Bihar: Violence against the Poor", *Economic and Political Weekly*, Vol. XII, No. 15 April 8, 1977, pp. 2037-40.
98. Sharma, K.L., op.cit., 1980, p. 176.
99. Mukherjee, K., "Peasant Revolt in Bhojpur", *Economic and Political Weekly*, Vol. XIII, No. 34, August 26, 1979, pp. 1536-39.
100. Ibid., p. 1537.

101. Sharma, K.L., op.cit., 1980, pp. 178-79; and Morkhandikar, R.S., "Marathwada Riots: The Background", *Economic and Political Weekly*, Vol. XIII, No. 4, January 24, 1979, pp. 1461-62.
102. Reports of the Commissioner for Scheduled Castes and Scheduled Tribes, Part-I, 1975 and 1976 (24th Report) and Part-II, 1977-78.
103. Srinivas, M.N., "Future of Indian Caste", *Economic and Political Weekly*, Vol. XIV, Nos. 7 and 8, 1979, pp. 237- 242.
104. Rosen, G., *Democracy and Economic Change in India*, Berkeley: University of California Press, 1966; and Marriot, McKim, "Multiple Reference in Indian Caste System", in James Silverberg (ed.), *Social Mobility in the Caste System in India*, The Hague: Mouton Publishers, 1968, pp. 103-114.
105. Srinivas, M.N., op.cit., 1979, p. 242.
106. Leach, E.R., op.cit., 1976, pp. 19-20.

12

The Harijans and Class Stratification

Untouchability is an age-old phenomenon. It has been said that the untouchables of India occupied the lowest position in the *varna* or caste system, hence untouchables and stratification were correlated. But this statement does not stand valid today in India to a large extent, and it was not completely true in the past as well. The untouchables were a highly differentiated category of people, and they had a hierarchy of their own, and therefore their relations with caste Hindus were not of a similar nature. In other words, different castes and subcastes of untouchables had differential relations with different caste Hindus depending upon the ranks of both the untouchables and the *swarnas*. Some of the families of the untouchables found positions of respect in the courts of the feudals while others did 'forced labour' during their life-time. Some untouchables were close to the upper caste families, while others were not so. Some castes and subcastes were less impure than others, and therefore, they had different relations with the caste Hindus.

Such a situation was not just due to the notions of pollution and purity of birth ascription. Distinctions among various castes and subcastes of untouchables were of a wholesome nature as they were reflected in their styles of life, traditional callings, relations with 'clean' and the upper castes and opportunities for mobility and migration etc. The situation of untouchables today cannot be understood without viewing the stratificational relations which they had in the past. Today, all types of Harijans are not equally victims of atrocities of the landlords, rich peasants and the upper castes. Why some of the families of Harijans are tortured and exploited? Why the Harijans of a particular village, who have generally a low and poor status among the Harijans, are victimized? Why only certain sections of Harijans have extracted most of the benefits extended to them by the central and the state governments and voluntary agencies? Why some castes and groups have advanced in the field of education and others have migrated to towns from their native places just for bare survival? These are some of the very relevant questions for understanding of the problems of the Harijans of India today.

The institution of untouchability is functioning selectively, but quiet effectively, in certain arenas of our social relations. It has eroded in regard to its pollutional aspect to a large extent, but it does not show encouraging trend of decline in regard to its social and economic dimensions. This shows that the institution of untouchability has been a dynamic institution of Indian society. Changes in the institution of untouchability have occurred from time to time corresponding with the changes in other institutions such as caste, property, land tenure, hereditary occupations etc. Some of the ex-untouchables are not strictly 'untouchables' today, and some others continue to sail in the same boat. Such a situation demands an analysis of structural factors which have brought about mobility, migration and awareness among the Harijans of today. Secondly, untouchability is a contextual and relational phenomenon. The untouchables are treated as 'untouchables' in a given context, and they are treated like 'non-untouchables' in some other contexts. We could call these as 'sacred' and 'mundane' contexts, respectively. Thus, the view that an untouchable must not be 'touched' physically, has no meaning in a secular context. For example, when the upper caste Hindus work with the untouchables on their farms, or when they wish to extract work from them, or when they visit Harijan houses during elections, we could refer these as secular contexts. However, the untouchables are treated as 'polluting creatures', when they are invited to eat at the patron's houses on certain occasions. The discriminatory treatment meted to them is an ample testimony of the 'sacred' context. It could be said, therefore, that all untouchables are not equally 'untouchables' among themselves, and also in relation to the caste Hindus. Further, it could be said that untouchability is not the sole criterion of untouchable's status in our society. Since untouchability and caste stratification are closely interrelated and caste has been a dynamic and adaptive system, untouchability should be studied through a processual perspective.

There are different views regarding untouchability. First, the functions performed by the untouchables are considered necessary, useful and important for the entire society. In other words, untouchability would continue so long as the untouchables performed these functions. Contrary to this is the view according to which untouchability refers to a situation of exploitation, suppression and powerlessness. The untouchables are pauperized and the wretched of the earth. They are the lowliest of the lowest. Their exploiters are the well-off caste Hindu landlords and big peasants. However, both the views do not explain singularly or together the position of Harijans in relation to other castes. The positions of Harijans as well as caste Hindus have changed to a large extent, hence no traditional web of relations between the two. For example, the upper castes do not continue to be landowners, and the Harijans do not work on the traditional basis. The intermediate castes have gained the status of landowners, and the Harijans work on their fields as agricultural labourers on a daily wage basis. When the poor Harijans refuse to work due to some genuine reasons including less wages, they become a target of the fury of the landlords. Bihar, Uttar Pradesh, Haryana and Rajasthan have this sort of conflict between the Harijans and the rich peasants, and the latter are generally from among the intermediate peasant castes.

According to a third view, violence and insecurity are an offshoot of the elite sponsored developmental system. In such a situation, which we have, violence by elites on Harijans, and 'violence of protest' by Harijans are found simultaneously. However, the elites always get an upper hand even after the violence is deciding the affairs of the society and fate of the downtrodden. It is quite foolish to expect justice from the vested interests.

The institution of untouchability has changed in recent years, not due to the Untouchability Offenses Act of 1955, but due to the pragmatism of the upper and upper middle castes and classes. They have realized lately that observance of untouchability might be quite disadvantageous for them economically and politically in the changed circumstances after independence. It is felt that without working with the Harijans on farms, in factories or in elections, the upper castes cannot continue to dominate or reconsolidate their position. This has been acquired due to some of the structural changes initiated since independence to bring down the age-old ascriptively determined monolithic dominance of the upper castes. However, partly due to legal loopholes and other lacunae, and partly due to pragmatic stratagems, the upper and the upper middle castes and classes have remained in positions of power, both politically and economically. Today, therefore, one finds dissonance between the formal and the real status of the Harijans, and there is also a hiatus between the form and the content of their position and standing in Indian society. One cannot understand the position of Harijans in terms of the existing legislation, constitution and other governmental measures.

The untouchables suffer a number of disabilities ranging from their most personal relations to the utterly formal and latent actions. These disabilities have been noted in regard to recruitment to army and police, admission to schools and colleges, bondage to the land, denial of services by Brahmins and other upper castes, use of sacred places and temples, and entry into shops and tea-stalls etc. The disabilities are not the same for all the untouchables as differential treatment given to the Harijans by the caste Hindus is found on the basis of their economic condition, education, occupation etc. Mahar observes that the nature of untouchability is too variegated in social and cultural phenomena and diversity of groups subsumed under such labels. Thus, there is no single measure or uniform criteria for identifying an 'untouchable'. Apparently, untouchability is a stigma, but in reality, it is a contextual phenomenon and a behavioural norm. It is not, therefore, just a cultural entity. The untouchables have complained against the upper castes on account of discrimination meted out to them, and the upper castes have complained against the Harijans as they have interfered in their exclusiveness of practices etc. The law does not provide a satisfactory solution to this antithetical, but apparently legitimate situation of self-righteousness.

Why there are atrocities only on Harijans and not on their other non-untouchable counterparts from among the caste Hindus? An answer to this question could explain the role of 'untouchability' as a factor responsible for the exploitation of the 'untouchables' by the *svarnas*. A number of studies have shown that the policy of preferential treatment has not given its desired fruits. The Harijans have not changed their traditional callings, nor they have acquired formal education to the extent caste Hindus have acquired. Moreover, these developments have created cleavages also among various scheduled castes. The Mahars, the Malas, the Balais, etc., are ahead of other scheduled castes of their respective regions. Thus, certain new forms of inequalities have emerged among the scheduled castes themselves. The caste Hindus and the Harijan elites have combined, may be unwittingly, to prevent the flow of facilities and new opportunities to the rank and file of the Harijans just to safeguard their vested interests or to promote further their own interests by directly or indirectly diverting the resources for sabotaging the welfare plans meant for the scheduled castes. The crux of the problem is that an equalitarian structure cannot be built without removing the structural bottlenecks of the already existing unequal groups.

We know that the Harijans earn their livelihood by working on land, and they are deprived of control over the land on which they have been working. The incidence of landlessness is more among them compared to other groups. The size of their landholdings is also smaller than that of caste Hindus. As many as 33 per cent of the total agricultural labourers are from among the scheduled castes. Most of them have uneconomic landholdings. The Harijans have barren and fallow lands. The fertile and strategically important lands have been allotted to the caste Hindus with the connivance of the local leaders and district administration. Therefore, it is necessary to ask: What is the meaning of development for the scheduled castes? There is a need for a basic change among the planners, leaders, scheduled caste elites and administrators to ensure the filtering down of the benefits to the rank and file of the Harijans.

Eminent economists such as K.N. Raj, V.K.R.V. Rao, B. S. Minhas, Dandekar and Rath have shown that the planning has hit the poor badly, and they have become, indeed, poorer. The way modern education, technology and legislation have been initiated, has led to the breeding of inequality. The rich can escape, and the poor can be trapped. Consequently, the Dalits, the Chamars and Harijans are beaten, their houses are burnt and their womenfolk are molested and raped by the landlords and other caste Hindus. These victims are not the well-off Harijans, Harijan leaders and the Harijan white-collar workers. In fact, they are the people who could not have proper education, could not migrate to urban centres for better prospects, and who could not escape the fury of the landed interests. We have ample evidence to show that the poorest of the Harijans are dehumanized and oppressed by the caste Hindus.

In 1975-76, Uttar Pradesh had highest number of atrocities as reported by the state government. About 50 per cent of the total number of such inhuman incidents occurred in the most populous state of India. In 1976-77 also, Uttar Pradesh topped the list of atrocities followed by Delhi, Bihar and Madhya Pradesh. About 80 per cent cases were of beating, and only 10 per cent were of untouchability.

An overwhelming number of these clashes with Harijans are over land and agriculture. Atrocities by police have also been on the increase. However, the cases reported to the government are only a small fragment of the total atrocities which have been committed on the Harijans.

On June 22, 1974 two scheduled caste persons were killed by Kanbi Patels in Surendranagar district of Gujarat because they wanted to fetch water from a village well. The scheduled castes had a well, exclusively for themselves, but it had dried up. The Patels had to come to a compromise due to police intervention and allow the scheduled castes to draw water from the well during fixed hours of the day. However, the Patels did not tolerate the decision and considered this as their direct insult, and hence planned murder of two scheduled caste men who had raised voice for fetching water from the village well.

In 1976, a study was conducted by the Harijan Sevak Sangh in 179 villages of nine districts of Madhya Pradesh. It is mentioned that "important programmes, like land distribution, irrigation, distribution of homestead plots, debt redemption, freeing of bonded labour and financial help schemes were only marginally implemented." Most of the 54 lakh Harijans in the state are agricultural labourers or landless peasants, and their future is in the hands of a few big farmers. They were paid as low as Rs. 1.50 for a day's labour. The Harijans were terrorized by anti-social elements belonging to the upper castes. Their crops were destroyed or looted, houses were burnt and womenfolk were raped. All the Harijans suffered from one or another disability. Uttar Pradesh tops the list of atrocities on the Harijans, and Madhya Pradesh comes next to Uttar Pradesh. During 1972-73, 200 cases of atrocities were reported in Madhya Pradesh. In the first half of 1973-74, 254 cases were reported, and 18 of these were murder, 37 rape, 38 arson, and 81 grievous hurt cases, and 80 offences under the Untouchability Act. During 1974-76, 11,812 cases were registered.

Arun Sinha, while commenting on Bihar situation, observes that it is 'class war' against Harijans, and not atrocities. In 1977, Bihar, among all states, accounted for the largest number of cases of atrocities against Harijans. The outrages occurred in Kargdhar, Belchhi, Pathadda, Chhaundadano, Gopalpur and Dharampur. The people were killed or persecuted not because they were Harijans and the actions of the landlords were not just atrocities. The issues behind these happenings were struggles for minimum wages, the occupancy rights of the sharecroppers, and a challenge to the absolute feudal power of the landlords. Therefore, such atrocities could be against non-Harijan proletariat as well belonging to the non-scheduled castes, the backward castes, the intermediate castes and even the upper caste proletariat. However, this view is only partially true. There is an element of Harijanness in the atrocities committed by the caste Hindus on Harijans. We could explain this point by making a distinction between a situation of atrocity and that of exploitation. It is true that all proletariat, irrespective of their caste background, are subjected to inhuman treatment by the caste Hindus. But there is a difference between a Harijan proletariat and a caste Hindu or a Brahmin proletariat. The differences between the two are found in regard to their occupational background, prestige of occupation, numerical strength in their respective castes, patronage from caste dominants and cultural milieu. The fact is that a Harijan becomes a target of landlord's fury, but a proletariat belonging to his own class does not get the similar treatment even if he works on his farm as an agricultural daily wage labourer. This is, what we would like to call as 'Harijanness' in the phenomenon of atrocities on Harijans.

We find somewhat different explanation of the atrocities on the Harijans. On May 27, 1977, in Belchhi, a village in Bihar, one villager was shot and 13 others were burnt alive. This was assessed as 'systematic harassment' of the Harijans by the upper caste Hindus according to one political party. However, the Janata Party maintained that the murders were the culmination of a feud between two groups of criminals, each including Harijans and upper caste Hindus. We do not have to enter into the controversy regarding the veracity of the incident, but it was said that the Bharatiya Lok Dal-Jana Sangh combine in eight of the Janata ruled states in 1977 encouraged the upper caste Hindus to persecute the Harijans. In other words, it was rumoured that the Harijans would remain defenseless so long as the Janata Party remained in power. A section of the Harijans made a demand for arms to protect themselves against the toughs and anti-social elements of the upper and upper middle caste Hindus. Thus, the emergence of Janata Party with BLD and Jana Sangh as its two important constituents was characterized as "the rise of the Kulak power at the centre and in the states." Oppression of the Harijans was considered a logical consequence of this change of power in the country.

The Atyachar Virodh Samiti recently made an analysis of riots in the Marathwada region of Maharashtra. The massacre, loot and rape of Harijans in this region have been quite frequent like Uttar Pradesh, Bihar and Madhya Pradesh. The Samiti observes that caste represents a specific form of oppression at the level of relations of production. There are both class and caste issues, because caste divisions persist beyond purely economic classes. A link should be established between fights against caste oppression and class exploitation, that is, caste discrimination and caste oppression are, in effect, representative of class hegemony of the upper castes.

It is reported that during 1966-76, 40,000 cases of atrocities were recorded. During the 19-month rule of Janata, the cases of atrocities were more than 17,000. Regarding the cases of atrocities (only murder and rape), Uttar Pradesh (183) tops among the states, followed by Madhya Pradesh (100), Bihar (100) and Rajasthan (78).

In Marathwada, the riots began due to renaming of Marathwada University as Dr. Babasaheb Ambedkar University in July 1978. The Students Action Committee launched an agitation against the change of the name of the university. The violence against the *dalits* took many forms which continued for more than two months. The Protection of Civil Rights Act did not help the victims in getting out of the inhuman situation prevailing in the region. The violence was of a wholesome nature. It included killing of people, molestation and rape of Harijan women, burning of their houses and huts, pillaging their *basties*, evicting them from their houses and villages, killing of their cattle, denying them drinking water and refusing them work, etc. It is reported by the Atyachar Virodh Samiti that 1,200 out of 9,000 villages of Marathwada were affected by the attacks of the caste Hindus, 5,000 people became homeless and stateless, and 2,500 became totally demoralized and helpless. This was an offensive launched by caste Hindu capitalist landlords with the help of police, patels, sarpanchas and anti-social elements. Breasts of one woman were cut off after raping her. Those who had left their homes were not ready to go back in spite of starvation.

The Samiti observes that renaming of the Marathwada University was only a pretext; the real issues were different. These included preferential treatment given to the *dalits*, namely reservations in educational institutions and jobs, the policies and character of *dalit* movement itself and its leaders, the increasing unity among the *dalits* themselves and between *dalit* and *swarna* agricultural labourers, and the linkages between the rural and the urban *dalits*. Thus, the issues such as language, separate statehood, caste exclusiveness, communal freedom, establishment of steel plants, and opening or renaming of a university, etc. are only apparent causes of the atrocities on Harijans. The real cause of all this is the desire of the upper castes and the landlords to maintain their monolithic control over the resources of the society, and to keep the Harijans and other proletariat as their servants and slaves. As such, caste becomes a mechanism of exploitation of the poor people, particularly the Harijans. It is, in effect, a system of relations of production; it promotes conservatism and helps the rich and the entrenched few in Indian society.

Charan Singh when he was Home Minister of India said that the caste system was the root cause of the problems of the Harijans. Atrocities on Harijans would continue so long as the caste system continued. He made the suggestion that the preferential treatment should be given to those marrying outside their own caste. Attitude of the persons towards caste should also be considered while giving them jobs. Jagjivan Ram, an acknowledged Harijan leader, observed regarding molestation and rape of Harijan girls: "Why did such things happen? Harijan girls were not known for their beauty and there were far more beautiful girls in other communities. The reason was economic weakness of the victims. They would not put up a fight against the 'ruffians', whether they belonged to the police force or other communities."

The backward class movement particularly in Bihar and Uttar Pradesh has further sharpened caste divides in the countryside. Brahmins, Rajputs, Kayasthas and Bhumihars who comprise about 7 per cent of total population, hold 75 per cent of government jobs. In Karnataka, the backward classes constitute 38 per cent of the population, but hold only 12 per cent of the jobs. Besides this discrimination, the backward class people like Harijans are kept at a distance in social and cultural arenas by the upper castes. Parvathama observes:

The Indian social structure itself is based on graded hierarchy of status where religious, economic, educational, political and judicial powers increase in the ascending order thus directly limiting the status of lower castes. While the instances of disabilities and backwardness are in the descending order, they are thinly spread over a whole range of Sudra castes, but greatest concentration obtains with reference to the untouchables who fall traditionally outside the *chaturvarna* scheme and thus constitute a class of *avarnas* called as *panchvnas*.

Thus, we must search for an explanation of the position of today's Harijans in the social structure of Indian society. The causes of their exploitation, oppression and intimidation are not casual, short-lived and contingent in nature.

Our study of educational inequalities among Rajasthan's scheduled castes shows that their alarmingly backward condition is connected to the deprivation they suffer in relation to the higher status groups and to the differential treatment they receive from the power elites from among themselves. We have found that the distributive disparities affecting the scheduled castes are at three levels: between the scheduled castes and the general population; between the various scheduled castes; and among scheduled castes in a particular district or area. Emergence of inequalities among scheduled castes has become a new stratificational problem, and this has accentuated class distinctions within the scheduled castes. Such a phenomenon would give a setback to unity, mobilization and movement among the scheduled caste people.

Available data reveal that the lowest castes, namely, Harijans, become the targets of violence. Such violence has very frequently occurred in Uttar Pradesh, Bihar, Maharashtra, Gujarat, Tamilnadu, and Andhra Pradesh. Atrocities on Harijans are inflicted both by upper and upper middle castes in these and other states. Our view is that caste divisions in Indian society are not outside the purview of class divisions. Since caste and class coexist, class consciousness and class unity are hampered by norms of caste divisions. It is, therefore, necessary to give a proper attention to the factor of 'caste' in the analysis of class relations, and also to see caste divisions from the class point of view. In fact, caste is a double-edged weapon being used against the Harijans by the caste Hindus, and to oppress them in the name of their exclusiveness and freedom. Resilience of the caste system has promoted the interests of the upper castes and suppressed the Harijans and other lower castes to a great extent. In other words, the processes of social change initiated after independence have helped the upper castes in the fields of education, politics and jobs. Violence against the Harijans is an expression of the hostile attitudes of the upper castes towards the Harijans, as this results into suppression of class consciousness among them and promotion of the vested interests of the caste Hindus.

Index